Moving to Maine
THE ESSENTIAL GUIDE TO GET YOU THERE
& WHAT YOU NEED TO KNOW TO STAY

MOVING TO MAINE

Updated and Expanded 2nd Edition

THE ESSENTIAL GUIDE TO GET YOU THERE & WHAT YOU NEED TO KNOW TO STAY

Victoria Doudera

DOWN EAST BOOKS
CAMDEN, MAINE

To Mom, Will, and Lucia—three magnificent new Mainers

Printed and bound at Versa Press, East Peoria, Illinois

5 4 3 2 1

Down East Books
Camden, Maine
A division of Down East Enterprise
Book orders: 1-800-766-1670
WWW.DOWNEASTBOOKS.COM
Distributed to the trade by National Book Network

LIBRARY OF CONGRESS CATALOGING-IN-PUBLICATION DATA

Doudera, Victoria, 1961-
  Moving to Maine : the essential guide to get you there
& what you need to know to stay / by Vicki Doudera.
      p. cm.
  Includes index.
  ISBN 978-0-89272-728-5 (trade pbk. : alk. paper)
  1. Maine--Guidebooks. 2. Moving, Household--Maine--
Handbooks, manuals, etc. I. Title.
  F17.3.D68 2007
  974.1--dc22
                              2007011656

Contents

Introduction: You're Moving *Where?*

Recently, I was riding the subway in New York City when a woman asked me what Maine was like. Her eyes widened as I described the coastline, mountains, forests, clean cities, and neat, small towns. "It sounds like paradise," she said wistfully. But then she gave me a knowing smile and nodded her head. "It must be very lovely in Maine, but it snows all year long, right?"

Let's face it: outside of northern New England, you tell people you're from Maine and you get some pretty comical responses. Although national weather information is just a click of the mouse away, the notion that Maine is locked in the icy grip of winter for most of the year persists. You'd think this was the United States' version of the Arctic by the shivers Maine can elicit. And then there is the geographical confusion. Just where in the world are we, anyway? A group of Italians I encountered in Florence had no reference point for Maine, and kept insisting the state was part of Vermont, despite my efforts to convince them otherwise. Finally, one of them had an epiphany. "Jessica Fletcher?" he queried, referring to Angela Lansbury's character on a popular television show from the 1980s called *Murder, She Wrote.* Wearily, I nodded and headed off to buy a gelato, leaving the group to reminisce about Hollywood's Cabot Cove and its many mysteries.

Maine isn't on the rest of the world's radar screen, except perhaps in TV reruns. Watch a game show and you'll see our fellow Americans scratching their heads, trying to place it. (I've had some people insist we're really part of Canada . . .) Tucked way up in the northeastern corner of the country, Maine isn't a place you drive through, fly over, or happen upon unintentionally. So why in your wildest dreams would you ever want to live here?

In the twenty-odd years since I moved to Maine, I've learned that people come for as many reasons as there are lobster pots in Penobscot Bay or potatoes in an Aroostook field. An unsurpassed natural environment, a lifestyle that encourages a slower pace, a low crime rate, and an economy that values creativity and entrepreneurship are just some of the lures. Affordable real estate, especially when compared to other coastal states, is another.

There are people who move "back" to Maine, too. I think of them as wild salmon, swimming against the current to return to their roots and family. There are those who spent their college years here, or a military tour, and just never got the state out of their system. And then there are those who can't explain their reasons – they just know Maine is the place for them.

If you have recently relocated to Maine, are thinking about it, or have packed and labeled your boxes, this completely revised edition of *Moving to Maine* is for you. You'll find the answer to the big question (Why am I doing this?), as well as to many others, such as:

- Is Maine part of mainstream America?
- Are there good-paying jobs up there that offer rewarding work?
- Can I live in a remote, rural state?
- Will my business still prosper?
- Is there enough cultural and ethnic diversity? Is there any?
- Are there decent doctors? Schools? Restaurants?
- Can I survive the winter?
- Will my family find things to do?
- Will I ever really fit in?

Here is the scoop on what it's really like to live here. The biggest advantages. The surprising benefits. And even the pitfalls. With loads of useful information, helpful hints, and tips from those who've already blazed the trail, you'll learn how to manage in Maine before you step foot in the Pine Tree State.

If you've already made up your mind and taken on the 207 area code, you'll find the following chapters to be a useful guide to your new state. The information you need to get acquainted is here, including tips on everything from registering your car to eating a lobster, to rafting your first North Woods river.

My Story

Did I mention that some people move to Maine almost on a whim? Maybe it's the benefit of hindsight, but when I look back at our reasons for moving north more than two decades ago, they seem pretty thin to me. Yes, I love the outdoors and knew I'd appreciate Maine's clean, natural environment. And yes, my soon-to-be husband and I thought small-town living in a close-knit community would be ideal as we started our life together. Did we know anyone in Maine? No. Had we taken several scouting trips, done our homework ahead of time? No. We'd been to Maine together only once, on a spontaneous drive up the coast to the fishing village of Corea, to rent a cottage I saw advertised in the *Boston Globe.* (Talk about a whim! Take a look at your Maine map and you'll see how far we drove . . .) We didn't have jobs, or even a modest nest egg, or any real ties to the state. But we had something that many new Mainers possess: a spirit of adventure. Along with that, we shared a willingness to work hard and keep our minds open. We knew we were choosing the road less traveled, a path that not everyone would understand right away, but we felt in our hearts that it was our destiny. Thanks to the feedback I've received from readers of the first edition of *Moving to Maine,* I know that many of you took similar leaps of faith in coming here.

Our sense of adventure prompted us to drive from Boston to Maine on one of the coldest weekends of the winter in January 1986. The mercury hovered in the single digits (Fahrenheit) as we purred along in Ed's aging Datsun 280Z, weaving our way up the coast, bundled in down and polar fleece as if on an expedition. We'd decided to look for a business and had even taken a class at Boston's Center for Adult Education on inn ownership. The teacher of the workshop was himself an innkeeper who did his best to prepare participants for the pitfalls of the hospitality industry. "You'll get divorced and become an alcoholic," he warned. "That's what happened to me."

Despite his precautions, we made appointments and toured several turn key properties in different parts of the state. Our intention was to buy a business, but it was a forlorn Victorian, empty and unkempt, that captured our interest. Beneath the house's grime and through the myriad cobwebs, we spied ornate plaster moldings and peeling tin ceilings, lovely old floorboards, and deep parlor fireplaces. Underneath it all we could see a lovely inn that we could breathe life into. As we stood shivering in the damp chill, that mysterious alchemy between old homes and romantic souls worked its magic, and we succumbed to the Victorian's hidden charms. Three months later, the house belonged to us and our Maine adventure had begun.

We barely had time to think about our new lives that first year. Renovating the house took months of sawdust and sweat, and then we were thrust headlong into the role of innkeepers. Ed baked muffins and flipped flapjacks and, in his spare time, passed the Maine bar exam. He opened a law practice in a pretty tin-ceilinged room at the front of the inn. We joined town committees and the church down the street, adopted a black Lab puppy, and began to feel at home.

Yet it wasn't long before we noticed there were palpable differences to living in Maine, differences that went beyond the physical surroundings.

One day I was running some errands in the village. As I slowed for a blinking yellow light, a car horn began honking insistently at me. In a flash, my Boston-driver instincts kicked in. "Give me a break," I muttered. I scanned the streets for the offending car, ready to give its obviously obnoxious driver a nasty look—at the very least. There, idling on a side street, I found the culprit: an enthusiastic woman I'd met the day before, smiling and waving while sounding her horn.

Another day, I was in the supermarket check-out line with my cart full of inn supplies, when I realized my meager amount of cash wasn't nearly enough. I'd forgotten my checkbook and credit cards, and I was ready to put the groceries back when an employee handed me a fifty-dollar bill. I thanked him and asked if he wanted my name and address. "Nah," he said. "You'll pay me back."

These are the kinds of stories all newcomers tell, the kinds of tales that demonstrate the unexpected richness of life in Maine. When Ed and I fell under the spell of that old house years ago, we really became part of a place with much more to offer than we could ever have imagined. A place with people—some of them "natives" and some (like us) "from away"—who've become good friends. A state where our children are valued members of the community. A place where I can enjoy the outdoors to my heart's content. Personally, I couldn't agree more with the tourist slogan—Maine: The way life should be.

Nevertheless, the nation's most northeasterly state is not for everyone. Living in the more remote sections or weathering the sometimes long winters can be a challenge. Making a living here takes some real resourcefulness. Taxes can seem comparatively high, and ethnic diversity disappointingly low. Maine isn't perfect—what place is?—although some of us consider it much closer to perfection than anywhere else.

This Book

To get perspectives other than my own, I spoke with new residents who've moved here from all over the United States within the past few years. These kind souls shared their biggest challenges and rewards as new Mainers. "What do you wish you had known before you moved here?" I asked. Their thoughtful answers to my many questions helped enormously in creating what I hope is a truly useful and informative guide.

In writing this updated edition, I've also had guidance from my readers. I truly appreciate the kind comments and constructive feedback you've shared, and I've done my best to incorporate your thoughts. One of the best conversations I had about the book was with a new Mainer who said he felt I had written *Moving to Maine* from my heart. I think he's correct. My heartfelt advice and those of others is within these pages.

Updating this book has also meant looking back at recent history. Much has occurred in the seven years since the first book's publication in Maine and in the nation as a whole. The stock market declined, a recession occurred, and a rash of corporate scandals unfolded, eroding both the economy and our trust. And then the biggest impact of all: the attacks of September 11, 2001. Just like the rest of the country, these events, including the ongoing wars in Iraq and Afghanistan, have had a sobering effect here.

What you'll find once again in *Moving to Maine* is a broad overview of the state, with as much specific information as possible on key topics like tax rates, medical centers, insurance, and schools. Where I have not provided specifics, I've given several paths to find them. In many cases, I've directed readers to websites, which are a wonderful way to research an area. Maine in particular has an overwhelming amount of quality information online, including several superb sites I've listed throughout the book and in the Virtual Maine chapter. For the more traditional researcher, phone numbers are listed. Although automated systems are, unfortunately, on the rise, real people pick up the phone here more than in other places, and chances are that person will be both helpful and polite.

Timeliness and accuracy have been my goals; but please forgive me if I've omitted something or if information has evolved since publication. Even in Maine, things do change. Take my husband and me, for instance. After running our inn for twelve years (and somehow staying married and sober), we sold it to a lovely couple and started new careers. Our children changed from toddlers to teens, with our eldest now a student at the University of Maine. Our network of family members expanded as first my mother, and then my brother and sister-in-law, relocated to the state.

Maine is basically one big small town, a place where connections to others truly matter. One of the best things about writing a book is connecting with readers and I hope I'll hear from you. When you have a chance, please visit my website at www.vickidoudera.com to send me an e-mail or see some of my other writing (such as gardening and home-improvement articles) online. I welcome and thank you for your comments and time.

I'll close with what I wrote back in 2000: moving anyplace is an undertaking that requires courage, energy, creativity, and faith. For your move to this great state, you might want to bring along bug spray (for our notorious blackflies) and a warm jacket as well. Best of luck to you as you begin your adventure in Maine!

1 The Spirit of Maine

"I felt like I'd been misplaced in the cosmos and I belonged in Maine."

—TERRY GOODKIND*

What is it about this state that pulls people here like metal to a magnet? For many, it's the state's beauty—the rough-hewn coastline and rugged islands, the spruce-filled forests and towering mountains, the clean rivers, lakes, and streams. Others, like Dottie Paradis of Cornish, cite the relaxed pace of life in Maine. "I automatically shift into low gear the minute I cross the border into Maine," she says. "I love wearing shorts and sandals to work, seeing lots and lots of green, and making my own rules, hours, and goals."

For some, it's Maine's inhabitants who make the difference. "We also chose Maine for the people," says Lynda Chilton, who relocated from Virginia with her husband and children. "In the little bits of time we spent here, we made good friends. People I would have kept in touch with, even if we hadn't decided to move up. When you live in a metropolitan area, you get used to not having time for close friends, and the people you come in contact with in stores, restaurants, and in business are stressed out, and often surly and rude. Road-rage invades all parts of life. In Maine, people take the time to be nice—you feel you are part of the community."

While I was drawn here by all of these things, I never dreamed I would discover an overriding state spirit, what former Governor Angus King calls "that indefinable attitude that won't take 'no' for an answer, that says yes

---

*Author Terry Goodkind, quoted in an interview by Lynn Flewelling in the *Bangor Daily News,* November 1995.

to life and its infinite possibilities." Although I had canoed down the Saco River and fished in Rangeley Lake, I thought of the state in a fairly stereo-typical way: a vast expanse on top of New Hampshire, full of moose, lob-sters, and tight-lipped New Englanders. Maine seemed too big and too wild to have its own distinct identity.

I settled in Maine and soon discovered—as do all newcomers who don't already know it—that Maine is a place with a soul, something that is felt more than seen. An attitude, a mystique, summed up in the sigh that es-capes the lips when crossing the Piscataqua River at Kittery, regardless of how many times you've done it before.

The Essence of Maine

There is a palpable Maine spirit, no matter where in the state you go, a mixture of pride and perseverance sprinkled with independence and old-fashioned neighborliness. Mainers have "moxie," a term from the late 1800s meaning nerve and verve (and also the name of a century-old bever-age, still popular Down East). Like the state's heroes—Civil War General Joshua Chamberlain, pioneering Senator Margaret Chase Smith, and for-mer Governor Edmund Muskie, to name just a few—Mainers may be hum-ble, but they aren't afraid to stand up for what's right.

Businesspeople who relocate to Maine from other states are often amazed by the strong work ethic here. The sun rises early in the Pine Tree State, and most Mainers have already had a mug or two of coffee before the rest of the country is out of bed. They also are exacting, and believe in qual-ity and workmanship. Whether their field is biotechnology or blueberries, residents here comprise the best workforce in the country.

The Maine spirit creates an indelible impression on those who adopt the state as their home. Most newcomers find the indefinable attitude conta-gious and take it on themselves. Others see it as a precious commodity that might spoil if not tended: "Be prepared to be a part of Maine," advises new-comer Carol Doherty-Cox, who moved to Port Clyde from Westchester County, New York. "Don't bring your old life with you. The value of Maine is in its identity. We don't need to inundate the state with people who want to remake it in their image."

The Maine mindset and lifestyle can come as a bit of a shock to newcomers. The rhythm of life is slower, and the frenetic pace of large cities (and even most suburbs) is not commonly found. "People aren't living off their calendars here," says Thad Chilton, a Virginia native. "Nobody pulls out their date book to make an appointment." Catching up on the latest news at the post office is viewed as more important than merely processing people through a line. Cashiers at stores—even large department chains—take time to chat or offer helpful advice about purchases. Newcomers who are used to a faster pace will find that patience is a virtue that can often come in handy here.

Maine is old-fashioned in other ways as well. Deals may still be sealed with a handshake, and issues are often worked out over the backyard fence rather than in the county courtroom. This is not a cynical, world-weary place—honesty and integrity are assumed to be part of everyone's makeup. "No one seems to be uptight about anything," says Jane Dahmen, a resident of Newcastle since 2005. "People have a good handle on what's important in life—but they are bright, interesting, talented, and they love living here. They are great neighbors."

The ways of the village flavor life even in the urban areas. When in need, Mainers depend on one another. Neighbors drop off fragrant chicken pot pies or hearty casseroles when a new baby comes; community suppers are held to raise money for families struggling with an illness or unexpected accident. This willingness to lend a hand was demonstrated to the rest of the nation during the state's great ice storm of 1998. Crews from as far away as North Carolina, here to fix downed lines, were astounded at the warm welcome they received from victims of the storm, many of whom had been without power for several days. Congressman Thomas H. Allen, who represents the First Congressional District of Maine, sums it up this way, "While Maine is populated by people who pride themselves on their self-reliance, we are also quick to help a neighbor or even a stranger in need."

In many ways, the state functions as one big community. But despite this closeness, newcomers are warmly welcomed.

"We were concerned about being seen as outsiders, especially since that was how we were treated in South Carolina," says Mary Griffin of Orono. "But the Bangor region really welcomed and embraced us and made us feel as though we were part of a great community."

Kathleen and Robert Hirsch, former Pennsylvanians, concur. "We had always heard that if you weren't born in Maine you would always be 'from away.' Not only were we not natives, but we didn't even have a history of spending a lot of time in Maine. My big concern was whether we would ever be accepted. I even considered creating a tale about great-grandparents and grandparents living and vacationing in Maine to give us more credibility, but I never got that story concocted. So, here we were living in Maine and the question everyone seemed to ask was, 'whatever brought you here to Maine?' There is no good answer to that question other than to say that Maine 'felt' like the right place for us to be. And now that we are here, we can actually say that it is a great place to be. My fears of not being accepted were ill-founded. We have found the people here to be warm, welcoming, and helpful."

Schooners such as the *Grace Bailey,* built in 1882 to carry lumber, now offer sailing cruises along the coast from May to October. *Photo courtesy of Maine Windjammer Cruises.*

Something for Everyone

Maine's natural assets have always been its greatest attraction to vacationers, and they are a big lure for new residents as well. "One of the biggest advantages to living in Maine is the beautiful natural environment," says Lynda Chilton, a native of Virginia. "When I go anywhere here, my views are of beautiful mountains, oceans lapping at rocky shorelines, charming old homes, and comfortable farms."

Maine offers something for everyone, largely because of its size. Measuring 320 miles long by 210 miles wide, the state encompasses 33,215 square miles—about as much land area as all of the other five New England states combined. Its famous rocky coastline curves in and out for 3,478 miles, from York to Washington counties. It comprises 16 counties with 22 cities, 424 towns, 51 plantations, and 416 unorganized townships. One county, Aroostook, is so big that it alone is larger than Connecticut and Rhode Island combined. Distances between Maine towns can be vast for travelers used to the scale of southern New England. For instance, Portland, the state's largest city, is actually closer to New York City (328 miles) than to Madawaska, on the Canadian border (356 miles).

Maine boasts 542,629 acres of state and national parks, including Acadia National Park, Baxter State Park, and the ninety-two-mile Allagash Wilderness Waterway. The state's highest peak, Mt. Katahdin, rises almost a mile above sea level, while Acadia's Cadillac Mountain has the distinction of being the tallest mountain on the eastern seaboard.

Water abounds in Maine—on a map the state appears to be sinking, so frequently do blue patches interrupt the green! There are thirty-two thousand miles of rivers and streams, fifty-one lakes that have an area of at least five square miles, and, of course, the meandering coastline. More than three thousand islands dot the bays, making for spectacular sailing. Pleasure boats of all sizes ply the waters, as do working lobster and fishing vessels, ferries, and the beautiful historic wooden schooners called windjammers. "For me, spending time on the coast of Maine was truly magic," says Lynda Chilton. "I felt that this place was calling to me and my family."

The People of Maine

Ask new residents in Maine why they like living here, and, without fail, they will mention their neighbors. Mainers may be gruff or loquacious, natives or relative newcomers, yet almost all of them share a sense of community and a love for their state and its resources. "People here are friendly and supportive," says Dottie Paradis, who moved to Cornish from Massachusetts in 1999. "Not at all the staunch and rigid Yankees I imagined."

Even those who have been here for several decades cite Mainers themselves as a draw. "A few weeks ago I met a man who said he moved here twenty-five years ago," says Kathleen Hirsch, who headed north from Pennsylvania with her husband in June of 2005. "He said he chose Maine for the people and he has stayed here because of the people. That says you can't go wrong moving to Maine!"

Carole Brand, who also came in 2005, has formed a theory concerning why residents are typecast as rough-and-tumble woodsmen. "The stereotype of Mainers as mostly backwoods loggers in red flannel shirts living in drafty log cabins who drive trucks, drink beer, think ice fishing is the height of culture, and whose vocabulary consists of the all-purpose 'Ayuh' is locally promulgated as a way of keeping the tourist population in check. In fact, my immediate neighbors consist of a nuclear physicist, a retired pediatric oncologist, a pathologist, a former executive of Rockefeller Institute, a computer scientist, and a retired mathematics professor. The annual conference on foreign policy was sold out within days, and I am having difficulty finding a book group that has an opening. However, the local Shakespeare Society has been very welcoming."

Approximately 1,317,253 people live in the state of Maine in an estimated 518,200 households. The majority of them call the countryside home; while nearly 80 percent of the population of the United States lives in metropolitan areas, only 40 percent of Mainers live in cities, the major ones being Portland, Bangor, Augusta, and Lewiston-Auburn. Maine is the third most rural state in the nation, behind Vermont and West Virginia. People here like their personal space: the average population density in 2004 was 16 persons per square mile, and, in about half the state, this figure drops to only 1 person per 3 square miles. More than one-half the population of Maine lives in the southern/southwestern corner of the state.

Who Lives Here?

To better answer the question of who lives in Maine today, let's take a look back at the very first folks who took the Maine plunge. The earliest permanent European settlers here came from western England. They were soon followed by the Scots-Irish and by a number of Quakers, or Friends, from the other New England colonies. In the 1740s Germans settled in Waldoboro, and soon afterward many Irish Roman Catholics moved to York, Lincoln, and Cumberland counties. The French, who controlled much of Maine's territory until 1759, were not active colonists early on, although a number of families of French Huguenots settled along the coast.

The 1800s brought large-scale emigration westward as cheap land and gold strikes lured Mainers away. So great was the human "outflow" in 1870 that William W. Thomas, the state commissioner of immigration, brought over a group of Swedish immigrants who established the colony of New Sweden in northern Aroostook County. Although Maine has a slightly higher percentage of English, Irish, Scotch, Dutch, and German ancestors than the United States as a whole, one group of immigrants would arrive in the late 19th century to work in industry and forever alter the state's cultural mix: the French.

"The most outstanding feature of ancestral composition in Maine is the large percentage of French," says a 1994 report from the Maine Department

PROFILE

"I chose the state of Maine because of the skiing, and also because I was offered a good job with Carrabassett Valley Academy," says Peter Mahncke, who emigrated to Kingfield from Germany in 1997. "I think there are many benefits to living here," he says. "The slower pace, the relatively clean environment, the beautiful landscape, the good political leadership, and the balance between the state's economy and ecology are big pluses. And there is little suburbia and low crime, which I also like. If you enjoy living somewhat removed from corporate America and you are not looking for a fast-paced lifestyle with hectic people, this is the place for you."

of Labor called "Diversity and Community." "From a national point of view, this large French concentration is unique. Over time the French have shown the least inclination of all other European countries to migrate and have typically had the highest rates of return."

Today, there remain large numbers of people of Franco-American descent in much of Maine, particularly in the Lewiston-Auburn, Biddeford-Saco, and Augusta-Waterville areas. They were eventually joined in the industrial centers by Finns, Russians, Poles, Italians, and others from southern and eastern Europe. However, none of these settlers were the region's earliest modern inhabitants. The Wabanaki Indians, or "People of the Dawnland," first called Maine home. Their tribes include the Passamaquoddies, Penobscots, Maliseets, and Micmacs. Native Americans in present-day Maine belong to either the Passamaquoddy or Penobscot tribe, and comprise approximately .6% of the total population. The Penobscot reservation is on Indian Island, in the Penobscot River near Old Town, and the two Passamaquoddy reservations are in Washington County.

Mainers are very proud of their ethnic roots, and fairs, festivals, celebrations, and religious observances honor the origins of the state's many cultures. Bagpipes play at the Highland Games in Brunswick, and the lilting sounds of traditional French chansons fill the air in Lewiston and Auburn at the Festival de Joie. Midsommar Festival, held in the Aroostook County towns of New Sweden and Stockholm, commemorates that area's Swedish heritage, and a day honoring Maine's Wabanaki tribes occurs in April. Despite these celebrations, almost all newcomers, like Laura Read of Arundel, feel Maine is still rather culturally homogenous, lacking a blend of cultures, races, and religions. "There are very few people of color," she notes. Adds Peter Mahncke of Kingfield, "I love Maine's beautiful landscape, the slower pace, the tranquility, and the ability to use the land for recreational purposes. The only downside to living in Maine might be that the population isn't very diverse."

Growing Diversity

It's true that the face of Maine is largely white— 96.9 percent in 2000 —although that percentage is slowly changing. It may not appear so, but today the Pine Tree State is experiencing the greatest growth in racial diversity in its history. Between 1990 and 2000 for example, the Asian population grew from 6,683 persons to 9,111; the African-American population from 5,138 to 6,760; and the Hispanic population from 6,829 to 9,360. The Census Bureau predicts that this growth will continue, but the pace will be slow.

"Racial diversity has always existed in Maine," says a report that ran in the *Portland Press Herald* in 1999 called "The Changing Face of Maine." "Indians are the original inhabitants of the area, and blacks were living in Maine by the early 1600s. Racial diversity in Maine is growing today because of births in families of color and for reasons seen throughout history — people's migration in search of economic opportunity and a safe place to live and raise families. That migration includes foreign refugees who are settling here, as well as native-born people of color coming for jobs and Maine's quality of life."

Statistics show that much of Maine's recent ethnic and religious diversity has come through the United States Refugee Resettlement Program. Since 1975, Catholic Charities Maine, the major organization designated for refugee resettlement in the state, has assisted in the resettlement process for over 5,000 refugees from some 25 countries in Southeast Asia, Africa, the Near East, Eastern Europe, Cuba, and the former Soviet Republics, including Cambodia, India, Vietnam, Afghanistan, Somalia, Sudan, Democratic Republic of Congo, Iran, Iraq, and Russia. This program has considerably grown the cultural and religious diversity in Maine. In particular, Buddhists and Muslims from these countries have planted their roots, creating religious centers and participating in the civic, social, and economic life of Maine.

"Religious diversity can be increasingly found in the smallest and most unexpected pockets of America's geographic and civic landscape," says Colleen Rost-Banik, a member of the Pluralism Project, part of Harvard University's Committee on the Study of Religion. "Maine is one such pocket." She notes that, aside from refugees bringing their religious and cultural heritage with them, the landscape is also a draw for religious diversity. "Maine's beaches, mountains, and rolling hills have helped give rise to a number of religious communities—from Baha'is who began the internationally known Green Acre Baha'i School along the beautiful bank of the Piscataqua River; to the Buddhists, many of whom have moved to Maine from neighboring cities on the East Coast and started meditation groups in their homes so they can practice in a more relaxed atmosphere; to the Pagans, who have been supported in both solitary and community practice by the vast spaces of land and water all throughout Maine."

Colleen Rost-Banik authored the Pluralism Project's report (www.plu ralism.org), which notes that while religious diversity is on the rise all over the country, Maine is unique in the level of interconnectedness among religious and civic institutions. "Since there is such a small population in the state, many people realize that in order to coexist and accomplish the goals needed to move Maine forward, all groups of people must be actively engaged in the public square. The state of Maine, which is quite large in landmass, is actually a small community with few degrees of separation among people. When resources are limited, and when a community understands that all its realms are interconnected, they realize they must work together for their collective well-being."

Maine's service organizations, school systems, and religious communities collaborate to make sure that the various needs of people are met. Notes Rost-Banik: "In one instance, when the Portland Muslim community struggled to find a space that was big enough and willing to host their Eid al-Adha prayer, a local public school opened up their gymnasium to the community. Some might contend that this blurs the line of separation between church and state. But in reality, the public school system is working to ensure that underrepresented communities have the same resources afforded to more privileged groups in the area."

What about discrimination? It's hard to gauge racial attitudes, and few studies have been done addressing the issue. Mainers who are minorities report mixed reactions: some feel comfortable here, while others sense a lack of acceptance. The *Portland Press Herald* reported in 1999 that "Hate crimes based on a victim's race are the single largest category of bias incidents in Maine, according to the Attorney General's Office. Blacks alone represented 35 percent of the 1,110 incidents reported to the attorney general between October 1992 and June 1998, with additional victims who were Asian, Indian, or races other than white. The bias incidents included physical attacks, property destruction, death threats, and a cross-burning."

Attitudes toward issues of sexual orientation have been easier to measure, with Mainers rejecting an effort to repeal the state's gay-rights law, allowing Maine to join the other New England states in legally protecting homosexuals from discrimination. In November of 2005, Mainers went to the polls to approve the sexual orientation and gender identity non-discrimination bill, which had passed both houses of the Maine Legislature with strong bipartisan margins and was signed into law by Governor John Baldacci. However, the law exempts religious organizations that do not receive public funds, and is worded to say that it is not meant to address a right to marry. Maine is the 16th state to outlaw discrimination based on sexual orientation and the 6th to outlaw discrimination based on gender identity.

Like any other state, Maine is exposed to diversity as ethnic influences continue to permeate popular culture, music, current events, films, and television. "Maine is a state that embraces tolerance," Governor Baldacci has said, "and it will thrive based on a celebration of each individual's diverse strengths."

I thought of the Governor's words on a recent trip to Nashville, Tennessee. On the way to the airport, my cab driver saw my Maine sweatshirt and began telling me how much his relatives loved living in Portland. "Like me, my cousins are refugees from Somalia," he told me. "They say the people in your state are very, very nice. They say Portland is a city that acts just like a small village." Most Mainers—no matter what their ethnic origin—believe the state will benefit as diversity here grows.

Slow Population Growth

Maine's population on the whole is growing, albeit slowly. Over the 1990s, the population grew by 3.8 percent. Who's moving in? All kinds of people, really—young families, early retirees, skilled professionals, risk-taking entrepreneurs. They come from all over the map, although migration from southern New England and the mid-Atlantic region outnumbers other spots.

"If I had to rank them," says Valarie LaMonte, the director of the Center for Real Estate Education at the University of Southern Maine, "I'd say that the most common home states of new residents are Massachusetts, New Hampshire, Connecticut, New York, and Pennsylvania." A table produced by the U.S. Census Bureau that includes data on the largest migration inflow and outflow by state backs up her informal data. From 1995 to 2000, Maine gained nearly 20,000 residents from one state: Massachusetts.

The northeastern United States has historically been a source for Maine's new residents. Many Maine towns were settled in the 1700s by families from Massachusetts or New Hampshire seeking cheap land and abundant game. A century later, the so-called rusticators (moneyed summer residents of Bar Harbor, Kennebunkport, Islesboro, and other coastal communities) boarded steamships to escape the heat of their home cities of Philadelphia, Boston, and New York. And many of their families liked it here so much that they settled in Maine permanently.

But certainly not everyone is from the Northeast. Ruth Anne and Wesley Hohfeld came to Maine in 2001 from California. "We wanted to move out of the high-pressure San Francisco Bay area," says Ruth Anne. "We wanted a lower cost of living and fewer people."

Laura Read lived in North Carolina and came to Maine to work at a summer camp. "I loved the blunt personality of Mainers," she says. "So refreshing compared to the 'Southern Gals' I grew up with."

Jeff and Cathy Cleaveland moved to the small town of Appleton from Seattle. "We wanted to be on the East Coast, closer to family in Massachusetts," says Cathy. While she loves having lots of land and four distinct seasons, there's one thing Cathy misses about Seattle: "Drive-through coffee stands!"

Who Is a Native?

With new people coming to Maine from just about everywhere, some good-natured speculation goes on concerning who is rightfully a "native." Strictly speaking, Maine natives have ancestral ties to the state going back at least three generations. It gets confusing because sometimes folks will answer the "Are you a native" question with, "Yep. Born and bred." But to many sticklers, merely being born in Maine isn't enough. Here's the succinct explanation you're likely to encounter: Just 'cause the cat has kittens in the oven, that don't make 'em biscuits.

It's all in fun, though—after all, folks "from away" have been coming to Maine for centuries. I like the old joke in which the fellow from Massachusetts asks the Mainer, "Have you lived here all your life?"

To which the Mainer answers, "Not yet."

No matter where you live in the state, your neighbors may be from just about anywhere: Veazie or Virginia, Scotland or Scarborough.

A Safer Place to Be

In addition to scenic beauty and welcoming people, Maine boasts something that, unfortunately, few other states can claim: friendly streets and neighborhoods. "We haven't locked our car doors in three years," says a former Californian. "We feel safe when we're out with our kids. My internal early-warning radar system doesn't have to be on all the time. In fact, it's funny: every time I see a thriller or mystery at the movies, the setting is usually a gritty, urban environment. When I leave the theater, my city-tough attitude is on, and I look around corners for danger and generally have my bristles out. But then I quickly realize that's unnecessary and laugh at myself."

While law-enforcement officials are quick to recommend street smarts even in the smallest town, the fact remains that crime in Maine is tame compared with other places. The state consistently ranks among the top ten safest states, and in recent years, Maine has made the top three, coming in second (North Dakota was safest) in 2006. According to the Uniform Crime Reports, compiled by the FBI, the 2004 rate of violent crimes in Maine was 1 offense per 1,000 people. The 2004 national average was 4.6 violent crimes per 1000. Contrast that statistic with those of a few other states (Illinois' rate of 5.41 or Florida's of 7.1), and you get a sense why newcomers feel appreciably more secure in Maine. And the state seems to be only getting safer: in 2004, rates for crimes in nearly every category measured dropped from those of 2003.

A Four-Season Climate

Although some might shiver at the very thought of the long winters, there are plenty of people who consider the Pine Tree State's climate to be ideal, and consider it part of the appeal of living here. "Frankly, I think the weather is an advantage," says Carole Brand. "Summers are cool and winters are very manageable."

"Maine is recognized as one of the most healthful states in the nation," claims the state tourism bureau. Smog-free air and moderate temperatures (average 70 degrees in summer, 20 degrees in winter) benefit residents whether working or playing. "I love the change of seasons," says Elizabeth Burrell, of Rockland. "The weather in California was so predictable."

And what of the legendary winters? While they offer an excellent chance to wear colorful fleece jackets and down parkas while pursuing a wide range of cold-weather sports, winters here tend to be the victims of hazy memory and hyperbole. For the most part, the force of Old Man Winter in Maine has been greatly exaggerated. Data suggest that although the winters are frosty, prolonged severe cold spells are rare. "I find the winters invigorating," says Lynda Chilton, who moved here from Virginia. "Especially because I enjoy outdoor activities in all seasons."

We'll take a look at Maine's climate and delightful seasons (including winter) in more detail in Chapter 6.

MAINESPEAK

While only 7% of the population speaks something other than English at home, you may find your new neighbor's diction nevertheless different. Here's a little glossary of Down East expressions you won't find in your dictionary, as well as tips on how to master your own Maine accent:

A Piece: an undetermined distance, as in "down the road a piece."

Ayuh: okay

Bug: lobster

Chowdered Up: destroyed

Crittah: a furry animal

Cunnin': cute

Dooryard: front yard

Finest Kind: the very best

From Away: not from Maine

Gawmy: clumsy

Numb: stupid

Pot: lobster trap

Prayer Handle: knee

Quahog: thick-shelled clam (pronounced co-hog)

Scrid: a tiny piece

Steamers: clams

Wicked: very

The secret to speaking like a "Mainah"? Relax your jaw. Let your lower jaw drop on the second syllable, pronouncing "er" at the end of a word as "ah." While you're at it, drag out some one-syllable words into two syllables. ("Here" becomes "hee-ah.") Drop the "g" in "ing" so that "running" becomes "runnin'". Finally, broaden "a" and "e" sounds, almost like the Brits, saying "cahn't" instead of "can't."

ONLY IN MAINE

Maine towns often appear on lists of the best places in the nation to live and do business. Here are a few examples:

- Portland was chosen as a "North American Dream Town," by *Outside* magazine in 1999.

- Camden was called Maine's best small town by the *Maine Sunday Telegram* in 1997. Cornish came in second.

- Bath was selected as one of "The 100 Best Small Towns in America," in a 1995 book of the same name.

- Deer Isle was chosen as the country's fifth-best small art town by John Villani in *The 100 Best Small Art Towns in America*. Belfast ranked tenth, and Lewiston came in nineteenth.

- Brunswick was chosen as one of the top five places to retire by *Money* Magazine, June 2000.

- Portland made the list of "Ten Great Adventure Towns" in the

September 2004 issue of *National Geographic Adventure* Magazine. That same year, *INC.* Magazine included Portland in its listing of the top 25 cities for doing business in America.

• Bangor landed in the number-two spot in the 2004 edition of "Cities Ranked & Rated." Bangor was found to be the second-best location in the country among metropolitan areas with populations fewer than 100,000.

• Portland ranked as the number-one large market in the country for small business vitality by American City Business Journals in January 2005.

• Rockland is ranked among the top 100 best small towns to live in by *Outside* Magazine; and Lincolnville as one of the top 100 best small towns to recreate in.

• Portland was rated one of the top 10 cities to "Have It All" by the A&E television channel. Maine's largest city is consistently rated as one of the most desired cities to live in America.

• Camden was chosen one of the "50 Best Places to Live" by *Men's Journal* in 2006 for its growing cachet as a telecommunity.

2 Maine 101

"Maine should be a quick story—it's not a big or a populous place and nowhere near as old as any comparable site in Europe or Asia. But the historic flavor of this small corner of America needs room for its rich diversity to be explained, to be narrated, even to be sung in bits of poetry and scraps of fiction intermingled with the exposition of facts."

—NEIL ROLDE*

How does the Pine Tree State operate? A quick look at the geography and history of the nation's most northeasterly corner goes a long way toward understanding how the state functions on a day-to-day basis.

Maine Geography

Maine is diverse—geographically speaking—thanks to the work of massive glaciers long ago. As the slowly moving masses of ice crawled southeast, they scraped and softened the contours of mountains, gathered loose soil and stones, and broadened and deepened river valleys. When the climate warmed again, beginning fourteen thousand years ago, the glacier unloaded rocks, stone, and soil as it melted, creating moraines, eskers, and drumlins as well as the bodies of water dotting the state. Ancient river valleys were dammed up, forming chains of lakes, such as those in Belgrade. The weight of the mile-thick ice sheet had depressed the land, so when the glaciers melted and sea level rose, water flooded the sunken terrain, forming Maine's bays, inlets, and coves. Today's islands are the hilltops and ridges of this "drowned coast." Because of the glaciers, Maine contains the only fjord on

---

*Quoted from *Maine: A Narrative History,* by Neil Rolde. Gardiner, Me.: Tilbury House Publishers, 1990.

MAINE STATE FACTS AND SYMBOLS

Capital: Augusta
Population: Approximately 1.3 million
Gemstone: Tourmaline
Fossil: *Pertica quadrifaria*
Cat: Maine coon cat
Insect: Honeybee
Animal: Moose
Flag: The coat of arms of the State of Maine is placed on a blue field of the same shade of blue as in the flag of the United States. Adopted by the Legislature of 1909.
Motto: Dirigo—A Latin term that means "I lead."
Tree: White pine, adopted by the Legislature of 1945.
Floral Emblem: White pine cone and tassel *(Pinus strobus)*. Adopted by the Legislature of 1895.
Bird: Black-capped chickadee *(Parus atricapillus)*. Adopted by the Legislature of 1927.
Fish: Landlocked salmon

the East Coast—Somes Sound—and even, believe it or not, has its own stretches of "desert" in places like Freeport and Wayne, where erosion has exposed ancient deposits of glacial sand.

When the climate warmed, grasses grew, along with other plants, flowers, and, eventually, forests. Animals multiplied, and soon the first Mainers appeared.

A Little History

Prehistoric inhabitants of Maine included Paleo Indians, who lived here perhaps 11,500 years ago. Historians believe they were followed by the Archaic Indians, and finally by the Red Paint People, whose artifacts, colored with distinctive red ochre, have been found on North Haven Island and elsewhere.

Evidence indicates that these natives enjoyed many of the same pleasures that present-day vacationers do. They headed to the coast in the summer for cool breezes and hearty seafood feasts. The middens, or piles of shells, they left behind are remnants of ancient clambakes. In addition to shellfish, they enjoyed porpoise and seal meat—items that have not remained a part of our modern summer menu.

When the first Europeans arrived is still a controversial topic. Debate rages over whether or not Vikings had a settlement in Maine. W. Hodding Carter, trip leader of the 1998 *Snorri* expedition, which traced the Vikings' route in a replica of a Norse ship, says, "We know for sure they were in Greenland and Newfoundland. We aren't certain they sailed to Maine. But after three months in a replica of a Viking merchant ship, I'm convinced that any self-respecting Viking would have found his way to Penobscot Bay."

An ancient Norse penny found in Brooklin, Maine, adds weight to Carter's sentiments. Dating back to 1065 or so, it's the oldest European artifact ever found in North America. The coin resides at the Maine State Museum in Augusta, although it is currently on display at the Smithsonian Institution.

European Exploration

The first Europeans to "discover" Maine came in search of gold, spices, and the elusive Northwest Passage to the Orient, as well as more practical items such as fish, furs, and lumber. Beginning in 1524, Italian, Spanish, French, and English explorers traded along the coast, sailing home with full cargoes of valuable furs, cedar, and sassafras root, as well as stories of abundant fish and enormous lobsters.

Did the Vikings reach Maine? This eleventh-century Norse coin, found in a coastal Indian archaeological site in Brooklin in 1974, seems to indicate they did. *Photo courtesy of Maine State Museum.*

Maine's first European settlers were a band of eighty Frenchmen, led by Sieur de Monts and Samuel de Champlain. They landed on St. Croix Island in the St. Croix River (notable for having the highest tides in the continental U.S.) in late June of 1604. The area was part of the region known as La Cadie, today called Acadia. After a dreadful winter

HISTORIC MAINE FIRSTS

1604   The French explorers who settled on St. Croix Island near Calais, produce the country's first regularly issued newspaper, *The Master William*.

1604   This same hardy band stages the first Christmas revelries—complete with wine and feasting—in North America.

1620   The first water-powered factory in the United States is built on the Salmon Falls River in South Berwick.

1641   York becomes America's first chartered city (although Mainers hate to admit it was part of Massachusetts at the time).

1775   First naval battle of the Revolutionary War occurs when Machias rebels capture the British schooner *Margaretta*.

1851   Maine becomes the first state to prohibit the sale of all alcoholic beverages.

1853   Isaac Winslow, a sailor, is the first to pack canned corn.

1905   The Pastime, the first movie theater in the country built exclusively for the presentation of moving pictures, opens in Brunswick.

1948   Margaret Chase Smith, of Skowhegan, becomes the first woman to be elected to the U.S. Senate.

during which nearly half of the party perished, the Frenchmen pulled up stakes and headed to a more hospitable climate—Nova Scotia.

Throughout the seventeenth century, explorers came and went, including some of the more famous names from New England history, like captains John Smith and Miles Standish. Smith landed on Monhegan Island in Muscongus Bay in 1614. He made Monhegan his home base for several years, and penned a bestseller about the region's attributes. Smith was the first to refer to Maine and the environs as New England rather than New Virginia, as it was first designated.

Soon the wild mainland bordered by islands came to be known simply as "Maine," and no one has been able to definitively say where the name came from. Some suggest it was derived from the term "mainland," others that it came from a French province. Although few Europeans lived here, the

The craggy cliffs of Monhegan have changed little over the years. The photo above, from the collection of the late Frank Claes, depicts men seining for fish in 1926. Nearly eighty years later, a group of lobstermen head past the same spot. *Both photos courtesy of the Island Institute.*

region was carved into huge tracts of land that were granted to wealthy English noblemen by the King. These land grants remained virtually unpopulated until the mid-1600s, when the successful Massachusetts Bay Colony began expanding, first into New Hampshire, and then northward into the "Province of Maine." In 1641, York, located on Maine's southern coast, became the first chartered city in America.

The hardy families who cleared the land, fished the sea and lakes, and began new lives in Maine were technically part of the colony—and later, state—of Massachusetts. From the beginning, though, their lifestyles and attitudes exhibited the independent spirit that is still strong in Maine. Native Americans, lumberjacks, mill owners, ice cutters, sea captains, fishermen—their colorful stories unfold in museums throughout the state (see Chapter 8).

Maine remained part of the Commonwealth of Massachusetts until 1820, when papers were signed in Freeport to make it into a separate state. The twenty-third state, Maine came into the Union as part of the historic Missouri Compromise, a turning point in the nation's ongoing debate over slavery. (The "compromise" provided that Maine would be admitted as a free state, balanced by Missouri as a slave state.)

Statehood marked the beginning of another chapter in Maine's history, a story as rich and colorful as a prize-winning blueberry pie. To savor more than this small slice, try historian Neil Rolde's highly readable history, *Maine: A Narrative History*, published by Tilbury House Publishers, of Gardiner, Maine.

A Quick Tour of the State

Maine is divided into sixteen counties. Although the county system is not as significant as town government, a glance at these counties, each of which has a distinct personality, is a good way to learn what's where. To best understand the state—and to get where you're going—you'll need a dependable map. The DeLorme Company's atlases, maps, and guides are known throughout the world for their reliability and quality—many Mainers consider them indispensable, especially the *Maine Atlas and Gazetteer*. Besides showing Maine in painstaking detail, down to the last logging road, the atlas is chock-full of information, from driving distances to state parks and canoe routes. It's available throughout the state at bookstores, supermarkets, and sporting-goods stores, or directly from the Yarmouth company at (800) 452-5931. Drop by their headquarters and see the massive globe *Eartha* or visit their website at www.delorme.com for more information.

ANDROSCOGGIN COUNTY

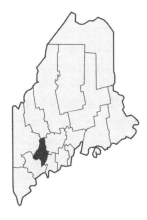

This south-central county of 105,259 residents is named for the state's third-largest river. Although its waters were once so toxic that the river was said to glow in places, the Androscoggin is now the healthiest it has been in a century and is a prime spot for kayak and canoe enthusiasts, some of whom paddle in the Great Falls Canoe Race held each June.

The Androscoggin winds through the county's two biggest cities, Lewiston, home of Bates College, and Auburn. The friendly burghs are so entwined they share two nicknames—"L-A" and "the Twin Cities"—and they rival Portland in their combined size and economic importance. Auburn is a city of about 23,000 people, while 35,700 or so folks call Lewiston home.

Lewiston and Auburn are busy centers of commerce and cultural activities, favored by many companies because of their prime location, which is nearly smack in the middle of the most populous part of Maine. Once an industrial area full of mills and factories, which attracted a large French-Canadian population, the pair enjoyed a great rebirth in the late nineties, retrofitting office centers into these old mills and attracting new businesses of all sorts. Though they are bustling, the Twin Cities are ringed with bucolic villages, among them Leeds (population 2,000), Poland (4,800), and Turner (4,700), and they are only an hour or so from the heart of the western mountains. Androscoggin County is also dotted with crystal-clear lakes, ponds, rivers, and brooks, including Lake Auburn. Nearby Lost Valley is a popular ski area once the snow flies.

AROOSTOOK COUNTY

Maine's largest and northernmost county is unspoiled and unpretentious. Jutting up into the Canadian provinces of New Brunswick and Quebec, this

beautiful, rolling area is often called simply "the County" due to its vast size. Lumber barons and lumberjacks are the stuff of local legends, and towering timber still stretches for miles in the western and northern parts. More than two thousand lakes, rivers, and streams (including the legendary Allagash Wilderness Waterway) dot the countryside, home to scores of old-fashioned fishing and hunting camps. (Some are so remote that float planes or snow-mobiles are the only way in.) The rest of the County has an almost Midwestern feel, with miles and miles of agricultural fields, most of them devoted to potatoes—a breathtaking sight when in bloom. During the fall harvest, schools are closed for three weeks so children can help dig for spuds.

Picturesque and remote, Aroostook is referred to (even by Mainers) as "the other Maine." It seems almost untouched by the faster pace of life to its south. The population has declined somewhat due to a lack of jobs, a condition the state's Northern Maine Development Commission is working hard to improve, but the County is as real and unspoiled as Maine gets.

Major cities in Aroostook include Presque Isle, home to about 9,500 residents, a branch of the University of Maine, a shopping mall that is popular with Canadians, and a neat old downtown. With a population of 8,000 or so, Caribou is another hub, located on the shores of the Aroostook River. Madawaska (a Maliseet Indian word meaning "land of the porcupine") is the

Built in 1902, Houlton's Cleveland House is a blend of Queen Anne, shingle, and colonial revival styles. It was the residence of Edward L. Cleveland, one of Aroostook County's leading potato merchants. *Photo courtesy of Maine Historic Preservation Commission.*

northernmost town in Maine and a major port of Canadian entry, with approximately 4,300 residents. Other communities in the region, most of them potato-powered, include Fort Kent (home to 3,800 and another branch of the University of Maine) and Fort Fairfield (population 3,400). Houlton is the county's oldest community and the seat of government, with more than 6,000 residents. A number of its beautiful, rambling old homes and a whole section of the brick downtown are on the National Register of Historic Places.

CUMBERLAND COUNTY

The most populous county, at 273,505, Cumberland contains the cities of Portland, South Portland, and Westbrook, and it is the fastest-growing area in Maine.

With a population of 64,000, Portland is big enough to offer a wealth of cultural and recreational activities, yet still be of a size where folks know one another. A bustling haunt for locals and tourists alike is the Old Port, a quaint section of shops, restaurants, and offices by the waterfront, with Victorian brick buildings, wide sidewalks, and narrow cobbled streets.

Casco Bay wraps around the city, dotted by the Calendar Islands, which were named in the 1600s by Captain John Smith, who marveled, "there are as many islands as there are days in the year." (He was off slightly—there are only 136.) The city's waterfront bustles with activity. Lobstermen and fishermen off-load their catch, among the biggest in New England, and cruise ships and pleasure craft dock at the Maine State Pier and Long Wharf.

The major island closest to Portland is 720-acre Peaks, home to a year-round population of about 1,500. Chebeague Island is the largest island in Casco Bay, supporting a year-round population of 400. Both have the remoteness and romance associated with islands, but are within commuting distance of the city.

South Portland, one of Maine's largest cities in its own right, is home to the Portland Jetport and the Maine Mall, the state's largest retail area, full of big chain stores. Classic New England villages and wide sandy beaches surround both South Portland and Portland. The residential towns of Cape Elizabeth (more than 9,000 people), Scarborough (16,900), North Yarmouth (3,200), Falmouth (10,300), and Cumberland (7,000) are still fairly rural, but the pace of new home construction is brisk. Farther up the coast is Freeport, home of the renowned sporting-goods retailer L.L. Bean, as well as numerous factory outlets, restaurants, inns, and 7,800 residents. Brunswick, a community of more than 21,000 people, has a college-town atmosphere thanks to historic Bowdoin College, but it also is the site of a major military base, the Brunswick Naval Air Station (which has been slated for closure by 2010).

Inland, Sebago Lake is the second-largest in Maine and the source of much of southern Maine's drinking water. Ringed with camps, motels, and resorts, Sebago is enjoyed year-round by residents of the neighboring towns of Windham (14,000), Raymond (4,300), Naples (3,200), Bridgton (4,800), and Standish (9,285). These small towns are rapidly developing, too, and are host to thousands and thousands of summer visitors.

FRANKLIN COUNTY

Franklin County rises from the central upland portion of Maine to a more mountainous region in the north. In population, Franklin is one of the state's smaller counties—about 28,000 people living in twenty-two towns and plantations. There are no cities in Franklin County, and Farmington, a town of 7,883 people with a University of Maine campus, is the county's shiretown and commercial hub. The University of Maine at Farmington was Maine's first public institution of higher education, and was recently chosen one of the top public liberal arts colleges in the nation by *U.S. News and World Report*. Known for its brick downtown and quick access to the woods, Farmington is also enjoying a quiet renaissance as a retirement center.

Beautiful and unspoiled, Franklin County is an important center for tourism. Here you'll find many outdoor recreational areas, including the Carrabassett Valley, home of Sugarloaf/USA, a popular ski mountain; Saddleback Mountain, another popular skiing destination in Rangeley; the Bigelow mountains, and more than a hundred lakes and ponds, including those in the magnificent Rangeley Lakes region. Franklin County straddles two major watersheds, with the Dead, Carrabassett, and Sandy rivers draining into the Kennebec River, and the Rangeley Lakes pouring westward into the Androscoggin. Rangeley Lake alone is 149 feet deep. The town of Rangeley is a nifty place, with a bustling downtown, remarkable mountain vistas, and easy access to the lakes. It's easy to understand why it was one of Maine's earliest resort areas.

Towns in Franklin County include Wilton, population about 4,000—home of the only fiddlehead canning factory in the country as well as lovely Wilson Lake—and Weld, a small community of 500 or so, site of eight-mile-long Webb Lake and stunning Mount Blue State Park, where the peaks climb and the water is clear.

HANCOCK COUNTY

The resort town of Bar Harbor (year-round population about 4,800) and extraordinarily popular Acadia National Park are the best-known features of Hancock County—between them the pair sees more than three million visitors a year. Bar Harbor has all the inns, shops, and restaurants one would expect of a national-park gateway, and it's also home to a highly regarded environmental school, the College of the Atlantic.

Hancock County's Mount Desert Island (pronounced as either "desert" or "dessert") contains most of Acadia, the oldest national park east of the Mississippi River. Cadillac Mountain, the tallest peak on the eastern seaboard, dominates the island's eastern side. If you explore south from Ellsworth to Deer Isle, you'll find the picturesque seaside towns of Blue Hill (population 2,300), Brooklin (900), and Stonington (1,200), as well as Castine (1,300), home of Maine Maritime Academy and one of the most beautiful villages in the state.

The county is named for John Hancock, the first governor of Massachusetts, who wrote the largest signature on the Declaration of

Sand Beach, a popular site in Acadia National Park, as seen from the Beehive, one of the park's many hiking trails. *Photo by Nate Doudera.*

Independence. Hancock's largest city is Ellsworth, which has approximately 6,300 year-round residents, a pretty, old downtown, and a long stretch of strip malls. Tiny Frenchboro, on Long Island, is Hancock's smallest town, with—at last count—43 hardy souls.

KENNEBEC COUNTY

Maine's capital city, Augusta, straddles the banks of the river for which this county is named. Once a trading post for the Pilgrims, Augusta is today a city of 20,000 or so, and provides a wealth of cultural and recreational activities as well as the workings of Maine's government. Nearby are the charming cities of Gardiner (6,100) and Hallowell (2,400) as well as the towns of Farmingdale (2,800) and Monmouth (3,700). The Belgrade and Winthrop lakes regions are popular residential and recreational areas.

In addition to the mighty Kennebec River, Kennebec County is home to scores of lakes and ponds, including the county's largest, eight-mile-long China Lake. Not far away is the city of Waterville, population 16,000, and home to Colby College, one of the country's top private liberal arts institutions.

KNOX COUNTY

Established in 1860, Maine's youngest county is named for General Henry Knox, George Washington's Chief of Artillery during the American Revolution and, later, His Secretary of War. A replica of General Knox's mansion, Montpelier, stands in the coastal town of Thomaston (population about 3,700). The largest city is Rockland, an eclectic mix of working waterfront and artsy downtown, which is currently enjoying great prosperity thanks to the Farnsworth Art Museum, one of the nation's best small museums. Rockland is home to about 8,000 people. In recent years this part of Maine's midcoast region has experienced growth due to the major expansion of the credit card bank MBNA, and then uncertainty as the company first downsized and then was sold to Bank of America.

Several communities in Knox County, including Rockland, Rockport (population 3,000), and Owls Head, flank Penobscot Bay, world renowned for its fine sailing. The Camden Hills, a ridge of low mountains that stretch along the coast, offer sweeping views of Penobscot Bay and its 200-odd islands. Snuggled between the mountains and the sea is the town of Camden, a vacation hotspot.

Knox County is a mix of bustling tourist towns, quiet fishing villages, rural inland communities, and hundreds of islands—some of them inhabited year-round. North Haven and Vinalhaven, known together as the Fox Islands, are both serviced by ferries from Rockland. A genuine working island, Vinalhaven has approximately 1,300 residents, while the more genteel North Haven has about 300. Matinicus, about twenty miles offshore from Rockland, is Maine's most remote inhabited island, with a year-round population of about 50.

LINCOLN COUNTY

Most people think this county is named for our country's sixteenth president, but actually it is a tribute to Thomas Pownal, a Massachusetts governor whose home was Lincoln, England. Lincoln County is home to approximately 30,000 Mainers and is a mix of coastal and inland towns and offshore islands such as the artist colony of Monhegan.

Lincoln County contains no cities, and the area's largest town is Waldoboro, with a population of about 5,000. Waldoboro was settled around 1740 by German families who were brought to America by General Samuel Waldo. Wiscasset (accent on the second syllable) is the next largest community, with about 3,000 residents. This town bills itself as "the prettiest village in Maine," and it is indeed a charming place of fine architecture, nestled alongside the Sheepscot River. Other communities in Lincoln County include Boothbay (population 2,800), well-known resort Boothbay Harbor (2,300), and Newcastle (1,700). Damariscotta (1,800), located between the ocean and lovely Damariscotta Lake, is a bustling place during the warmer months and has seen an influx of retirees in recent years.

Monhegan, reached by ferry from Port Clyde, New Harbor, or Boothbay, is probably Maine's most famous island, thanks to the work of such internationally known artists as Rockwell Kent, Edward Hopper, and Jamie Wyeth. Located about ten miles out to sea, Monhegan is less than a mile wide and about two miles long, yet seventeen miles of trails wind around its nature preserves and spectacular cliffs, including the legendary Cathedral Woods. The island has a year-round population of about 75 and no automobile traffic.

OXFORD COUNTY

Oxford County sits smack in the middle of Maine's western mountains, and part of the White Mountain National Forest is located in this region, as are lovely lakes, ski areas, and resorts that draw tourists year-round. Bethel, called the classic New England village by many, is nestled in the Oxford Hills, along the Androscoggin River. About 2,500 people live in Bethel's

pretty old homes and farms. Close by is the
Sunday River Ski Resort and the Sunday River
Bridge, one of the most photographed covered
bridges in the state. The foreign-sounding
Maine towns of Norway (4,900), Mexico
(3,300), Denmark (900), Sweden (240), and
Paris (4,600) are all located in Oxford County.

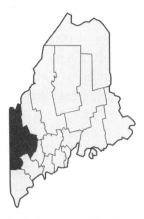

Rumford, with a population of nearly
7,000, is the largest community in Oxford
County and the home of Mead Publishing Paper
Division, a massive paper mill. Rumford has a
97-bed community hospital, as well as the small Black Mountain Ski Area.
Rumford and nearby Mexico are part of the scenic River Valley, so named because it is where the Androscoggin and Swift rivers converge.

PENOBSCOT COUNTY

Penobscot County was named for the mighty
river that meanders through the region. One of
Maine's prime whitewater rafting areas is on the
river's west branch. Also situated along the river
is one of the state's largest cities—Bangor.

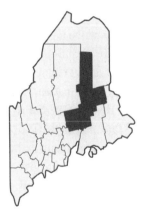

Once known only for its colorful history as
a logging town (a thirty-one-foot statue of Paul
Bunyan welcomes visitors), Bangor today is a
city of 31,000 residents and boasts a lively arts
scene, state-of-the-art health care facilities (in-
cluding Eastern Maine Medical Center), and a growing importance in foreign
trade and travel thanks to Bangor International Airport. It is home to the
Bangor Auditorium—a 6,000-seat hall hosting everything from concerts to
garden shows—as well as the Bangor Civic Center and the Bangor
Fairgrounds.

Bordering Bangor is Orono, population 9,200, home to the main campus
of the University of Maine. The University is a city within itself, comprising
more than 8,000 acres and 158 buildings, and featuring the Maine Center for
the Arts, a concert hall that brings many national acts to the area.

The working city of Brewer (8,684 inhabitants) and the charming riverside town of Hampden (6,200) are nearby communities, as is the city of Old Town (8,000), famous for its finely crafted Old Town Canoes. Millinocket (population 6,600) is located about seventy miles up the Penobscot from Bangor, at the northern end of the county. Known for its huge paper mill, it's also the gateway to the extraordinary wilderness area called Baxter State Park.

PISCATAQUIS COUNTY

Piscataquis County takes its name from the Abnaki term meaning "at the river branch," and it is Maine's third-largest county. Within its boundaries are 200,000-acre Baxter State Park, as well as Maine's highest mountain, Mount Katahdin. The park was a gift to the people of Maine by Governor Percival Baxter, who stipulated that it be kept "forever wild." Excellent fishing, mountain climbing, and hiking are found on its 175 miles of trails. Piscataquis County also contains much of the Allagash Wilderness Waterway, a nationally known canoe route.

Heavily forested, with a low population density, Piscataquis has about 18,000 residents. The town of Dover-Foxcroft, with 4,272 people, is the largest community and a business center for the surrounding area. A pretty town of graceful old homes, it is situated on the Piscataquis River. Greenville, population 1,800, is on the bank of 75,000-acre Moosehead

The bold hump of Mount Kineo, rising 1798 feet above the shore of Moosehead Lake, has a stark beauty in the winter. *Photo by Victoria Doudera.*

Lake, the biggest lake contained in one state this side of the Mississippi. The town is a wilderness outpost, known for moose and four-season outdoor recreation. A spectacular site at Moosehead is majestic Mt. Kineo, which rises out of the water and forming a sheer 700-foot cliff.

SAGADAHOC COUNTY

With only 257 square miles, this is Maine's smallest county. Bath, located along the Kennebec River, is Sagadahoc's largest city, with a population of 10,000. Bath has been a shipbuilding center since the eighteenth century, and the tradition continues today at Bath Iron Works, where massive ships are constructed for the Navy. Bath boasts handsome homes and a brick downtown, as well as the Maine Maritime Museum.

Topsham, with about 9,000 residents, is the next-largest community, as well as the area's fastest-growing town. The towns of Bowdoin (2,700) and Bowdoinham (2,500) are bucolic villages near massive Merrymeeting Bay, where six rivers meet and where migrating ducks and geese rest en route to and from warmer climes. Woolwich (2,800) is a rural town located across the Kennebec from Bath.

SOMERSET COUNTY

The land area of Somerset county—3,903 square miles—makes it Maine's

second-largest. Extending from the Canadian border all the way to Fairfield in central Maine, the area is almost 90 percent forested, and borders Moosehead Lake and the Allagash Wilderness Waterway. Flagstaff Lake, as well as much of the Dead River, a popular rafting spot, are located in Somerset County.

Skowhegan is the largest community, with a population of 8,800. The home of the late Margaret Chase Smith, the first woman to serve in both the U.S. House and Senate,

Skowhegan is also the site of one of Maine's largest agricultural fairs and a prestigious school of painting. Fairfield (6,700), Pittsfield (4,100), and Madison (4,600) are other sizable towns in Somerset County. The Forks and Caratunk, tiny villages both, are at the epicenter of Maine's whitewater rafting industry.

WALDO COUNTY

Belfast (population about 6,500) is the largest community in Waldo County, and its only city. Once known more for its chicken-processing plants than its lovely harbor, Belfast today is a mix of lively downtown shops, businesses, and elegant homes from the 1800s. Deemed "culturally cool" in *USA Today*, the city is home to a number of artists, has a theater troupe, a huge health-food co-op, a dance studio, and a movie theater that shows art films.

Waldo County's coastal towns include Lincolnville (2,000) and Searsport (2,700), famous for its sea-captain's homes. Several of its small inland communities bear patriotic names: Liberty (804), Freedom (699), and Unity (about 2,000). Waldo County has grown in recent years, thanks to the expansion of credit-card giant MBNA (now Bank of America) and smaller local heroes such as Moss, Inc. There is a small but excellent hospital—Waldo County General, in Belfast. Islesboro (population 600) is home to a tony island community where actor John Travolta has a summer place.

The new $84 million Penobscot Narrows Bridge and Observatory links Prospect and Verona Island. The name was chosen after the original moniker, "Downeast Gateway Bridge," created an uproar in eastern Waldo County towns. *Photo by Victoria Doudera.*

WASHINGTON COUNTY

The easternmost county in the nation, Washington is nicknamed "The Sunrise County" because many argue that the sun hits here first as it wakes up the United States. A trip through this part of Maine reveals rocky and sandy beaches, dramatic oceanside cliffs, the highest tides in the country, and acres and acres of windswept blueberry barrens, home to Maine's thriving lowbush-blueberry industry. Nature preserves dot the landscape: Petit Manan in Steuben, Great Wass Island in Beals, Roque Bluffs State Park, near Machias, Cobscook Bay State Park in Dennysville, and Moosehorn National Wildlife Refuge, near Calais—all set before miles and miles of glorious oceanfront.

This is the quietest coastal region in Maine, a place where tradition still reigns and where tourism is welcome but not counted upon. Fishing and blueberrying are the major industries. The primary city is Calais (pronounced CAL-us), which has about 4,000 residents and is connected by a bridge to St. Stephen, New Brunswick. Eastport (population about 2,000) is the easternmost city in the United States, and it has a lovely and historic brick downtown. Because of its situation on Moose Island, just about every house in Eastport has a fantastic view of Passamaquoddy Bay. Other important towns in the county are Lubec (2,000) and Machias (2,500), home to a branch of the University of Maine.

YORK COUNTY

Maine's oldest and most southerly county was created in 1652 as Yorkshire Province. This stretch of Maine is famous for its broad white beaches and picturesque New England towns. York County's coast is the home of the famed villages of Kennebunkport (population 3,700) and Ogunquit (1,200), where tourists flock by the thousands in the summer. From Kittery (9,500) in the south, known for its outlet shop-

47

ping, to Old Orchard Beach (8,800) in the north, a beachfront boardwalk community famous for its honky-tonk atmosphere, the southern Maine coast is popular both with vacationers and new Mainers, many of whom commute to Portland, Portsmouth, New Hampshire, or even Boston for jobs. Some of Maine's wealthiest communities are in York County, as well as many of the fastest-growing towns.

The neighboring cities of Biddeford and Saco (with populations of 20,000 and 16,800 respectively) together make up York County's largest center of commerce. The towns of Sanford (20,000) and Wells (9,400) are other notable spots.

Politics

STATE GOVERNMENT

Like many states, Maine has three governing branches: executive, legislative, and judiciary. The head of the executive branch is the governor, elected to a term of four years. The governor can serve no more than two consecutive terms, and the state does not have a lieutenant governor. If the governor dies or becomes unable to govern, the succession passes to the president of the senate and next to the speaker of the house.

The Maine legislature is composed of the house of representatives and the senate. The Maine House of Representatives consists of 151 members (one of the largest in the country), plus two nonvoting members representing the Penobscot Nation and the Passamaquoddy Tribe. Each house member represents a district of approximately 8,132 people.

The Maine Senate is the upper chamber and serves as the final confirming body of all bills passed before they are sent to the governor. There are thirty-five senators, and at this writing, nineteen are Maine natives and sixteen

Maine's capitol building was constructed in 1910.
Photo courtesy of Maine Office of Tourism.

are women. Maine ranks second in the nation for the percentage of women elected to the senate (45 percent—Washington state has 46.9 percent) and is the only state to have three women holding senate leadership positions during the same session.

Elected to two-year terms, the legislators pass the laws, confirm judges, and choose four constitutional officers, who also serve two-year terms: attorney general, secretary of state, state treasurer, and state auditor. The effect of this procedure is to allow the majority party to control the constitutional offices.

Maine is one of three states with a joint standing budget committee system. The state budget must receive a two-thirds vote of the legislature, and the governor does not possess line-item-veto power.

The judicial branch is headed by the Supreme Judicial Court, with a chief justice and six associate justices to handle appeals from lower courts. Criminal and court cases requiring a trial by jury are heard by the Superior Court, while civil actions, traffic infractions, juvenile cases, and small claims are heard in Maine's thirty-three district courts. Each county has a probate court to handle wills, estates, adoptions, and appointment of guardians. Probate in Maine, unlike in other states, is considered a simple, prompt, and relatively inexpensive process.

LOCAL GOVERNMENT

Government in Maine, as in much of New England, has a strong local bias, with the town unit at its foundation. Towns (currently there are 424) must be incorporated, requiring a legislative act but not a charter. Towns are governed by the quintessential example of direct democracy—the annual town meeting and elected officials called selectmen. Since 1970, towns in Maine have operated under home rule, which means they may make many of their own decisions without going before the state legislature.

Maine's cities, numbering twenty-two, must be chartered by the legislature. All have a representative form of government called the city council. Population size doesn't always indicate city or town status. Eastport, in Washington County, for example, is a city of about 2,000 citizens, while Brunswick, with a population of more than 20,000, is a town.

In addition to cities and towns, Maine still has examples of plantations, an archaic form of local government used centuries ago in Massachusetts.

Plantations are mini-towns, usually populated by fewer than one hundred people, incorporated by the commissioners of the county in which they are located. Although Maine's fifty-one plantations have fewer rights than do towns, and do not operate under home rule, they are governed in much the same way, with an annual meeting and elected officials called assessors. Monhegan Island is probably the best known of Maine's plantations.

In addition to plantations, Maine has another unique twist: 416 unorganized townships. Almost half the state's land area falls in this category. These very sparsely populated townships have no local government. They are supervised and taxed directly by the state. Some have regular names—Attean Township, Chain of Ponds Township—but many are identified only by their location in a surveyor's grid: T5 R17 or T3 R12, for example.

Maine's sixteen counties are governed by commissioners who are elected by the people. County budgets are determined by the legislature. In some states, county government is very powerful, but this isn't really true in Maine. Counties are primarily responsible for running jails and sheriffs' departments, and county offices house registries of probate and deeds.

"Democracy is alive and well and living in Maine," says Carole Brand. "Town meetings, church meetings, local meetings are all held and are well attended to decide even the smallest issues. Should we buy a new fire engine? The whole town weighs in. Should we paint the church steeple? Let's have a congregational meeting to vote. As a result, locals are far better informed about local, state, and national issues, and politicians stay very close to their constituents."

POLITICAL PARTIES

The independent Maine spirit is especially apparent at the voting booth, where people tend to vote their conscience rather than their party affiliation. In the past twenty-five years, Maine has had two independent governors: James Longley, elected in 1974, and Angus S. King, Jr., elected to a first term in 1994 and reelected in 1998 by one of the largest margins in Maine's history.

The newest political development is the legitimization of two additional political parties. Thanks to a recent state law, The Green Independent and Reform parties are now listed on state income tax forms for donations, as well as on voter registration applications. These parties may also join with Maine

Democrats and Republicans in presidential primaries and other elections.

Taxes

"Maine's low tax base means a high tax burden," observes Gary Swanson, who moved here with his family from Oakland, California, in 1998. Most Mainers agree, and various forms of tax reform are in the works. Spending limits for state government and caps on municipal and county tax levies were approved by the Legislature in 2006; a Taxpayer Bill of Rights appeared on the November 2006 ballot but was defeated by referendum.

With regard to state and local taxes, Mainers shoulder a heavy load. According to The Tax Foundation, residents of Maine bear the highest state and local tax burden in the country, largely due to high property taxes, the lion's share of which go to pay for public schools. The U.S. Commerce Department reports that, in relative terms, Mainers pay the fourth-heaviest property levy in the country, averaging fifty-two dollars in property tax for every one thousand dollars earned.

PROFILE

Jay Culberth and Lynn Johnson moved to Maine from Minnesota and Ohio, respectively. They lived in Portland for a few years before moving to Poland in 1998. "We wanted to live on a mountain or lake, and our real-estate agent found us a place on a lovely little pond," Lynn explains. "The house is a fishing shack from 1940, and it sits on a peninsula. We love watching the water and the wildlife."

Jay works for the American Skiing Company in Bethel and is also a member of Poland's planning board. Lynn is employed by Idexx Corp., a biotechnology firm in Westbrook. Androscoggin County has worked out well for their respective commutes. "Poland is real small-town living," says Lynn. "It's one of those towns where, if you blink, you've missed it. We appreciate the quiet and the friendly townspeople and neighbors. We absolutely love living here."

In an effort to soften the tax blow, Maine has trimmed its sales tax (in July 2000 the rate dropped from 5.5 percent to 5 percent), increased personal exemptions on the state income tax, and offered property tax breaks to homeowners. A new program that reimburses businesses for property taxes on new equipment saved Mainers about $42 million in 1998. Tax reformers believe more relief is in sight.

But tax bites depend on many factors, including income brackets and which taxes are considered. A recent Citizens for Tax Justice analysis suggests that for middle income Maine people, state and local taxes are actually the same or lower than the national average. Their analysis places greater weight on Maine's progressive income tax structure, which requires wealthy people to pay more here than in other states.

According to a U.S. Census survey, residents paid $2,223 on average in state taxes in 2005, ranking Maine 19th nationwide. Governor Baldacci has said that Maine's stigma as a highly taxed state must be refuted. Depending on how one looks at the numbers, some Mainers agree.

One reason for high local taxes is that traditionally Mainers have balked at consolidation of services on the county model, preferring instead a type of government that is close to the people. However, this means that individual towns are expected to provide a high level of services, including police and fire protection, road maintenance, and public assistance.

Tax burdens are relative, depending on your point of reference. Retirees Bill and Allie Lou Richardson, of Islesboro, find Maine's taxes significantly lower than what they paid in New York. Ruth Hohfeld, who moved from California, says she continues to compare her property taxes to California private-school fees and feels blessed.

The next section explains how some of Maine's state taxes break down. For more information, call the Maine Revenue Service at 207-626-8475, or try its website at www.maine.gov/revenue.

PROPERTY TAXES

All real estate and personal property of Maine residents is subject to local and, if authorized by the legislature, state property taxes. Local property taxes, based upon assessed valuation, are assessed, levied, and collected by municipalities. Much attention has been focused on the burden of property taxes in Maine. Calls for legislative action, citizen referenda, consideration of tax and spending caps, and broader discussions of tax fairness and tax reform, are all attempts at addressing this heavy load. It seems you can't go anywhere without property tax reform coming up as a major topic of debate.

According to the Maine Center for Economic Policy (www.mecep.org), the median household in Maine pays about 4 percent of their income in property taxes, yet the variability in property tax burdens across households is considerable. Roughly one third of Maine homeowners pay less than 3 percent of their income in property taxes; about a third pay between 3 and 6 percent of their income; and a third pay more than 6 percent. At the extreme, about 11 percent of households pay between 10 and 20 percent of their income in property taxes; and 7 percent pay more than 20 percent of their income. Tools such as the Maine circuit breaker program, also known as the Property Tax and Rent Refund Program, make refunds available to most resident homeowners who are paying more than 4 percent of their income in property taxes. (Renters who pay more than 20% of their income may receive refunds as well.) Homestead and veteran's exemption programs, administered by the state, are also available to reduce property taxes for those who qualify.

The Homestead Exemption program provides a measure of relief for certain individuals that have owned homestead property in Maine for at least 12 months and make the property they occupy on April 1 their permanent residence. Property owners receive an exemption of $13,000 on the assessed value of their home. A veteran exemption of $5,000 is available to those who served during a recognized war period, are 62 years of age or older, are receiving 100% disability as a veteran, or became 100% disabled while serving. Exemptions are also available for paraplegic veterans and persons who are legally blind.

INDIVIDUAL INCOME TAX

Maine has a graduated individual income tax rate, similar to the federal tax structure. Tax rates are 2 percent, 4.5 percent, 7 percent, and 8.5 percent. The applicable rate depends on marginal income. For example, a single taxpayer with $20,000 of taxable income would pay 2 percent on the first $4,150; 4.5 percent on the next $4,100, 7 percent on the following $8,250, and 8.5 percent on the final $3,500 of taxable income.

For 2006, the personal exemption amount was $2,850; and standard deduction amounts began at $4,850 for single filers and $8,150 for married joint filers. Additional amounts are allowed for taxpayers over age sixty-five.

Income tax revenues go into the state's general fund.

CORPORATE INCOME TAX

Maine imposes an income tax on all entities organized as corporations (except S corporations) that have Maine-source income. The corporate income tax is graduated, with rates ranging from 3.5% (for income up to $25,000) to 8.93% (for income in excess of $250,000). A number of tax-credit programs have been established to spur investment, including the High Technology Credit, the Research and Development Expense Super Credit, and the Maine Seed Capital/Venture Capital Tax Credits.

REAL ESTATE TRANSFER TAX

A real estate transfer tax is imposed on both the seller and buyer at the rate of $1.10 per $500 of property, including the value of any mortgage or other encumbrance. Half of the money raised benefits the state's general fund, the rest goes to the county in which the sale occurred.

REAL ESTATE WITHHOLDING TAX

Non-Maine residents who sell property located in Maine are subject to a withholding from the total sale price of the property, to be used as an estimated tax payment towards any Maine tax liability on the gain realized from the sale. The buyer of the property will withhold and remit this money to Maine Revenue Services, and the amount to be withheld is equal to 2.5% of the sale price.

Some individuals may be eligible for an exemption or reduction of this payment, and can apply using a form submitted at least five business days prior to the closing.

INHERITANCE AND ESTATE TAXES

There is no inheritance tax in Maine. Maine imposes a tax on estates (gross estate plus prior taxable gifts) valued at $1,000,000 or more for all decedents with property taxable to Maine. The amount of tax due will normally correspond to the proportion of property located in Maine, compared to all property of the estate. This tax is applied even if there is no federal estate tax. For those estates that are below the taxable threshold and that have real or tangible personal property in Maine, you may obtain a lien release for that property.

MOTOR VEHICLE EXCISE TAX

"The tax on our cars was an unpleasant surprise," recalls Jan Njaa, who moved to Belfast from Chicago in June 1999.

Maine's motor vehicle excise tax is based on the manufacturer's list price of a vehicle, including all options, at a rate ranging from 24 mils ($24 per $1,000 in value) for new vehicles, down to 4 mils ($4 per $1,000) for older models. The tax base is the purchase price in the original year of title, applying to motor vehicles, aircraft, camper trailers, truck campers, and mobile homes used on public roads. For example, the owner of a three-year-old car with a manufacturer's suggested retail price of $19,500 would pay at the .0135 mil rate, or $263.25. This tax is paid prior to registering your vehicle every year at your local town office. The town that collects the excise tax can use it as revenue. Monies from this tax go towards the annual town budget and are typically spent on local road maintenance, construction, and repair.

GASOLINE EXCISE TAX

Mainers pay a tax of 27.4 cents a gallon on gasoline and 27 cents a gallon on diesel fuel. Monies raised go to the highway and general funds.

SALES TAX

The general sales tax was reduced to 5 percent from 5.5 percent in 2000. On lodging and prepared food the tax is 7%; on short term auto rentals it is 10%. Grocery food items are not taxed.

Highest Individual Income Tax Rates

Montana	11.0	Iowa	8.98
Vermont	9.5	Maine	8.5
Dist. of Columbia	9.5	No. Carolina	8.25
California	9.3	Hawaii	8.25
Oregon	9.0	Minnesota	7.85

MAINE TAXES AT A GLANCE

Sales Taxes
- State Sales Tax: 5.0% (food and prescription drugs exempt)
- Gasoline Tax: 27.4 cents/gallon
- Diesel Fuel Tax: 27.0 cents/gallon
- Gasohol Tax: 27.4 cents/gallon
- Cigarette Tax: $2.00/pack of 20

Personal Income Taxes
- Tax Rate Range: Low–2%; High–8.5%
- Income Brackets: Lowest–$4,449; Highest–$17,700 (For joint returns, the taxes are twice the tax imposed on half the income)
- Number of Brackets: 4
- Personal Exemptions: Single–$2,850; Married–$5,700; Dependents–$2,850
- Standard Deduction: Single–$4,850; Married filing jointly–$8,150
- Additional Deductions: Single or head of household over 65–$1,150; One spouse over 65–$950; Both over 65–$1,900
- Medical/Dental Deduction: Federal amount
- Federal Income Tax Deduction: None
- Retirement Income Taxes: Social Security is exempt. $6,000 exemption for pension income, but not IRAs, minus amount of Social Security benefit. Out-of-state government pensions qualify for the $6,000 exemption.
- Retired Military Pay: Follows federal tax rules.
- Military Disability Retired Pay: Disability Portion–Length of Service Pay; Member on September 24, 1975–No tax; Not Member on September 24, 1975–Taxed, unless combat incurred. Retired Pay–Based solely on disability: Member on September 24, 1975–No tax; Not Member on September 24, 1975–Taxed, unless all pay based on disability and disability resulted from armed conflict, extra-hazardous service, simulated war, or an instrumentality of war.
- VA Disability Dependency and Indemnity Compensation: Not subject to federal or state taxes.

See the Maine Revenue Services site: www.maine.gov/revenue for more information.

3 Economy and Work Opportunies

"Just as the Red Sox proved the critics wrong,
Maine can compete and can win."

—GOVERNOR JOHN BALDACCI*

What is it like to get a job or start a business in Maine? Clay and Maggy King are massage therapists who came from Atlanta in August of 2002 hoping that their new practice would thrive. "We moved here with no hesitation or worries," says Maggy. "I suppose we should have been concerned about making a living here, but we just crossed our fingers and believed that we'd do just fine, and we have." Not everyone has the faith of the Kings, and even they admit it wasn't easy those first few years. "There were times in the beginning that we'd open the appointment book and shake our heads, but those times quickly passed. We were always very optimistic and confident that we'd be okay." Unless you are retiring here, it's likely you're asking yourself how you'll earn a living in your new state.

The Maine Economy

For hundreds of years, Maine's economic lifeblood pulsed thanks to the state's tremendous natural resources. Fishing, lumbering, farming, trapping, and shipbuilding put supper on the table for Mainers of the 18th and 19th centuries. In the late 1800s, the Industrial Revolution took hold in Maine, and mills and other manufacturing centers sprung up along the

---

*Governor John Baldacci in his State of the State Address, January 25, 2005.

state's mighty waterways and in remote northern towns. Soon shoes, clothes, textiles, paper, and other products were produced in all corners of the state. Fifty years ago, manufacturing was so important here that as many as one out of every two Mainers worked in the industry. In this economy of yesteryear, landing a job in a mill following grammar or high school ensured a fairly decent standard of living.

In the second half of the 20th century, the economic climate began once more to change. While manufacturing remained the biggest source of employment, jobs in this sector began to decrease, falling 14 percent between the early 1980s and the early 1990s. Meanwhile, the number of jobs in the service industries and retail trade began to inch upward, and soon tourism took hold as the state's number-one industry.

Despite the decline in the manufacturing sector, employment is up overall. From 2003 to 2004, Maine's overall employment grew 1.2 percent. Today, statewide employment in Maine numbers about 613,900 people, and of these the largest share—38 percent— punch their time cards in the service industry, doing such things as data processing or running a deli. About one-fourth of workers toil in the wholesale or retail trade; 5 percent in federal, state, or local government, including those in the military; 15 percent in manufacturing; 5 percent in finance, insurance, or real estate; 5 percent in construction; 5 percent in transportation or public utilities; and 1 percent in farming (including agricultural services), forestry, or fishing.

Keeping the economy strong is a challenge in a state of 1.3 million people living in an area roughly the size of the other five New England states combined. Factors that have had the most impact on Maine's economy in recent years include globalization of the marketplace, development of new technologies, the influx of women into the workforce, and an aging population.

Recessions, of course, pose special challenges, especially in rural states. Experts say Maine weathered the most recent economic downturn (which most feel ended in 2001) fairly well, and the state's economy has improved, albeit at a relatively modest pace. According to the Federal Reserve Bank of Boston, "Maine proved to be resilient in the face of recession, suffering less severe consequences than the rest of the region, so now it is enjoying milder gains." And yet those gains are pretty impressive. The Bureau of Economic Analysis reported that Maine's Gross State Product grew 10.6% between 2000 and 2004. The state regained all jobs lost and job

A MAINE SUCCESS STORY

The world's leader in the outdoor-specialty field, L.L. Bean, is headquartered in Freeport in a 109,000 square-foot Main Street store and the adjacent 17,000 square-foot L.L. Kids store. To glance around at the more than sixteen thousand items in the main store alone, amongst the more than 3.5 million customers who flock there each year, you'd be hard pressed to believe it all started with one humble shoe and one entrepreneurial Mainer.

The company was founded in 1912 by Leon Leonwood Bean, who developed the gum-soled Maine Hunting Shoe to avoid soggy feet when traipsing through the woods. Initially, his product was manufactured in one room and sold exclusively through catalogs to other hunting enthusiasts. Today, "Bean's" sells to 147 countries around the world, with annual sales totaling more than $1 billion, produces approximately fifty different catalogs each year, and has nine locations in the United States and more than a dozen retail stores in Japan. L.L. Bean employs more than ten thousand workers during the peak holiday season and is Maine's third-largest employer.

The original L.L. Bean retail store as it looked in the 1930s.
Photo courtesy of L.L. Bean, Inc.

growth is projected to continue, with the unemployment rate remaining below the national rate. Personal income increased, closing part of the gap with national figures, and the state's exports reached an all-time high. To cap off these achievements, Maine received an "A" on the Corporation for Enterprise Development's Assets and Opportunity Scorecard.

Even with these positive trends, some new Mainers find it a challenge to make a living. "We've always believed that it was important to live where and how you wanted to, and that the economic aspects of life would tend to take care of themselves if you were doing what you wanted," says David Cherry, who moved with his partner from Northern California in 2002. "In truth, had we realized just how poor (and poorly managed) the state's economic outlook was before we moved, we probably would not have come. It is extremely non-business friendly and seems to be trying to go back to the industrial 1800s rather than moving forward."

By all indications, Maine is heading forward, but the pace is slower than many would like. Job growth in Maine has outpaced both the New England region and the U.S. for the last seven years, and yet the gains are modest when compared to states such as California. There are disparities in income

Although horses have been replaced by machines, logging is a traditional occupation that remains vital to Maine's economy. *Photo courtesy Maine State Museum.*

distribution, too, and the current growth doesn't benefit all of Maine. Realities such as the closing of the Brunswick Naval Air Station, one of the state's largest employers, will have major economic and social impacts on neighboring towns and the state as a whole. As a mill worker of a previous generation might have said, Maine has its work cut out for it. But rather than confounding Mainers, these challenges have spurred them to use the Yankee ingenuity and solid work ethic for which they're famous to adapt and begin to thrive in the face of change.

The Good News

As the Maine economy recovers, new jobs are being created, and innovative new businesses are taking the state in new directions. Along with jobs, wages and production continue to climb. Other indicators of a growing economy, such as retail sales, construction contract awards, and building permits, have all risen significantly. Under the leadership of Maine's previous governor, Angus King, the state mounted an aggressive economic development strategy aimed at creating new jobs, cutting workers' compensation insurance costs, lowering electric utility rates, reforming taxes, and building a state-of-the-art telecommunications infrastructure. The impact of these achievements still resonates, and provides an excellent base upon which the current leadership is building.

Is the Maine economy a glass half full or half empty?

"Half full," writes Jack Cashman, Commissioner of the Maine Department of Economic and Community Development, on the Department's website (www.econdevmaine.com) "It's time to focus on filling it rather than dwelling on why it is not already full. We are all working toward the same vision: An economically prosperous Maine. If we work together, we will make greater progress. Let's concentrate on the many good things that are happening in our state and use those good things as a foundation upon which to build our success."

The 2006 "Measures of Growth in Focus" report, prepared by the Maine Development Foundation, says that although the economic challenges are considerable, there are reasons for optimism. For instance, Maine is on the right track, investing considerable resources in research and development. The state takes care of its citizens, as demonstrated by the high rate of health insurance coverage. On-the-job injuries have dropped consistently over the past several years, and the death rate from cardiovascular disease is coming down. Conservation and well-managed forest lands are increasing, too. "The bottom line is that the state must continue to focus its energy and resources on building its base of talent. Maine must also improve its business climate, strengthen its urban areas, and effectively manage the development of its natural environment. Through these steps, the state can position itself favorably in the new economy in which it operates."

Why Do Business in Maine

Maine in the new millennium offers many advantages to businesses, starting with Mainers themselves. Maine's people are dependable, hardworking, and willing to master new skills. Employers praise the state's customized approach in developing programs and training initiatives that meet business demands for a highly skilled, technical workforce.

For instance, in November 2004, T-Mobile USA, Inc. announced their decision to locate their newest Customer Service Center in Oakland, Maine. Although T-Mobile had considered several locations nationwide, Maine was chosen because of the quality of the workforce.

"Our customer service employees play a vital role in our company's success," said Sue Nokes, senior vice president of customer service. "That's why we selected Maine. The culture and residents of Maine are very much service oriented, which is a perfect match with T-Mobile's values. This was reinforced in our interactions with state and local government officials throughout the site selection process."

Vitally important to any company is a state's telecommunications network. Maine is considered by many to have the best in the nation, with more than 110,000 miles of fiber-optic cable and 100 percent digital phone-switching technology in place. The state's location is a boon for international trade, not only because it is coastal, making for easy shipping, but also its border with Canada, an important trading partner. Finally, the state's transportation infrastructure (roads, airports, freight lines, and ports) offers uncrowded, high-quality avenues to quickly move products. Add these advantages to a business climate that fosters risk-taking and entrepreneurial efforts, and you have a winning combination.

Maine offers business incentive programs to help spur new investments; a list of public and private capital funding programs designed to help start-up and expanding businesses; and a growing list of venture capital funding sources. (See the state's official website for more information at www.maine.gov/portal/business.)

Speaking of funding, how expensive is it to do business in Maine? According to the Milken Institute's 2005 Cost-of-Doing-Business Index (www.milkeninstitute.org), Maine offers the lowest cost of doing business in the Northeast. A decrease in the tax burden and a reduction in electricity cost by more than 40 percent when compared to the national average were cited as factors in the recently released report. Maine also ranked well below the national average for industrial and office rental costs.

In the study, Maine improved its position to the 19th most expensive state in which to do business, down from its ranking of 16th in 2004. This three-point change represents the second-greatest drop in the U.S. According to the index, Hawaii is the most expensive state in which to do business, with New York, California, Massachusetts and Connecticut rounding out the top five.

Telecommunications

It may not mesh with the state's moose-and-mountains image, but Maine boasts a new high-tech telephone system that is, according to the president of Verizon, "the best in the United States, if not the world." Completion of the fiber-optic system in autumn of 1999 linked Aroostook County with an existing system of lines in other parts of the state, assuring that phone connections across Maine are top of the line.

The one hundred thousand or so miles of fiber-optic cable in Maine's system mean more than just clear conversations with Aunt Elsie. The system is capable of carrying millions of voice, data, and video signals daily and includes 100 percent digital phone switching technology as well as self-healing technologies in the event something goes awry. In short, the $100-million investment puts Maine solidly in the forefront as a telecommunications leader. (see Chapter 11, Virtual Maine, for more information.)

According to a March 2000 report from the Federal Communications

Commission, Maine ranks second in the nation in the percentage of households with telephone service. An estimated 97.6% of Maine households have phones, well above the national average of 94%. (Delaware ranks first, with 98.2%.) Twenty-two phone companies keep connections clear and crisp, with Verizon—serving 85% of the state—the largest. Local companies, although small in comparison, are no lightweights when it comes to telecommunications. "All of Maine's phone companies, including the twenty-one independent local companies, are tied in to the inter- and intrastate fiber-optic network," says Phil Lindley of the Public Utilities Commission. "Regardless of size, they have state-of-the-art technology and, in many cases, can connect people to the Internet with a local phone call." Smaller phone companies, says Lindley, are linked to the folks they serve in more ways than one. "Local phone companies tend to be community-minded," he notes. "And since they truly know their customers, they offer exceptional customer service."

Maine is already home to a number of businesses that rely on this sophisticated and reliable telecommunications infrastructure for their call centers and communication networks. L.L. Bean, EnvisionNet, and Auto Europe all maintain large and complex call centers that serve a global customer base.

Health Care

Health care is a growing industry in Maine, and an increasingly important force in the economy as well. According to the Maine Hospital Association, health care directly accounts for sixty thousand full- and part-time jobs and up to thirty-five thousand related jobs. Indeed, the health-care industry is responsible for roughly 10 percent of all jobs in the state and 15 percent of the private sector's payroll.

Through a well-designed website (www.themrc.com), as well as more traditional methods, the Maine Hospital Association's Recruitment Center actively courts health-care providers, especially physicians. The center offers the latest information about health care opportunities and provides confidential job searches, all with the aim of attracting top-notch professionals to high-tech hospitals in Maine's pristine, low-key setting. "Maine's hospitals offer health-care professionals a special 'quality of life'," claims the website. "Our hospitals are community focused and committed to ensuring that every patient receives personal attention and high-quality care. Hospitals are located in virtually every type of environment in which you'd like to live and work. Maine's famous coastline is dotted with hospitals located a stone's throw from the ocean. Inland hospitals are in communities close to peaceful lakes, fishing, ski resorts, and hiking trails. Our largest medical centers are in small, manageable cities with an urban flavor and plenty of cultural activities." It's true, and many health-care providers find the lure irresistible.

Howard Jones practices internal and occupational medicine in the midcoast. "I went online during the summer of 1998 and made a connection with Waldo County General Hospital in Belfast. They invited me up, and when I arrived it was a beautiful August day. Everything looked like the cover of a *Down East* magazine. I liked both the hospital and the people I met. That winter, my family and I left North Carolina for Maine.

"Those of us in the medical field are fortunate, because we can live just about anywhere and make a decent living," Jones continues. "Practicing medicine in Maine is really nice. You have a different kind of relationship with patients than in other places, because you'll actually see them again in the community. There's a wide cross-section of people, and not very many managed-care companies to put a wall between you and your patients. And I think the people in Maine are hardy, healthy souls."

Biotechnology

Maine's emerging biotechnology industry is one of the fastest-growing sectors of the economy, offering more than 650 different products and services to national and international markets. According to the Biotechnology Association of Maine, a trade association representing the growing community of biotech companies, more than forty-seven hundred Mainers are employed by biotech companies, nonprofit and government laboratories, and educational institutions throughout the state. Industries as diverse as aquaculture, diagnostics, immunodiagnostics, marine science, microbiology, and pharmacology are part of this new force in the Maine economy, and its steady growth has been a focus of the state's economic planners.

That focus is paying off. Biotechnology employment in Maine has

65

Lobstering then and now. The photo below was taken in December 1999, on Monhegan Trap Day, the time when local lobstermen set out traps for the island's special winter season. *Photo by Bill MacDonald, both photos courtesy of the Island Institute.*

tripled in the last ten years, with notable non-profit institutions such as the Foundation for Blood Research and the Maine Medical Center Research Institute joining successful for-profit biomedical businesses such as IDEXX Laboratories, ViroStat, Binaxx, and PharmX. If it all seems like *Brave New World*, keep in mind that biomedical research and development has actually enjoyed a long and significant history in Maine. The Jackson Laboratory, located in Bar Harbor, is an internationally respected, non-profit biomedical research institution, founded in 1929. Today, the organization has grown to become the largest mammalian genetics research laboratory in the world. As one of eight Cancer Centers, designated by the National Cancer Institute, the Jackson Laboratory performs research to discover genetic factors related to cancer. The laboratory also offers a variety of educational programs, ranging from high school internships to a cooperative Ph.D. program with the University of Maine.

In addition to this initiative, Maine has put in place other programs to enhance the future of its biotechnology industry. Programs such as the Maine Science & Technology Action Plan and the Science & Technology Report Card initiate and evaluate the effects of science and technology on the state economy. The Maine Experimental Program to Stimulate Competitive Research (EPSCoR) fosters collaboration between the university system, local business, and the federal government to invest and influence funding in building Maine's research and development infrastructure. Its projects include the Center for Technology-Based Business Development, which promotes technology transfer.

Maine is home to several bioscience and technology incubators, such as the Maine Applied Technology Development Centers, encompassing the new 20-acre, $2.5 million Thomas M. Teague Biotechnology Center, currently under construction in Fairfield; the Loring Applied Technology Development Center in Limestone, which focuses on forestry and agriculture; and the Center for Environmental Enterprise in South Portland, which focuses on environmental technology.

Biotech experts say the main problem facing the Maine biotechnology industry today is a lack of funding. However, the state has increased its research and development funding in an effort to improve the future of its economy and encourage venture capitalists to do the same. Although Maine still falls below the national average in many indicators, current trends indicate that Maine is well-positioned to become an industry leader.

Natural Resources

Magnificent natural resources have long been the backbone of the state's economy. Fishing, hunting, rafting, skiing, snowmobiling, and forest-based manufacturing industries are all dependent on Maine's woods, waters, and wildlife. In 1996, fishing, hunting, and wildlife observation produced $1.1 billion in economic output, supported 17,680 jobs, and generated $67.7 million in state tax revenues.

Although hunting and fishing might spring to mind as Maine's top outdoor industries, wildlife-watching is actually the leader of Maine's recreation industries. In a national survey conducted by the U.S.Census, 778,000 Americans participated in wildlife-watching in Maine in 2000, compared to 164,000 who hunted and 376,000 who fished. According to chamber of commerce data, in 1996 nature observers in Maine spent $224.6 million and put 6,020 people to work, generating $111.4 million in wages.

Maine's acres of trees are the basis for the largest manufacturing industry in the state. Forest-based manufacturing (stumpage, harvesting, sawmills, pulp and paper, furniture and fixtures, and other wood products) contributed $5.2 billion in value of shipments to the econ-

Aquaculture takes many forms. Here, oysters are being graded for size using a mesh screen. *Photo by Bill MacDonald, courtesy of the Island Institute.*

68

omy in 2001, or 36% of the state's total manufacturing sales. According to the North East State Foresters Association, this industry provides employment for 21,692 people and generates a payroll of over $1 billion.

Forest-based recreation and upcountry tourism—hiking the peaks, rafting the rivers—provide employment for more than 12,000 residents and generate payrolls of $145 million. Other revenues from Maine's "Evergreen Empire" include maple syrup (112,000 gallons of the sweet stuff, valued at nearly $1.9 million), wreaths (more than one million valued at $6 million), and more than three hundred thousand Christmas trees, worth $5.25 million to Maine's economy.

Tourism

Tourism is a traditional Maine industry that is still thriving. From small inns to large resorts, trendy restaurants to wharfside lobster pounds, cruise ships to canoe rentals, many Mainers make a good living off vacationers, 70 percent of whom are out-of-staters. In terms of employment, tourism is the largest industry in Maine, with more than 122,000 jobs generated in 2003 and a payroll of $2.6 billion. And many other businesses profit indirectly

PROFILE

Dottie Paradis was born and raised in Farmington, but left the state in 1973. "My life in Massachusetts became incredibly stressful," she says, "and with my children both grown, I needed a change." She moved back to Maine in May 1999, leaving a successful career in sales to open an ice cream parlor in Cornish. She chose the state for its affordability and the calming effect of a rural location. "I love running my own business and being closer to family," she says, "and I've found people to be friendly and supportive. Nevertheless, I've been lonely at times, and I miss my friends in Massachusetts." Dottie thinks retirement in Maine would be easier because expectations are lower. "Never move alone," she advises. "It's got to be an adventure you can share with someone you can depend on."

through the influx of visitors year-round. The state is the biggest beneficiary—tax revenues from tourism in 2003 were $208 million in sales tax; $103 million in personal income tax, and $73 million in gasoline tax.

Can you make a decent living in a seasonal industry such as tourism? That's what Dottie Paradis asked herself before she moved back to Maine in 1999. "I was expecting a lot more foot traffic," she says of her ice cream parlor in the small inland York County town of Cornish. "I've taken a huge salary cut from what I was making in Massachusetts. But I love running my own business and making my own hours."

Many Mainers agree. "It's difficult at first to adapt to the 'feast or famine' income swings, but eventually you do, and come to enjoy the down time," says Maggy King. Whether your dream is to run a cozy bed-and-breakfast inn or sell handmade decoys, chances are, you can do it in Maine. For more specifics about tourism, contact the Maine Office of Tourism: 207-623-0363 or www.mainetourism.com.

WAGE Clubs

The WAGE Project, a collaborative grassroots program designed to help close the wage gap between women and men at work, has come to Maine. "Maine has one of the most progressive equal-pay laws in the fifty states, so it only makes sense that Maine again would be on the forefront of the movement to get women paid fairly," says Sarah Standiford, executive director of the Maine Women's Lobby. The idea of WAGE (stands for Women Are Getting Even) Clubs began with former Massachusetts Lieutenant Governor and economist Evelyn Murphy. For more information, see their website at www.wageproject.org.

A Bevy of Small Businesses

The entrepreneurial spirit is alive and well in Maine. Small businesses of all types seem to thrive. Nearly 90 percent of Maine companies employ fewer than twenty people, and seventy thousand Mainers describe themselves as self-employed. The state sponsors many initiatives to help small businesses, and maintains seven SBDCs, or Small Business Development Centers.

A good source of information, if you are thinking of starting a Maine

MAINE WORKFORCE FACTS

- According to national standards, 83 percent of Maine's workforce is skilled.
- High school or post-secondary degrees are held by 83 percent of the one hundred thousand job seekers registered for work.
- Maine recently ranked number one in the nation in increasing its level of investment in higher education.
- More than 60 percent of Maine students pursue post-secondary education each year.
- Maine is the first state in the country to have every school and library—nearly twelve hundred facilities—linked by an advanced telecommunications technology called Frame Relay.

BUSINESS AND TRANSPORTATION FACTS

- Totaling thirty-two thousand miles, Maine's roads and bridges were ranked seventh-best in the country by a 1996 University of North Carolina survey.
- Interstate 95 runs nearly the length of the state, and Route 1 is the major artery serving the coast.
- More than 450 trucking firms provide intrastate service.
- Maine has a twenty-year highway maintenance and improvement plan.
- Most of Maine is relatively congestion-free; business here is not slowed down by traffic jams.
- The Maine Department of Transportation is doubling the biennial investment in bridges.
- Seven short-line railroad companies operate fourteen hundred miles of track.
- Maine has seven strategically located seaports.
- The largest cargo shipping ports are in Eastport, Searsport, and Portland. They can handle most types of cargo and provide regular service to Europe, Asia, and Canada.
- Eastport is New England's fastest-growing international cargo port, annually shipping more than two hundred thousand tons.

business, is the state's official website at www.maine.gov. Under the "Business" tab, you can access an online Business Answers service. Provided by the Department of Economic & Community Development, the service provides free information about doing business in Maine. The online Business Licensing Assistant will lead you through a series of questions about the type of business you are trying to start, and provide a list of licenses, permits, or qualifications you need. The site also answers frequently asked questions. Business Answers staff can send you resources, permit applications, and other follow-up information that you need to get your business running in Maine. Also available are customized packets offering information about self-employment, hiring employees and labor standards, and a Business Start-Up Kit, which includes *A Guide to Doing Business in Maine.*

The Maine Office of Business Development provides comprehensive financial, management, production, marketing, and other technical assistance to help Maine businesses launch and prosper, and is another great resource. On their website (www.mainebiz.org) you'll find a wealth of business knowledge—information on financing, workforce training, licensing, grants, tax incentives—almost anything related to doing business in Maine. They have many links to other great resources as well.

Family Ties

Maine also has a high percentage of independently owned family businesses. These range from first-generation "mom and pop" operations to sophisticated multi-generational corporations. The Institute for Family-Owned Business at the University of Southern Maine (www.usm.maine.edu/ifob) estimates that of the state's businesses, some 90% are family owned. Some, like Thos. Moser Cabinetmakers of Auburn, are first-generation businesses owned and run by their founders and family. Others, like The Smiling Cow, a retail store overlooking Camden harbor, are into their third generation, and an impressive number of Maine businesses go back as many as four or five generations.

The Oakland House Seaside Resort on Eggemoggin Reach in Brooksville is a Maine business with real family longevity. "My daughter

Sally McGuigan is a fifth-generation innkeeper here," says Jim Littlefield. "And she's the ninth generation on the property." Jim's ancestor (take grandfather and put five "greats" in front of it) acquired the land in 1767 through a grant from Britain's King George, and the property has been handed down to direct heirs since then.

United States Senator Susan Collins, herself the child of a multigenerational Maine business (S.W. Collins Lumber Company in Caribou), is a strong advocate for small businesses. She has sponsored bills providing estate-tax relief for family-owned businesses and farms. She believes family businesses can be the strongest, because family bonds create a strong commitment to employees and communities that might otherwise be lacking.

Moving a Business to Maine

A wide range of incentives and benefits are offered to businesses that decide to move to Maine through the Department of Economic and Community Development's Office of Business Development. These programs include business property-tax reimbursements, job and investment tax credits, and

Camden's Main Street in 1945. Today The Smiling Cow is a third-generation business that is still going strong. *Photo courtesy of Meg Quijano.*

sales tax exemptions. Check out their website at www.econdevmaine.com for more information, or call 207-287-2656.

The State of Maine is committed to the development of its rural areas, and offers several initiatives. First, the Employee Tax Increment Financing (ETIF) program enables employers hiring at least fifteen new employees over a two-year period to receive a tax reimbursement for a portion of the employees' state withholding tax. The company would receive a 30%, 50%, or 75% reimbursement of the state withholdings for eligible employees. Any qualified job creation in an area with 150% of the state unemployment rate is eligible for the 75% reimbursement. Since all of Maine's high unemployment areas are rural, this initiative benefits companies locating in Maine's rural areas.

In some parts of the state, Maine has established Pine Tree Development Zones to offer additional resources to companies locating in these areas. In a Pine Tree Development Zone, the ETIF program is enhanced to 80% reimbursement for eligible employees. Additionally, a company receives a 100% corporate income tax credit for the first five years, and a 50% credit for years six through ten.

Maine & Company is a private, non-profit corporation that provides free and confidential site-selection assistance to out-of-state companies considering Maine as a business location. Its services include real estate site searches, data collection and analysis, incentives identification and valuation, and site visit coordination. The website (www.maineco.org) is listed along with other resources in the Business Development Assistance Chart.

Probably the biggest incentives for moving a business here, however, are Maine people themselves. Ask just about any employer in the state, and you'll surely hear that the Maine worker is a highly valued asset. Mainers are well known for their strong work ethic and commitment to delivering top-quality work. Labor disputes here are rare—in fact, only one Maine company experienced a work stoppage in the past three years.

In addition, Maine offers a comprehensive workforce-development system should the need arise to upgrade worker skills. When businesses in the state venture into an area that requires new skills among their workers, Maine's community colleges and universities work closely to provide the needed training and education.

The Finance Authority of Maine

Maine's business-finance agency is the Finance Authority of Maine. FAME supports start-up and expanding businesses by working closely with Maine banks to improve access to capital. It offers a wide array of programs, ranging from traditional loan guarantees for small and large businesses, to tax credits for investments in dynamic manufacturing or export-related firms. FAME has also established taxable and tax-exempt bond-financing programs that provide loans to creditworthy firms at very favorable rates and terms. Some of the authority's many programs are:

- The Commercial Loan Insurance Program
- Export Financing Services
- Investment Banking Service
- Maine Seed Capital Tax Credit
- Occupational Safety Loan Program
- Plus 1 Computer Loan Program
- Rapid Response Guarantee
- Regional Economic Development Revolving Loan Program
- Small Business and Veterans' Small Business Loan Insurance Program
- Small Enterprise Growth Fund Bond Financing Programs

For more comprehensive information, including eligibility criteria, please call 207-623-3263 or visit FAME's website at www.famemaine.com.

Maine in the Global Marketplace

According to the Maine Department of Economic and Community Development, Maine businesses are participating in the global marketplace in record numbers, exporting nearly $1.5 billion worth of goods a year. International exports are growing, and Maine is increasing its profile as a trading partner with the Canadian Maritimes.

The Maine International Trade Center offers businesses and organizations international assistance working to expand the state's economy through increased international trade in goods and services and related activities such as trade missions, training programs, and conferences. For more information, check out its website at www.mitc.com.

The Creative Economy

In 2005, Governor Baldacci created a new Creative Economy Council, charging it to advise, support, and advance public and private initiatives building Maine's creative economy. The council is made up of a statewide slate of advisors drawn from technology companies, universities, Native American tribes, arts institutions, venture capital firms, design firms, and more.

"The creative economy is a catalyst for the creation of new jobs in Maine communities," said the Governor. "People who create jobs want to live in places that have a diverse cultural mix and an innovative and educated work force. Maine will be competitive economically if we continue to capitalize on the synergies between entrepreneurship, education, the arts, and quality of life."

Indeed, the creative sector is a major growing factor in Maine's economy, generating an estimated $6.6 billion in cultural tourism dollars. New England and Maine have a higher concentration of creative workers than other parts of the country, artists like Jane Dahmen who moved here in 2005.

"Everything we could ever need is here—services, shops, people, culture, etc. I do have my art supplies shipped up from Boston, but it's the perfect place to paint and show work. There are lots of artists living in the area, and many galleries." Dahmen says that she and her husband had visited Maine for years before pulling up stakes in Massachusetts. "We wish we had known how much we would like living here because we would have come sooner. Interestingly, we never knew all those years of visiting and sailing here how great it would be to live here."

As an artist, Dahmen is inspired by the beauty she sees all around her. "I've painted landscapes of Maine for years, and, yes, the light is different here, probably because there is less pollution. You really can see the stars at night."

The Maine Arts Commission does not specifically help artists relocate to Maine, but it does have a number of services in place for resident artists. Four programs are available: the Individual Artist Fellowship Program, the Traditional Arts Apprenticeship Program, the Maine Artist Roster, and the Maine Artist Registry. There is a formal application process, with paperwork due annually on February 2.

The commission's newest initiative, the Contemporary Artist Development Program, was adopted in June 1999. As an umbrella for a variety of services, this program provides reliable information, training, and funding support that responds to the artist's particular discipline, career stage, and professional aspirations.

Maine also supports an innovative "one percent for art" program, which sets aside an amount equal to one percent of the construction budget in a new or renovated public building to purchase original works of art. For further information on funding, residencies, or employment in all disciplines, contact the Maine Arts Commission at 207-287-2750, or visit its website at www.mainearts.com.

Living Here, Working Elsewhere

With Maine's superior telecommunications system, plus good airports, e-mail, scanners, fax machines, and next-day delivery services, it's hard to think of a job that can't be done here. Given this same scenario, it's possible to imagine many situations involving folks who live here, but actually service clients somewhere else.

"Neither of us works in Maine," says Jan Njaa, a graphic designer who recently moved with her family to Belfast. "David's a pilot, and he flies out of Minneapolis, and my clients are still in Chicago. We needed to make sure David would have a fairly easy commute to the airport, and Bangor turns out to be very convenient. I needed access to good Internet service and overnight deliveries for my business. Maine's got it all."

Attorney Dana Strout moved east from Colorado. Although his office is located here, his clients are still in the Rocky Mountains. "It's much more profitable for me to work out of state. I can charge more, for one thing, plus it's easier to practice law in Colorado. The Maine judicial system in my opinion is antiquated and disrespectful of lawyers' time. In Colorado, I can do hearings by telephone, and I can send pleadings, briefs, and motions by fax. It's far more convenient to practice law there."

Strout travels back to Colorado to meet with clients nine or ten times a year. "It's actually less traveling than what I did when I lived there," he says. His move to Maine in 1994 was, in fact, a homecoming. "I'm a Mainer,

WEBSITES FOR BUSINESS DEVELOPMENT ASSISTANCE

- Venture Capital in Maine: www.famemaine.com
- Maine Department of Economic &
        Community Development: www.econdevmaine.com
- Maine International Trade Center: www.mitc.com
- Maine Procurement Technical
        Assistance Center: www.maineptac.org
- Maine Small Business Development Centers:
        www.mainesbdc.org
- Maine & Company: www.maineco.org
- Active Capital: http://activecapital.org

Lafayette Center in Kennebunk, the administrative building for Tom's of Maine, international manufacturer of natural personal-wellness products. *Photo by Herb Swanson, courtesy of Tom's of Maine.*

and I've got more relatives in Maine than you can shake a stick at." He hadn't lived in the state since his teens and is happy to be back. "The lifestyle and the people here are great. I missed Maine terribly. In Denver, I was robbed ten times in fourteen years. It was time to come home."

TOP 20 LARGEST EMPLOYERS IN MAINE

As of December 2005. Compiled by the Maine Depart. of Labor.

1. L.L. Bean Inc, Freeport, 9,000
2. Hannaford Bros. Co., Scarborough, 7,000
3. Wal-Mart, Statewide, 6,000
4. Bath Iron Works, Bath, 5,000
5. Maine Medical Center, Portland, 5,000
6. Shaw's Supermarkets, South Portland, 3,000
7. Eastern Maine Medical Center, Bangor, 3,000
8. Unum, Portland, 2,500
9. MBNA Marketing Systems Inc., Statewide, 2,500
10. Banknorth N.A., Portland, 2,500
11. Mainegeneral Medical Center, Augusta, 2,000
12. International Paper Co., Statewide, 2,000
13. Central Maine Medical Center, Lewiston, 1,500
14. Home Depot, Statewide, 1,500
15. Pratt & Whitney Aircraft Group, North Berwick, 1,500
16. Mercy Hospital, Portland, 1,200
17. S.D. Warren, Westbrook, 1,200
18. Rite-Aid of Maine, Statewide, 1,200
19. Jackson Laboratory, Bar Harbor, 1,000
20. Verizon New England Inc., Portland, 1,000

4 House Hunting

" One of the nicest things about moving to Maine was finding just the right house. It quickly became apparent, as we inspected a number of candidates, that this state is ripe with wonderful choices—Victorians, Capes, shingle-style, some new and some historically recognized. A cornucopia of choices and most with basements! As former residents of Texas, we found underground storage a real plus. The fact that our search took place in June, when the weather in Maine is glorious, made our quest that much more enjoyable."

— JO STAGE*

Maine is a rich mixture of architectural styles and types of dwellings: grand old sea-captain's homes gazing out to the ocean, elegant Federals lining a village square. There are raised ranches where yards are strewn with toys, and tidy Capes in new subdivisions. Picturesque villages shelter lobster shacks stacked high with traps, and comfortable condominiums with water views. You'll find quiet cabins lining lakefronts and cozy apartments topping downtown shops. There are gleaming new retirement villages as well as trailers that have seen better days. And Maine is home to new houses of every imaginable design: modern, post and beam, solar, and manufactured.

Older Homes Abound

Few states have as many different types of houses as Maine, according to a 1999 report from the Maine State Housing Authority, and few states have as many historic homes. Almost 35 percent of Maine's homes were built before 1940, representing tangible ties to the past that few states can match. They

----

*Jo Stage and her husband Key bought a lovely Colonial (with a basement) in Camden in 2006.

John P. Nichols, one of Searsport's most financially successful sea captains, went to sea at age eleven and took charge of his own ship when only twenty-one years old. He commissioned this house, one of the finest Italianate-style homes in Waldo County, upon his retirement. *Photo courtesy Maine Historic Preservation Commission.*

are part of a landscape that, in many cases, seems to have changed little over time—proud white Colonials, extravagant Victorians, rambling farmhouses with attached outbuildings and lofty red barns.

According to the Maine Historic Preservation Commission, nearly twelve hundred properties in Maine—many of them private residences—are listed in the National Register of Historic Places. There are 130 historic districts in Maine, each with dozens—or hundreds—of properties. Portland, Castine, Bangor, and Bath all have large historic areas, as do Rockland, Farmington, Norway, Houlton, Belfast, and Thomaston. Even Maine's more remote corners—Chesuncook Village, in Piscataquis County, for instance, a lakeside community that can only be reached by boat—have homes of significant historical importance.

Maine has scores of Federal, Greek Revival, Italianate, Queen Anne, shingle style, and Colonial Revival–Style homes, but it also contains large numbers of post–World War II ranch houses. Architectural historian Kirk Mohney says that most of the state's communities exhibit a variety of styles, however he notes that the St. John River Valley is unique because of the distinctive early houses built there by Acadian settlers.

The Maine Historic Preservation Commission conducts surveys to identify important historic properties, and keeps an extensive library relating to technical preservation matters. Should you fall in love with an old Maine house, the folks at the commission may have some material relating to it, or they may be able to put you in touch with someone who does. And don't forget local historical societies—often fascinating sources of information. For further data on historic homes (or to see if an old Maine house meets the National Register criteria), contact the experts at Maine Historic Preservation Commission, www.maine.gov/mhpc, or call them at 207-287-2132.

The Housing Market

While Maine real estate is most expensive in the southern part of the state —think Portland or York County—and along the coast, inland and northern areas are starting to detect a similar trend. Residential real estate prices in the Bangor area had held to a steady course for years, climbing only slowly even amid the housing boom in York and Cumberland counties, but this began changing in 2002–2003.

The median home price in Maine increased 15 percent between the first quarter of 2004 and the first three months of 2005, to $187,500, according to the Maine Real Estate Information System. In Penobscot County, the median price increased 20 percent, from $112,500 to $135,000. Other big in-

PROFILE

David and Jan Njaa moved to Maine in 1999, fifteen years earlier than they'd originally planned. "Even though we loved Chicago, every time we left Maine we looked at each other and wondered why we were going back. There is no other place we feel so in love with or connected to," explains Jan. The Njaas love the landscape of Maine, the people they've met, and the low crime rate. "We love looking out the window and not seeing a brick wall." Jan advises those interested in Maine to "visit during the off months, so you know what it looks like at its worst. If you can make a living here, do it sooner rather than later. There is so much available to have a life rich in nature, culture, and community."

creases were recorded in Washington County (25.5 percent), Piscataquis County (28 percent), Knox County (19.5 percent) and Hancock County (54.8 percent).

Rising home values aren't the norm for the entire state. Prices actually declined in Aroostook County and appear to have stabilized, at least temporarily, in Waldo, Lincoln, and Oxford counties. And not everyone sees current prices as high—Maine still seems like a bargain to most out-of-state buyers.

Raw house lots—those with no improvements—containing up to two acres and located away from the salt water are selling for $35,000 to $50,000, and buyers like Jeff and Cathy Cleaveland, who moved to Maine from Seattle, had to tromp through parcels in several communities before finding their dream property of fifty-plus acres.

What about demand? Even with interest rates beginning to inch upward, it's still pretty high, say realtors around the state. Almost 25 percent of the homes in Greater Bangor sell within fourteen days, according to the Maine Real Estate Information System. One-third sell within three weeks, and only about one home in twenty takes more than six months to sell.

Several factors have fueled the rapid increase in prices: historically low interest rates; the trend for baby boomers to " trade up" to nicer homes or to condos; and the expanding second-home market.

Seasonal Homes

David and Nancy Weil are residents of New Jersey who purchased a vacation home in the midcoast in 2005. Nancy grew up in Presque Isle, attended the University of Maine, and has family in Scarborough and Damariscotta, as well as children at two private schools here. Nevertheless, the couple did their homework and considered several parts of the state before buying.

"We looked at a lot of properties and asked a lot of questions," says David. "It's important to spend as much time as possible in different seasons of the year in the communities you are considering before making a firm commitment, and talk to a lot of people—both year-round residents and summer folk."

People like the Weils have given Maine a higher percentage of seasonal and recreational housing than any other state in the nation. Nearly 16 percent of Maine's housing stock consists of beach cottages, ski retreats, lakeside camps, and hunting lodges that are used by folks who call somewhere else home. For resort towns, these part-timers can be a plus, because they inject money into local economies. The state benefits from the additional sales tax revenue, and municipalities reap more in property taxes without having to pay more for big-ticket items such as schools.

The flip side to this seasonal migration manifests itself in congested streets, overwhelmed merchants, and inflated real estate. Says David Weil, "The downside to living here is that it creates greater awareness of what Maine offers to others and increases the risk that the very special atmosphere and surroundings that attracted us may be diluted over time."

Building a Home

Home construction in Maine has been rising since 1998, and contractors are enjoying calendars with few empty slots. Maine leads New England in the rate of housing-permit growth, with 40 percent of Maine's construction dollars going toward residential development. While this has made builders happy, not everyone is enamored with all of the new growth. Communities around Maine have begun to address the specter of sprawl, taking preventative steps to keep their precious open space and the character of their towns.

GrowSmart Maine, an advocacy group based in Yarmouth, is one group addressing the environmental and economic impact of this issue. Building houses with big yards and long driveways not only threatens the state's natural resources, but pushes up property taxes and makes it difficult for Maine to attract businesses. Their goal is to build a statewide coalition and promote a vision for " smart growth" that calls for focusing growth in town centers on small house lots rather than letting it gallop along willy-nilly. Recently the organization sponsored a major study conducted by the Brookings Institution to look at Maine's economy, cost of government, and patterns of development, today and tomorrow. For more information see its website at www.growsmartmaine.org.

Many newcomers—especially retirees—decide to build houses in Maine, some because they are seeking a special style, others because they desire certain amenities not usually found in older homes, still more because they want to build the dream house with the dream view for which they've long planned. Maine is one of the few places left in the country with reasonably priced shoreland still available.

"It took us twelve years of coming up on weekends from New York to build our house," says Allie Lou Richardson, of Islesboro. "It was worth it, because we wanted to be on the water."

Marlene Kinlin, who moved to Jonesport from Massachusetts, echoes her sentiments: "My husband and I chose Maine for peace of mind as well as the gorgeous, affordable seaside property." The Kinlins retired to Maine in 1994 and built a home with views of lobster buoys and spruce-topped islands.

One thing to remember when considering a coastal site for your dream home, though, is Maine's shoreland zoning law. This regulation places restrictions on a structure's proximity to a body of water, on the clearing of vegetation near the shore, and on types of buildings that can be located on the immediate coast. More information on the law can be found at any town office.

And what about "McMansions"? With very few exceptions, Maine has not yet succumbed to the epidemic wreaking havoc with communities in other states, in which older, smaller homes are torn down so that expansive new structures can occupy the lot. Instead of tearing down a vintage house, bring that old gem back to its glory days and bask in the admiration of all your new neighbors. If you buy a vacant lot on an established street (planners encourage this practice, called "infilling," because it helps to prevent

Striking examples of classic architecture, such as this beauty in Boothbay Harbor, are common sights in Maine.
Photo courtesy of the Maine Office of Tourism.

sprawl), choose a design and a scale that will fit with the integrity of the existing neighborhood.

New Housing Styles

While Maine has a varied mix of housing styles, there are some that seem to naturally fit into the landscape. Cottage and shingle style houses, post-and-beam homes, Capes, and even homes built of Maine cedar logs look quite at home.

The Richardsons of Islesboro chose to build a post-and-beam house, a style characterized by large open spaces and cathedral ceilings combined with the beauty of exposed wood. According to Paul Meynell, of Acadia Post & Beam in Sorrento, this type of construction is a favorite among retirees and young families alike.

"Post-and-beam construction has been around for over four thousand years," Meynell says. "The timbers come together using rugged mortise-and-tenon joinery secured with wooden pegs. Most structures over a hundred years old still standing today boast some form of post-and-beam construction. I think this type of house suits Maine because of its beauty and authenticity. Plus they are energy efficient and comfortable homes."

Log homes are another popular choice for new residents. One company, Maine Cedar Log Homes, located in Windham, has manufactured this style since 1926. Their homes feature hand-shaved white-cedar logs for a natural look with low maintenance, and R-26 walls for energy efficiency.

Choosing a Builder

If you decide to build, keep in mind that buying land within the traditional village setting, on established roads, will help keep Maine from succumbing to the suburban sprawl that is eating away at much of the country's rural areas. Whatever style of house you consider, it's wise to take the time necessary to carefully choose your construction team. Mark DeMichele, of Maine Coast Construction in Camden, offers these tips:

▲ Set aside a minimum of 10 percent of your total budget during the planning stages to give yourself the ability to consider upgrades in

Post-and-beam homes feature timber framing and are energy efficient.
Photo courtesy of Rockport Post & Beam.

materials or compensate for other undetermined costs as the new
home takes shape.

⬧ Get the best value for your construction dollar by interviewing archi-
tects and builders. Check their financial and client references and
look at their past projects and works in progress.

⬧ Choose a "team" that can best assist you in achieving your specific
goals within your budget. Remember, the whole process is about
working, communicating, and making sound decisions together.

⬧ Another important consideration is your building site. "One formid-
able surprise that's often found when building in Maine is the condition of and difficulty in developing building sites. Land with the
presence of ledge and rock, extreme slopes, poor drainage, and
environmentally sensitive issues require more costly solutions for
development. Be sure the builder you choose is aware of issues
associated with site development and can suggest appropriate steps
to surmount specific obstacles."

This elegant Queen Anne–style home in Skowhegan is one of the finest in the state. It was built in 1887 for Samuel Wadsworth Gould, a local lawyer and businessman. *Photo courtesy of Maine Historic Preservation Commission.*

Manufactured Housing

Approximately 13.6 percent of Maine's housing stock is mobile homes, the highest rate in New England. Mobile homes—single and double-wide—have played a big role in Maine's housing growth in the last decade, with one mobile home added for every two site-built homes. Affordability plays a big part: they are a relatively inexpensive match for the relatively inexpensive landscape. The average price of a new double-wide home (not including the land) was $43,000 in 1997.

Since national standards were developed in 1976, mobile homes have become safer and better built. As a result, loans for mobile homes are available on terms only slightly more expensive than those for site-built homes. New mobile home insurance policies are also available.

Another type of manufactured housing is the modular home. Unlike mobile homes, which are placed on a cement slab, modular homes are built on a poured cement foundation and look similar to stick-built structures. They can be custom built to suit just about any style: Cape, ranch, even Colonial.

Al Benner, of East Holden, has been in the manufactured-housing business for thirty-four years. He says modular homes are popular—particularly with first-home buyers—because they are affordable and can be readily financed. "A modular home runs about 15 to 20 percent less than a stick-built or traditional house, and they can be constructed in five weeks' time or less," he notes. Quality has improved dramatically over the years, too, says Benner. "Maine was the first state to create a construction code for manufactured housing, which became a model for other states. It used to be that banks didn't want to finance these homes, but as the code has improved, so has the quality."

The Maine Manufactured Housing Board regulates the industry in Maine as it relates to construction safety, parts, and licensing of mobile and modular home manufacturers, dealers, and mechanics. By law, every municipality must allow manufactured homes to be installed in their town or city. However, Patrick S. Ouillette, Executive Director of the MMHB, notes that zoning restrictions are acceptable by state law and are common. For more information, call the Maine Manufactured Housing Board at 207-624-8612. Contact Al Benner Homes at 1-800-287-1071 or visit the website at www.albennerhomes.com.

Retirement Communities

The newest developments on the housing scene are retirement communities. As of March 2000, there were thirty-five privately developed retirement centers in Maine offering living units of various types—cottages, independent apartments, and facilities with assisted-living and long-term-care options. More units are being built all the time. See Appendix 5 for addresses and other details.

Located both along the coast and inland, retirement villages offer maintenance-free living and a lively social scene. Many are affiliated with health-care providers through which residents can quickly gain access to an entire continuum of care.

Retirement communities are set up in several ways. For instance, at Avalon Village, a retirement community on the bank of the Penobscot River, only five minutes from Bangor, the home buyer receives a share of stock representing the value of the residence. The equity in your new home belongs to you and your estate. In contrast, Schooner Estates, a retirement community nestled in a country setting near Auburn, offers independent-living apartments, assisted-living studio apartments, and a residential-care living center, but all are rental properties.

Condominiums

After years of little activity, the market for condominiums in Maine is booming. "We can't keep condos on the market," says a broker in Bangor. "The more mature population wants to be free of maintenance."

Sales of condos are stronger than ever, and in some parts of Maine it is difficult to find condo properties at any price. Developers have begun to respond to the demand for these low-maintenance homes, popular with both first-time buyers and retirees. If you are in the market for a condo and can be patient, your timing may be right, as the next few years will undoubtedly bring more condominium projects.

In Portland and other Maine cities, the trend toward "condo conversions"—the transformation of large private homes or apartment buildings into condominiums—has caught on. In 1999, there weren't any condo conversions in Portland; two years later, five buildings had been "condo-ized," creating 21 condominium units from what had been 25 apartments.

In more rural parts of Maine, condos are rarer than snowstorms in July. "You just don't see that type of housing in much of Maine," says a developer in Aroostook County. "This state is still heavily weighted toward traditional home ownership."

Apartment and House Rentals

In fact, the heads of three out of every four Maine households own their own homes, a remarkable statistic given the economic slowdown of the early 1990s. Depending on the community, renting a home or apartment in Maine can be next to impossible. High-growth areas, such as the coast and southern Maine, face a rental deficit that builders and municipal planners are trying to address. In communities where growth is not so rapid, rentals are both available and generally very reasonable.

Renters are in the minority in Maine, and sometimes feel at a disadvantage. "While I've met fabulous landlords here, there are no standardized landlord-tenant rules in Maine," says Dottie Paradis of Cornish. "I've never paid for water or sewer while renting in Massachusetts."

Looking at Property

Maine is a state of breathtakingly beautiful vistas: mountain ridges that reveal sparkling lakes below; glimpses through the pines of tranquil, rock-lined coves; acres of crimson blueberry fields, stark and austere. It's also a place where, just around the corner, you'll find a neglected trailer with a never-ending yard sale, a dilapidated barn ready to collapse in the next blizzard, or a working gravel pit. When you live here, you realize that conformity isn't what makes Maine special. Whether because of attitude or finances, things aren't "prettied up," and people hold their property rights and individuality close to their hearts. Sometimes out-of-staters look askance at what Laura Read calls "local flavor" and wonder whether any zoning laws apply.

"Readers of *Moving to Maine* should keep in mind that most villages on the coast are still active fishing communities," says real estate broker Laura Read. "I live and work in Kennebunkport. This summer, I had a half-million dollar house on the market in Cape Porpoise. It was a pretty yellow Cape with four bedrooms and plenty of yard for kids to run around in. However, to get to it, you had to drive through a lobsterman's yard, full of traps and discarded rope and lumber and buoys and plastic buckets and recycling cars. It took me forever to find a buyer. Everyone loves to eat lobster and to see the boats in the harbor, but they don't want evidence of the trade in the back yard. I finally did get a buyer from New Jersey who liked the local flavor and they are happily settled in."

Once you have scoured various communities and pinpointed the areas you like, it's time to find a house-hunting professional to help you look at property.

Real Estate Brokers

Maine's real estate professionals must be licensed by the Maine Real Estate Commission. Brokers and associate brokers have the most experience and training; sales agents must work under a designated broker.

A good real estate pro is an invaluable asset when moving anywhere. In Maine, they seem to often go above and beyond the call of duty, serving in many instances as a bridge to the new community. "Our real estate agent tried to inform us about Belfast as much as possible," says Jan Njaa, who moved here in 1999. "He really helped us make a smooth transition from Chicago to Maine, and even went the extra mile to show us around once we arrived."

Since a real estate transaction may involve one or more licensees, it's important to know whose interests are represented by each agent. At one time, brokers were understood to represent the seller, and this was true regardless of whether the broker was the listing agent or the selling agent. Today, that's not always the case. The Maine Real Estate Commission gives this advice: Buyers and sellers should not assume that an agent is acting on their behalf unless they have contracted with that person to represent them. Maine brokers are required to provide a form that explains the different types of agency relationships allowed in the state, and if you aren't clear who is representing whom, be sure to ask. Here's why: Maine law also provides that a real estate licensee may represent both the buyer and seller in the same transaction (this is called "dual agency"), but only with the informed written consent of both parties. Not all agencies practice dual agency, as it could create a real conflict of interest and may result in a loss of negotiating power for both parties. Broker Bob Fenton puts it this way: "I don't think dual agency makes sense. After all, would you hire a doctor who did podiatry one day and brain surgery the next?"

A better scenario is to find a buyer agent or "buyer's broker," a professional who helps a buyer find suitable property and acquire it at the most advantageous price and terms. Buyer's brokers can be a real boon to people hoping to relocate to Maine from far away, because they're familiar with the local market and can do much of the legwork.

Www.realtor.com can get you started on your search for a buyer's broker.

Home Inspections

Whether you are interested in a vintage Victorian or a new ranch, a total examination of the house from top to bottom is crucial. Love is blind, so it's a good idea, no matter what the age of the property, to go over the place thoroughly. An experienced and impartial home inspector can gave a visual examination of the physical structure and systems of a home, examining

Located in the Broad Street Historic District in Bethel, this house was once the home and clinic of Dr. John George Gehring, a well-known psychotherapist. It was constructed in 1896. *Photo courtesy Maine Historic Preservation Commission.*

the heating system, the interior plumbing and electric systems, the roof and visible insulation, walls, ceilings, floors, windows and doors, the foundation, and the basement.

Depending on where you call home, be prepared for some differences in what may be considered "standard" in other places. For example, thanks to Maine's very manageable summer temperatures, very few homes in the Pine Tree State have central air conditioning. Although some new homes are being built with Southern buyers in mind, it's likely you'll find few—if any—properties in which a flick of a switch generates icy air.

While you won't find cooling systems, be prepared to see several types of heating sources, some of which may be unfamiliar. Maine homes are heated using a variety of methods detailed in the Heating Your Home section of this chapter.

Although Maine does not have a termite problem like southern states, carpenter ants can be a nuisance. A professional can check for these and other pests, as well as conduct tests to check for the presence of harmful chemicals or elements.

Which tests are important in Maine? In addition to drinking-water tests, experts recommend lead and asbestos screening for homes built prior to 1978. Testing for radon, a naturally occurring gas produced by the breakdown of uranium in soil, rock, and water, is also important in this granite-rich state. Radon may be released into your home through air and water, and, according to the Surgeon General, is a leading cause of lung cancer. (The EPA publishes a number of informative documents about radon for consumers. Many of the radon-related booklets are available through the EPA's website, www.epa.gov/radonpro, or through state radon offices.)

Your real estate professional will know licensed inspectors in the area and can help put you in contact with one. If you can, it's wise to be there while he or she conducts the inspection and see firsthand any problems or concerns. Following the inspection, you'll receive a written report describing the house's condition in more detail than you ever thought possible.

Closing Costs

What does it cost to buy property in Maine? Here is a breakdown of costs to give you an idea.

Bank Charges: Banks require an application fee (approximately $350) to begin processing your mortgage request. This fee is applied to your closing costs, which generally include:

- Loan commitment fee (depending upon the interest rate charged)
- Underwriting fee: $100
- Document preparation fee: $150
- Recording fees (for the mortgage deed): $30
- Settlement agent fee: $300
- Credit report: $25
- Appraisal: $300
- Flood zone determination: $25
- Prepaid interest: interest from the date of closing to the day of the month on which your monthly payment will be due.

Real Estate Tax: In many Maine communities the real estate tax is determined on a tax-year basis running from July 1 through June 30. Make sure your contract provides that real estate taxes on the property will be prorated as of the date of closing. Generally, taxes for the current year are paid as part of the closing settlement process, even if some portion of the real estate tax is not yet due. (If a transaction closes before the tax rate for the current year has been established, it is customary to use the previous year's tax figure to do the proration rather than having to make further adjustments once the new tax rate is set. It's a good idea to address this issue in the purchase and sale agreement.)

Attorney's Fees: At closing, purchasers are generally required to provide and pay for a title-insurance binder with appropriate endorsements, generally obtained from an attorney. When you apply for financing, the bank will ask whether you want to select your own attorney or have the bank select one.

An attorney selected by the bank represents the bank—not you. Because of this, you may want to select your own attorney to do the title work and to certify title to the bank or to a land title insurance company. As long as the attorney selected meets the bank's requirements for liability insurance, you will not be charged any additional amount in connection with the title work.

Real Estate Transfer Tax: The state imposes a transfer tax on virtually all transfers of real property. The tax, which is paid by both buyer and seller, is $1.10 per $500, or fractional part thereof, of consideration or value. This tax must be paid at the Registry of Deeds as part of the recording process.

The Transaction

The process of buying a house in Maine differs from that in many parts of the country, especially out West. Here is a brief overview of the steps involved:

Once you have decided upon your property, your broker will prepare a purchase-and-sale contract that will include a number of standard clauses as well as some prepared with your needs and concerns in mind. Certain types of properties will also require the insertion of specific contract provisions.

For instance, if you are buying a shorefront property, you'll want to require that the seller provide a certificate indicating the condition of the septic system over the past 180 days. Also, you might want to include a clause providing for a review of the purchase-and-sale contract by your attorney before you need to sign.

The purchase-and sale-contract is not a contract until the sellers accept the buyers' offer and sign the agreement themselves. Generally a purchase-and-sale contract has a number of contingencies. The most frequent are: house inspection, financing, water safety test, survey or lot configuration, and radon test.

What's the role of the real estate professional during all this give and take? The brokers assist and monitor the activities necessary to fulfill the contingencies and then produce a document indicating when they are fulfilled. Now the buyer's attorney can perform the title examination. The results should be communicated to the buyers at the same time they are communicated to the lender, through a preliminary title certificate or a binder for title insurance.

Once the title work, appraisal, and other documentation required by the bank are assembled and approved by the underwriting department, the transaction is ready to be closed.

Title Insurance in Maine: Lender's and Owner's Policies

Virtually all banks making residential mortgage loans in Maine now require a title insurance policy to protect their interest in the property, which is generally the original amount of the loan itself. The basic cost of such lender's title insurance is $1.75 per $1,000 of loan. In addition to the basic premium, certain endorsements are required for different situations. Virtually every transaction requires a "secondary mortgage market endorsement" at a cost of $25, as well as an "environmental protection lien endorsement," also at a cost of $25. Endorsements for variable-rate mortgages, for condominiums, or for manufactured housing units also cost $25 each.

The lender's title insurance policy offers no protection to the owner even though the owner pays for the policy. If a title-related issue arises, for instance an ancient right-of-way that has not been mentioned in the chain of deeds researched prior to the purchase, the title insurer will not step in, for until the lender suffers an actual loss (foreclosure) it has no duty to intervene.

Fifteen or twenty years ago, title insurance in Maine was relatively uncommon and many purchasers and their attorneys didn't bother with owners' policies. Today, though, experts say it's a good idea. Title insurance protects your investment while you own it and also covers any warranty covenants you may offer in a deed to subsequent purchasers. If any of the covered situations arise, the title insurer will either correct the problem or reimburse you for insured losses up to the amount of the policy. You'll also be defended against any lawsuit attacking the title. The cost for title insurance is a one-time premium.

Loans

According to the Maine State Housing Authority, there is no shortage of capital for any form of housing activity in Maine for families with adequate incomes and credit eligibility. Home-improvement loans from Maine banks totaled an estimated $130 million in 1997, but this represents only a fraction of home-improvement activity, say experts. As with other parts of the country, a more popular way to finance home improvements is through an equity line of credit.

Heating Your Home

Even the Maine State Housing Authority admits that energy costs are high. "Electricity is expensive here," says Marlene Kinlin, who moved to Jonesport from Massachusetts in 1994. The high cost of heating a home is particularly unsettling for those who relocate from outside the Northeast, and many new residents are dismayed to find that natural gas, while now generally available inland, is not an option everywhere.

Far and away the most popular fuel in Maine is oil. "The cheapest thing is Number Two fuel oil," says Willard Wight, whose family has been in the fuel business in the midcoast since 1899. "Everything is on the expensive side—electricity is high, and so is propane. Kerosene, also called K-1, is a more refined oil used in certain types of units, but it's pricey. By far, the most efficient fuel in the state is oil."

Efficient, but in recent memory, expensive. In January and February 2006, the prices New England residents paid for oil reached their highest levels in at least twenty years, when a number of conditions coincided to boost demand and limit supplies. Instability in the Middle East, as well as a shortage of crude oil coming into the Northeast from overseas, combined to send retail prices skyward. Rates of $2.44 per gallon were all the more shocking when compared with 1999 prices, which were well below $1 per gallon.

The issue of Maine's dependence on overseas oil is a much-debated topic, particularly once the snow flies. The idea of creating an oil reserve for the Northeast is one response to shortages; alternative types of fuel are another. Approximately twenty-two thousand consumers currently are natural gas customers in Maine, and there are three proposals to construct natural gas pipelines and storage facilities in the Maine coastal zone. The largest of these projects would link gas resources offshore of Nova Scotia to the United States natural gas transmission system.

While solar energy warms other parts of the country, its future in Maine is still somewhat cloudy. "We can't rely on the amount of sunlight here," says Willard Wight, "And solar panels and the like are quite costly to install."

One thing we can count on—especially at higher altitudes—is a stiff breeze. Endless Energy Corporation, based in Yarmouth, is a wind energy development company working to bring New England the economic and environmental benefits of wind power. Incorporated in 1987, the company obtained the first permits granted in the state for a wind farm, at Sugarloaf Mountain, and was the first wind energy company in the U.S. to win a competitive bid with a utility. Learn more about their efforts to help build an environmentally and economically sustainable energy future at www.end lessenergy.com.

While windmills are still relatively rare, woodstoves are a common fixture in most Maine homes. Some households heat solely with wood (and to a lesser extent, coal), while others rely on woodstoves to supplement or back up a primary source of heat. Firewood isn't inexpensive—it usually runs between $130 and $200 a cord—cut, split, and delivered. It can be purchased in longer lengths for significantly less, if you're willing to do the final cutting and splitting yourself. How much wood does a woodstove burn in a typical Maine winter? An average homeowner, using wood along with another fuel source, will burn about two cords. Those using wood alone can expect to burn between four and five cords by the time warmer weather rolls around.

Direct-vent heating systems are another way Mainers heat their homes. These convenient, space-saving heaters can be up to 93% efficient, are inexpensive to purchase, and relatively inexpensive to operate. They use outside air for combustion and are fueled with kerosene, #1 oil, LP, or natural gas. Common name brands of these heaters include Monitor and Rinnai.

Many Mainers supplement their primary source of heat by burning wood.
Photo by Victoria Doudera.

Community spirit takes the chill off as well. Michelle and Bill Davis found that "after moving from Georgia to Maine, it wasn't the cold winters that took our breath away, but the warmth and small-town hospitality of the people here. Maine's relaxed pace actually allows time to really get to know your neighbors. There's something about being able to walk to dinner and running into a dozen friends and neighbors along the way. That would never happen in a huge metropolis like Atlanta."

# 5 Settling In

*"I write about Maine because it's what I know best,
but I also write about Maine because it's the
place I love best."*

—STEPHEN KING*

Most new residents find Maine communities surprisingly easy to slide into. "Our neighbors, even in this small coastal community, are friendly, and there's a real willingness to help others," says Carol Doherty-Cox of Port Clyde.

"Maine had a reputation for treating "people from away" differently," says Ruth Anne Hohfeld of Rockland. "We have found Mainers to be wonderfully welcoming people with little discrimination. People seem to have a deep belief that each person has a right to their 'idea-ahs.' Community is important."

Many new residents are amazed by the investment of time and energy Mainers make in their towns and cities. "I was surprised by the degree to which people are actively involved in the development of the community here," says Kristy Scher, who moved from Los Angeles to the midcoast in 1999. "It has been really wonderful and inspiring to see and work with a community of people who are so committed to living in a healthy, happy society. People are much less jaded in Maine—it's refreshing."

"I appreciate the level of involvement available in civic life," echoes Ruth Anne. "The excuse about 'they' doesn't work here. If one doesn't like something, one has to get out there and take action. At the same time, if one takes action, one can effect change."

---

*Stephen King, on Simon and Schuster's website to promote *Bag of Bones,* quoted in *Stephen King Country,* by George Beahm, Running Press, 1999.

Voting in many towns still involves the use of an old-fashioned ballot box. *Photo courtesy of the* Camden Herald.

Voter Registration

Voting is an important part of Maine citizenship. Turnout is generally strong, with the state consistently placing in the top five states—and often garnering first place—for voter participation. Presidential election years draw the most Maine voters, with an average of 65.8 percent of citizens casting ballots since 1980. Gubernatorial election years rank second with an average of 52.6 percent since 1978.

Maine is noted for its progressive voting laws. Maine was among the first states to adopt mail-in voter registration (possible up to two weeks before the election), same-day voter registration (bring proof of residence to voting place), and a motor voter program, which permits the Bureau of Motor Vehicles personnel to register voters. Maine law makes absentee ballots easily accessible—just contact your town office or city hall. Maine law also has special provisions to make registering to vote easier for those who have nontraditional residences. Most recently, the Maine Legislature protected the voting rights of stalking victims, by requiring their addresses be kept confidential.

Town offices such as the Cornish Town Hall are at the heart of Maine's small communities. *Photo by Ernie Rose.*

Spectators line the street to watch Camden's Memorial Day Parade. Community celebrations like this are a colorful part of small-town life. *Photo courtesy of the Camden Herald.*

Your Town Office or City Hall

People in Maine value local services, and pay for them (some think dearly) through local taxes. Nevertheless, your local town or city hall is a convenient source for just about any type of information you need. In addition, clerks at the office can issue landfill permits, birth and death certificates, dog licenses, fishing licenses, hunting licenses, building permits, motor bike permits, and permits for snowmobiles, boats, and ATVs. The town office or city hall is also where you pay your annual automobile excise tax.

Driver's Licenses

The Maine Bureau of Motor Vehicles (also known as the Department of Motor Vehicles) has offices in thirteen locations across the state where Maine driver's licenses are issued. Maine has just completed a switch to digital licenses, and they are valid for six years. To obtain one, you'll need your out-of-state license and one other form of identification. Unless you want to brush up on your driving skills, don't worry about studying—written tests are no longer necessary. (A national security check will be performed on your driving record.) You will be required to take an eye test, though, and pay a $40 fee.

BUREAU OF MOTOR VEHICLES LOCATIONS

Open 8 a.m. to 5 p.m., Monday through Friday. Closed on all legal holidays.

Augusta	285 State St.	207-287-3330
Bangor	Airport Mall	207-942-1319
Calais	204 North St.	207-454-2175
Caribou	159 Bennett Dr., Suite 1	207-492-9141
Ellsworth	24 Church St.	207-667-9363
Kennebunk	63 Portland Road, Suite 4	207-985-4890
Lewiston	124 Canal St.	207-783-5370
Mexico	Mexico Shopping Plaza	207-369-9921
Portland	312 Canco Rd.	207-822-6400
Rockland	212 New County Rd. (Thomaston)	207-596-2255
South Portland	364 Maine Mall Rd.	207-822-0730
Springvale	185 Main St., Rt. 109	207-490-1261
Topsham	49 Topsham Fair Mall Rd.	207-725-6520

Registering Your Vehicle

Cars are registered annually on a staggered basis. Generally, registrations expire one year from the month issued. You need evidence of auto insurance (see "Insurance," in this chapter) and your annual excise-tax payment to register a car. Registration can be done in person at a BMV office, through the mail, (Bureau of Motor Vehicles, Vehicle Services Division, 29 State House Station, Augusta, Maine 04333-0029), and, in some municipalities, on-line (www.maine.gov/sos/bmv). Many town offices also issue registrations and plates, so check first with your city or town to see if they participate in this program. If you choose to register your car in your new hometown, you may need to pay a small additional service charge, but since you'll have to go to city hall or the town office to pay your automobile excise tax anyway, it's convenient to renew the registration at the same time.

One interesting aspect of motor vehicle registration in Maine is that no notice of expiration or need for renewal is sent. Many a newcomer and old resident alike has sheepishly accepted a summons for driving an unregistered vehicle! Perhaps for this reason, the electronic registration renewal program is being piloted in several municipalities. Again, check to see if your community is one of the test cases for this new program by visiting www.maine.gov/sos/bmv.

Maine also requires an annual vehicle safety inspection. Most auto repair shops are also licensed inspection stations. The fee for the inspection is $12, pass or fail. If your vehicle fails, and you choose not to have the necessary repairs made, the shop is required to scrape half the current inspection sticker off the windshield, so other mechanics and the police will be aware that your vehicle has failed a state inspection.

License Plates, or, The Lobsters Return

Maine began issuing registration plates in 1905, with the state's first and only slogan "Vacationland" appearing on the plate in 1936. In July of 1987, the first of Maine's famous lobster plates (featuring a single red lobster on a plain white plate) appeared on Maine vehicles, the plan being they would help promote one of Maine's oldest resources. The crustaceans adorned everything from Cadillacs to Corvettes, until they were discontinued in June of 2000.

At that time a new design, showcasing the black-capped chickadee, Maine's state bird, flew off the assembly line and replaced the old lobster plates. But not long after the BMV terminated the production of the old lobster plates, members of the Maine Import-Export Lobster Dealers Association (MIELDA) rallied together in a three-year effort to bring back the lobsters with a brand new look.

With help from the Maine Lobster Promotion Council, a cleaner, clearer design for a specialty lobster plate was commissioned, and the winning image came from Karan McReynolds, a designer in Rockport. Cars began sporting the new plates in 2003, and by all accounts, the spiffed-up crustaceans are keepers. In addition to the obvious benefits of just having the lobster image on cars all over Maine, the industry receives some of the proceeds from the sale of the plates.

Other specialty license plates honor veterans, the Wabanaki culture, and University of Maine graduates. A popular plate features a loon and funds conservation efforts at state parks. The cost is an additional twenty dollars for most specialty models, and five dollars for a veteran plate.

Handicapped plates require a completed medical form that can be obtained from the BMV.

Vanity Plates

Vanity plates are available on selected plate types for an additional annual fee of fifteen dollars. Sally Littlefield of the Oakland House Seaside Resort in Brooksville says the vast numbers of humorous vanity plates on Maine roads is due to the free-thinking nature of Mainers. "We returned from a day trip to Kennebunkport via I-95, and what fun we had reading the "vanity" license plates on Mainers' vehicles. There is no end to the creativity expressed within the space of seven letters," she says.

"I hastily jotted down some of the more interesting ones spotted on our northbound trip: ALIENS, GO DRGNS, and DA TROLL. This was such fun that when I went to Bangor a few days later, I took my time, a piece of paper, and a pencil, ready to take notes. The wealth of creative vehicle registration lettering continued: VISTA, SLUDGE, SWEET-P, TANS VAN, LUNAR 76, MAINAH, B KEEPA (on a farm truck), BUILD (on a van parked at the local builder's supply store), SNOOP, HEAT IT (on a heating and plumbing truck), OLD BOY, RABIT, BLUE M&M, UH HUH, and DOO WOP."

Sally Littlefield does not attribute these whimsical plates to a dearth of activities during the long winter months, but finds them to be an expression of many residents' characters. "I believe Mainers are creative as a way of life. You have to be a jack of all trades, be resourceful, and inventive when you don't have the right tool to do the job and the hardware store is fifty miles away."

Whatever the reason, you can have fun crafting your unique message on the BMV's online search and order service for vanity license plates, on their website at www.maine.gov/sos/bmv. If nothing else, it's a good way to spend part of a winter afternoon.

Driving

Because Maine is a rural state, public transportation is largely limited to the big towns and cities. There are no commuter trains or subways in Maine. For most people, living in small towns means either walking for services or dri-

IN-STATE DISTANCES FROM PORTLAND

City	Miles	Kilometers	City	Miles	Kilometers
Augusta	57	92	Kittery	48	77
Bangor	129	208	Machias	205	330
Bar Harbor	162	261	Old Orchard	17	27
Bethel	66	106	Rangeley	118	190
Boothbay			Houlton	247	397
Harbor	56	90	Caribou	299	481
Camden	83	134	Fort Kent	313	504
Eastport	250	402	Madawaska	346	557
Freeport	13	28	Presque Isle	286	460
Greenville	154	248			

GETTING THERE FROM HERE

| Place | Mileage from | | | | |
	Portland	Bangor	Brunswick	Rockland	Rumford
Augusta	57	77	31	42	57
Boston	111	241	126	189	194
New York City	328	445	340	375	397
Philadelphia	421	537	447	480	502
Chicago	1053	1139	1106	1158	1075
Montreal	266	302	262	295	247

ving a car. But as newcomers quickly notice, driving about the state is relatively easy and often very pleasant.

"Driving here is much easier," says Lynda Chilton of Rockport. "There is no traffic and no sprawling generic suburbs. And Maine drivers are courteous. They stop for pedestrians and rarely honk their horns in anger."

Roads—with the exception of the Interstates and U.S. Route 1—are generally lightly traveled and fairly scenic.

A nationwide study released in 1999 reports that the average driver spends eighty-two hours a year in congestion in Los Angeles, seventy-six in the Washington, D.C., area, sixty-nine in Seattle, and sixty-six in Boston. Contrast that with the few minutes or so wait that Maine "traffic" sometimes causes. The only time that Mainers ever have to deal with traffic jams is in the summer, in such bottlenecks as the Bath and Wiscasset bridges and at various toll-booths on the Maine Turnpike.

"I have such a hard time driving back in New Jersey now," says Dan Barnstein of Bath. "The gridlock and road rage have only increased since we left five years ago. When people here complain about the traffic on Route 1, I just chuckle. It's so much more pleasant in Maine."

Despite the lack of public mass transit, those needing transportation assistance will find it. Services providing rides for seniors to doctors' offices, clinics, dining centers, government offices, and pharmacies are available even in the quietest communities. In Androscoggin County, for example, Community Concepts, Inc., offers free transportation to medical appointments for qualified residents. The Department of Transportation's Office of Passenger Transportation has a website listing public and fixed-route transportation providers by county (www.exploremaine.org), or check with local town offices for specifics.

Although rural, the state has launched an initiative to promote carpooling and alternative means of transportation. "Go Maine" is an offshoot of the Department of Transportation and it maintains a database of individuals who work in the state and have expressed a desire to commute to work via carpool, vanpool, transit, or bicycle. The group sponsors "Commute Another Way Day," an annual transportation event that promotes cost-effective, healthy, and enjoyable alternatives to driving alone to work. Register with them at www.gomaine.org.

Automobile Laws

Maine has some of the toughest laws in the country regarding operating under the influence (OUI). The legal blood-alcohol level is low—.08 percent—roughly equal to one cocktail consumed in an hour. (In some states the blood-alcohol level is .10.) And punishment for drivers deemed inebriated is swift and thorough: arrest at the scene, followed by courtroom penalties that include fines and license suspensions. Repeat offenders do jail time and risk losing their vehicle along with their license.

Maine has several new progressive automobile laws as well. Headlights must be on when using windshield wipers. Drivers must stop for pedestrians within any part of a marked crosswalk that is not regulated by a traffic light. Seatbelts are mandatory for all occupants in a car. And parents must follow safety precautions for children riding in automobiles. (See Chapter 9, Family Life.)

In 2002, Maine became the first state in the nation to mandate manufacturer responsibility for the removal of toxic mercury from vehicles. The law requires auto makers to create a system for removing and safely disposing of the mercury used in cars and trucks.

In 2006, Governor Baldacci signed a bill for a tough new regulation officially titled an "Act to Safeguard Maine Highways," but more commonly known as "Tina's Law" in memory of the victim of a fatal accident on the Maine Turnpike in 2005. The law redefines which violators are covered by mandatory minimum sentences, creates the crime of aggravated operation after habitual offender revocation, and imposes new penalties.

Car Insurance

The Bureau of Insurance notes that new residents should be aware of the state's financial responsibility-law for car insurance. Maine law requires that you buy liability insurance, uninsured motorist, and medical payments coverage. You cannot register your car in Maine without showing proof of insurance. Keep a proof-of-insurance card in your vehicle, too, because if you are ever stopped by a law enforcement officer, you will be asked to produce it.

The minimum limits (which all licensed insurance agents know) are $50,000 for the injury to or death of any one person; $100,000 for one accident resulting in injury to or death of more than one person; and $25,000 for property damage. Medical payments coverage is also required in the amount of $1,000. In addition, the state has mandatory uninsured-motorist coverage and the minimum for that is $50,000 per person and $100,000 per accident. Keep in mind that these minimum amounts may be low, depending on your situation, and you may want to buy more coverage.

The Bureau has an online "Consumer's Guide to Personal Auto Insurance" that will answer just about any question you may have. Check it out at www.maine.gov/pfr/ins/auto, or call them at 1-800-300-5000.

Registering Your Boat

Whether your taste runs to quiet kayaks, speedy J-24 sailboats, or steady fishing boats, there are plenty of ponds, lakes, rivers, and quiet coastal coves to explore. The Maine Department of Inland Fisheries & Wildlife in Augusta is the central office for boat registrations and registration records, but many municipal tax collectors or town clerks (and a few businesses) can do the job as well. If you are registering a watercraft at the Augusta office or in a town other than your own, you must first pay your annual excise tax in your town of legal residence. You must show the tax receipt in order to register your watercraft at another location.

Do all watercraft need to be registered? Motorboats of any size and non-motorized boats sixteen feet and longer do require registration, and your town office can give you the particulars. Another good source of boating information is the Inland Fisheries and Wildlife website at www.maine.gov /ifw, with registration details as well as tips on boating safety, a boating-supplies checklist, a list of which ponds and lakes prohibit personal watercraft and motorized boats, and much more.

Airports

The old Maine joke that "you can't get there from here" just doesn't ring true in this age of jet flight. If driving is not your style, Maine's airports allow you to whisk off to wherever in the world you desire. Smaller airports offer connecting flights to the state's international terminals as well as the chance to see beautiful scenery from the air. Many communities offer charter flight services as well.

Maine is served by two international airports, in Portland and Bangor, as well as more than 145 FAA-registered regional, municipal, and private facilities located throughout the state.

Incredible as it may seem for travelers accustomed to airport confusion, crowds, and long lines at security screenings, leaving on a jet plane in Maine is a pleasure. Both Portland International Jetport (www.portlandjetport.org) and Bangor International Airport (www.flybangor.com) provide true hassle-free flying. Parking is relatively inexpensive and easily available, crowded gates are nonexistent, and personnel are polite and pleasant, not to mention sharp as tacks. Another enjoyable perk: on nine trips out of ten you'll spot someone you know while strolling to the airport lounge. How often does that happen at Logan or JFK?

For a complete list of Maine's airports, along with which carriers they serve, see the Maine Department of Transportation's website at www.ex ploremaine.org.

Ferries

Living on an island means working around the arrivals and departures of the ferry. "It can be a challenge to find flights out of Portland that will also mesh with the ferry schedule," says Allie Lou Richardson of Islesboro. "We've become very relaxed about it, and I've found that professionals on the mainland are very understanding when I'm occasionally late."

Coastal Mainers are accustomed to taking ferries, whether for work or play. Private and state-run ferry services provide a vital link to Maine's many island communities, such as Islesboro, and international ferries provide service to Canada from ports in Bar Harbor, Eastport, and Portland. One of my sons remarked as a toddler that he wanted "to own the ferry that came and got your teeth." Only a child living near an island-dotted coast in an entrepreneurial state could hope to buy out the "tooth ferry!"

Good news for islanders and coastal travelers: in the coming years, speedier ferries will ply the high seas. The addition of new routes is part of an exciting plan by the state's Office of Passenger Transportation to increase the use of alternative transportation. A system of ferries linking coastal towns—from Boston to Eastport and into Canada—is being proposed as an alternative to driving Route 1 during the summer.

The Maine State Ferry Service operates most ferries; for general schedule information call 800-491-4883, or check the MDOT's website (www.ex ploremaine.org/ferry) for a link.

A quiet afternoon on Monhegan Island. *Photo courtesy of the Maine Office of Tourism.*

PROFILE

"We flew up to Bar Harbor to look at post-and-beam houses," remembers Allie Lou Richardson. "And on our return, flew over Islesboro and decided it looked like a great place to live." With a bird's-eye view of the island, the Richardsons began a twelve-year process of building their retirement home. "During that time we were too busy to have any concerns," she says. "The year before we moved, I began to panic. I wondered whether we'd find island living isolating, and I worried about health care and making new friends."

The Richardsons made the move to Islesboro in 1997, and found their fears to be unfounded. "There's plenty to do on the island, and our medical needs are well provided for by the local health center. We don't miss the mainland or New York. We do miss our children," says Allie Lou. "But then, we might move closer to them and they might move to Maine. It's kind of far for our friends to come visit, too." But by and large, the Richardsons' move to Maine has surpassed their expectations. "We wish we had done it sooner," Allie Lou says. "We've learned to make do and be much more relaxed."

STATE FERRY SERVICE

⚓ *Rockland to Vinalhaven,* 207-863-4421
Year-round service. 15 miles. Crossing 1 hr., 15 min.

⚓ *Rockland to North Haven,* 207-867-4441
Year-round service. 12.5 Miles. Crossing 1 hr., 10 min.

⚓ *Rockland to Matinicus,* 207-596-2202
23 miles. Crossing 2 hr., 15 min. Ferry service provided one day a month (more in summer).

⚓ *Lincolnville to Islesboro,* 207-789-5611 or 207-734-6935
Year-round service. 3 miles. Crossing 20 min.

⚓ *Bass Harbor to Swan's Island,* 207-526-4273
Year-round service. 6 miles. Crossing 40 min.

⚓ *Bass Harbor to Frenchboro,* 207-244-3254 or 800-491-4883
8.25 miles. Crossing 50 min.

OTHER FERRIES

⚓ *Monhegan Boat Line,* 207-372-8848
Year-round ferry service to Monhegan from Port Clyde.

⚓ *Northumberland/Bay Ferries,* 888-249-7245
Yarmouth, Nova Scotia, to Bar Harbor, Maine (seasonal).

⚓ *Prince of Fundy Cruises,* 800-341-7540
Yarmouth, Nova Scotia to Portland, Maine (seasonal).

⚓ *Casco Bay Lines,* 207-774-7871
Year-round service to Peaks, Chebeague, Long, Great and Little Diamond, and Cliff islands.

⚓ *The Cat,* 888-249-7245.
High-speed catamaran from Bar Harbor to Yarmouth, Nova Scotia, with new service from Portland, too.

Bus Services

Now that buses are smoke-free, they provide a healthy and enjoyable way to travel without having to take the wheel. You can even take in a movie on some routes. Here are the bus lines that serve Maine.

⚓ *Acadian Lines,* 800-567-5151. Service between Bangor and the

Canadian Maritime Provinces

⚑ *Concord Trailways,* 800-639-3317. Service to: Bangor, Bath, Belfast, Brunswick, Camden, Damariscotta, Portland, Rockland, Searsport, Waldoboro, and Wiscasset.

⚑ *Greyhound Bus Lines,* 800-231-2222. Service to: Bangor and Portland.

⚑ *Vermont Transit Lines,* 800-552-8737. Service to: Augusta, Bangor, Brunswick, Lewiston, Portland, and Waterville.

⚑ *West Bus Service,* 800-596-2823. Service to Bangor Airport, Bangor Greyhound Station, Calais, Ellsworth, Machias, and Perry.

⚑ *Zoom Shuttle Bus,* 877-THE-ZOOM, Service to: Biddeford, Old Orchard Beach, Portland, Saco, Scarborough, and South Portland.

Trains

After a thirty-year absence, passenger rail service is back in Maine. Amtrak's Downeaster (www.amtrakdowneaster.com; 800-USA-RAIL) provides service from Portland to Boston's North Station with stops in Wells, Saco, and Old Orchard Beach (and a few towns in New Hampshire as well . . .) The trip takes two-and-a-half enjoyable hours, and there are four round-trips daily, with a special late train for Red Sox fans. Amtrak is in the process of upgrading even more existing freight tracks to passenger rail standards, and communities as far north as Rockland are looking for ways to get on board as well.

Former Maine Senator George Mitchell got the project on track in 1993 when he sponsored legislation leading Congress to appropriate $39 million for track improvements. Because the initiative involved three states— Maine, Massachusetts, and New Hampshire—and many miles of old track, it took years to make Mitchell's dream a reality. But thanks to the perseverance of many dedicated train fans and a joint partnership between the state and Amtrak, riding the rails along the coast became possible once more in 2001.

At the time of the first "All Aboard!," former Governor Angus King said, "The initiative to restore passenger rail service has been in progress for more than ten years, beginning with the largest citizens' petition drive in Maine's history. Ordinary citizens demonstrated an extraordinary belief in the value of rail service in building our economy, reducing automobile emissions in our air, and providing a relaxing and picturesque travel experience to link great locations along the northern New England coast."

Bicycles

Maine is also actively pursuing bicycle travel, including rails-to-trails programs, bike and pedestrian paths, and bicycle tourism. Brunswick's new bike path, which follows the Androscoggin River for two-and-a-half miles, is a huge success, frequented by scores of joggers, walkers, skaters, and, yes, cyclists. There's talk of expanding the route to nearby Bath, and some hope it will one day link up with a network of trails that reach as far south as Kittery and as far north as Fort Kent.

Other communities are in the midst of creating bike and pedestrian pathways as well—Bethel, Augusta, and Old Town are just a few. The Department of Transportation has a new Bicycle/Pedestrian Coordinator, whose job it is to work on projects within towns as well as trails that connect communities in regions throughout the state. In the works are three trails—two of which are alongside railroad lines that will again operate—the department hopes to develop within the coming years. Combined, the trails will add up to an impressive 230 or so miles of bicycle routes that will help residents as well as tourists explore Maine from the seat of a bike.

The department provides a list of bike tours currently available in the state, including Maine's route for the "East Coast Greenway," the visionary "Urban Appalachian Trail" extending over 2,600 miles from Key West, Florida, to Calais, on the Maine coast. www.exploremaine.org. For more Maine bike info, check out the Bicycle Coalition of Maine's on-line newsletter at www.bikemaine.org. One final tip for bicyclists: Maine's new Bicycle Safety Act requires operators and passengers of bikes under the age of sixteen to wear bicycle helmets.

Health Care

"What about doctors?" One of the biggest concerns of people moving to Maine is the state and availability of health care. "I wondered about the quality of medical care, especially on the island we'd chosen," says Allie Lou

Richardson, who moved to Islesboro from suburban New York. Top-notch professionals and state-of-the-art facilities are important to all newcomers, especially those planning to raise a family or retire here.

The truth is that high-quality medical care is found throughout Maine for two different, yet complementary reasons: first, hospitals and medical practices still offer the kind of personalized care that has vanished in many big cities; and second, Maine's medical community actively recruits and attracts exceptional professionals from other states who are looking for a more relaxed lifestyle. In fact, Health Risk Management, Inc.'s, "Quality FIRST Index" ranks Maine one of the top ten states in health-care quality.

What about facilities and equipment? Although hospital costs per case remain less than the national average (and also less than the New England average), Maine's hospitals keep pace with their more expensive cousins in terms of up-to-date equipment and facilities. Administrators credit the state's Certificate of Need law, passed in the mid-1980s, with forcing hospitals to regionalize, promoting efficiency, and avoiding duplication of expensive gear.

While the regional approach helps keep costs down, it does create in-

Maine Medical Center, in Portland, is the state's busiest community hospital, as well as the area's leading provider of specialized services. MMC's open-heart-surgery program is the largest in New England.
Photo courtesy of Maine Medical Center.

PEDIATRICIAN DANA WHITTEN

A great example of the excellent medical care available in Maine is found in the pediatric practice of Dana Whitten, M.D. Raised in Massachusetts, Dr. Whitten has the kind of glowing resume you'd expect to see in the file of a prestigious big-city institution. His background includes education at Exeter and Harvard, medical training at the University of Pennsylvania School of Medicine, and residencies in Boston in pediatric hematology and oncology. In 1976, Dr. Whitten went from performing bone marrow transplants in Boston to diagnosing diaper rash in Belfast. It was a quality-of-life decision that he's never regretted.

"I hated my one-hour commute into Boston every day," he remembers. "My wife and I have always loved Maine, and we had ties to the state and friends here. We wanted to raise our daughter somewhere safe and beautiful. We came up to Waldo County with our three-year-old and discovered there wasn't a pediatrician in the area. I liked the hospital here in Belfast, so I started a solo practice with a great pediatric assistant—my wife—and fell in love with this kind of medicine."

The Whittens enjoy the benefits of a coastal lifestyle and can be spotted cruising Penobscot Bay in their sailboat. Their presence, in turn, has greatly enriched their midcoast community. "What's different about practicing medicine in Maine is that you know everyone," says Dr. Whitten. "There is a great patient–doctor relationship in a small town. I've kept some of my patients into early adulthood. I see parents everywhere, and they don't hesitate to ask me questions, even in the produce department of the local supermarket." He laughs. "I've even diagnosed a few things over the shopping cart."

His wife Diane, a registered nurse, is the same kind of caring practitioner. Ten years ago, she made a house call to check on a newborn and calm his worried mother. I was that new mom, and I've never forgotten the timeliness of Diane's visit and the competence of her care. It's what medicine in Maine is all about.

convenience for patients when they have to travel forty miles or more for treatments or diagnosis. At times, there's no other option than to get in the car and drive to one of the state's bigger institutions. Although annoying, this narrowing of focus has helped put some places at the forefront in certain specialties.

For instance, Portland's Maine Medical Center is recognized as a national leader in the field of cardiology, with outcomes for heart attack patients among the best in the country. The hospital was recognized by *Fortune* magazine in 1995 as one of the top eight hospitals in America for patients suffering heart attacks. Eastern Maine Medical Center, in Bangor, is another first-rate cardiology hospital. And the Joint Commission on Accreditation of Health Care Organizations ranks Central Maine Medical Center, in Lewiston, in the top ten percent of U.S. hospitals. It's hard to believe that a rural state can have such high-quality medical services, but it's true.

EMERGENCY MEDICAL SERVICES

In a vast state, emergency medicine is vital, and in Maine it's improving all the time. Paramedics and emergency medical technicians use the most sophisticated techniques available, and even the smallest of towns boast shiny new ambulances. Training is a constant focus, and even basic first responders are licensed to provide quick, life-saving care, involving the use of equipment like automatic defibrillators, crucial in the event of a heart attack.

Maine uses a unique Statewide Voluntary Trauma System linking hospital facilities with Emergency Medical Services. It's designed to very quickly move an injured person to the most appropriate hospital, no matter in what remote corner the injury may have occurred. And though the state may be rural, the roads tend to be less crammed with traffic, making for quicker emergency transport than in many cities and suburbs.

Maine's "LifeFlight" system, begun in 1998, is a key player in the voluntary Trauma System. LifeFlight's two new helicopters have already flown several hundred missions. One of the helicopters' more famous patients was author Stephen King, who was struck by a car while walking on a rural highway during the summer of 1999. The seriously injured writer was taken to Northern Cumberland Memorial Hospital, a small facility in Bridgton, where he was stabilized, and then flown to Central Maine Medical Center in

Lewiston. While the best-selling author certainly has the means to choose any facility in the world for his recovery, all of his treatment—including his follow-up and physical therapy—took place in Maine.

Knowledge can help in an emergency situation as well. In the spring of 2006, Governor Baldacci unveiled a first of its kind website, www.maine flu.gov, to provide information on pandemic influenza, also called avian or bird flu. In announcing the website, created through a partnership between five Maine state agencies and more than twenty diverse private-sector organizations and associations, Governor Baldacci explained, "This means that no matter what your questions or concerns are about flu, whether you are a physician, parent, or pandemic preparedness planner, this one website will provide a place for getting that information."

HOSPITALS

Thirty-nine acute care and specialty hospitals serve smaller communities throughout Maine. Most are private, nonprofit institutions with volunteer boards of directors made up of members of the very populations they serve. This local involvement keeps hospitals responsive to the community and fosters patient-doctor relationships. After all, it's difficult to give impersonal care to a patient whose son snowboards with yours.

There are also three government-run hospitals in Maine: the Augusta Mental Health Institute and the Bangor Mental Health Institute, as well as the Veteran's Administration Medical Center in Togus.

The small size of Maine's hospitals offers several advantages, one being that treatment often happens more quickly because there aren't as many distractions. When my daughter required emergency care at Penobscot Bay Medical Center in Rockport, a team was working on her before we could even take our jackets off. We knew the doctor on duty, who serves as a Cub Scout leader in town, and were able to call a specialist—another friend—who arrived promptly. While our daughter underwent surgery, my husband and I sat in the hushed waiting room, calm and quiet on a Wednesday night. We felt a rush of emotions, among them gratitude for the speedy, high-quality medical care available to us in our home area.

The state's two-tertiary care hospitals are Maine Medical Center in Portland, the largest hospital in northern New England, and Eastern Maine Medical Center in Bangor.

See Appendix 2 for a complete list of hospitals.

MAINE MEDICAL CENTER

Located in the heart of the city, Maine Medical Center serves as a community hospital for the Greater Portland area, as the medical hub for the southern half of the state, and as a center for health research and education for health-care professionals. Maine Med includes the Barbara Bush Children's Hospital (which added a brand-new inpatient unit in 1998) and Spring Harbor Hospital, a locally owned, not-for-profit mental health resource. Recently, Maine Med was named one of the Top 100 U.S. Cardiovascular Hospitals by HCIA Inc., a national health-care information company.

Maine Medical Center is a nonprofit institution dedicated to the highest quality of care possible for all Maine people. Along with additions to the Children's Hospital, Maine Med recently opened a new inpatient facility for the care of adult cancer patients, called The Gibson Pavilion. The research arm of the hospital, The Maine Medical Center Research Institute, is in the process of building a new home for its laboratory research divisions. This state-of-the-art facility will allow Maine Medical Center to expand research projects and attract new researchers.

EASTERN MAINE MEDICAL CENTER

Eastern Maine Medical Center (EMMC) is the specialty referral center for the northern two-thirds of Maine. Located on the bank of the Penobscot River since 1892, this 411-bed hospital provides full service cardiac-care, world-class cancer services, adult and pediatric intensive care units, as well as a level-three neonatal intensive care nursery. EMMC is the state's first trauma program verified by the American College of Surgeons, and serves as home base to one of Maine's two LifeFlight medical helicopters—flying more than 1,000 missions a year. EMMC's surgical weight-loss program was recently awarded the coveted status of Center of Excellence by the American Society for Bariatric Surgery, among the first programs in the country to offer surgical weight loss using robotic surgical techniques. On its three campuses and in its many primary-care offices, EMMC provides virtually any specialty medical service

EMMC is the flagship hospital of Eastern Maine Healthcare Systems. The system comprises seven non-profit hospitals, as well as community and allied health services spread across many hundreds of miles of central, eastern, and northern Maine. Connected by a vast network of clinical and informational technology, these hospitals together provide high-quality, state-of-the-art health services to the residents of the region. Visit www.emmc.org or www.emh.org for more information.

COMPLEMENTARY MEDICINE

In addition to traditional medicine, Maine offers a growing array of nontraditional and holistic care. Perhaps it is a reflection of the independent nature of Mainers, or their entrepreneurial spirit, but several communities offer a surprising variety of choice in what was once viewed as alternative medicine. Even smaller Maine towns feature wellness centers where treatments in disciplines such as massage therapy, acupuncture, and the ancient Japanese healing art of Reiki, can be found.

Statewide networks of hospice workers help the dying and their families as they go through the physical and emotional hardships of a terminal illness. Homeopathic practitioners across the state treat ailments from allergies to colic using natural substances. Certified nurse midwives and doulas assist in the births of hundreds of healthy babies. And Maine's 450 or so osteopathic physicians are trained and licensed practitioners who embrace a "whole person" approach to medicine that emphasizes the body's ability to heal itself. (Many of these D.O.s are graduates of Maine's medical school, the University of New England College of Osteopathic Medicine in Biddeford.)

Health Insurance

In February of 2006, *Down East* Magazine ran an article entitled "Maine's Insurance Mess." Unfortunately, the facts stated by author Jeff Clark came as no surprise to those who live here. As Clark explained, Mainers pay the second-highest health-insurance rates in the country after New Jersey; the state's taxpayer-funded Medicaid system is growing faster than almost any other state's; and the battles over Governor Baldacci's strategy to improve Maine's health-care system (Dirigo Health) have resulted in lawsuits and political wrangling. Newcomer Nancy Lawson of Camden says simply: "Health insurance is very expensive."

The current crisis started in 1993 when Maine, along with seven other states, passed laws stipulating that no one could be denied health insurance coverage no matter what his or her physical condition. A law limiting the amount an insurance carrier could charge for a health policy was passed at the same time.

The result? Health-insurance companies balked at the restrictions and began leaving the state. In 1993 there were more than a dozen carriers in the individual health-insurance market, but by 2006 more than 97 percent of the individual policies in Maine were written by one carrier: Anthem Blue Cross Blue Shield. Fewer carriers means less competition, and less competition has led to higher rates for everyone. As the cost of insurance has risen, Medicaid enrollments have grown, from 9 percent in 1993 to 21.4 percent in 2004. It's a vicious cycle.

I'd like to say something positive, but the truth is, Maine's health-insurance landscape is confusing and expensive. Reform is (hopefully) on the horizon. The good news is that just about everyone knows it is needed.

SOCIAL SECURITY OFFICES

- Auburn 207-782-5157
- Augusta 207-622-8348
- Bangor 207-990-4530
- Biddeford 207-282-5956
- Portland 207-780-3536
- Presque Isle 207-764-3771
- Rockland 207-596-6633
- Rumford 207-364-3731
- Waterville 207-872-2723

The toll-free number for all Social Security offices is 800-772-1213

Getting the News

Maine has seven daily papers: the *Portland Press Herald*, the *Bangor Daily News*, the *Kennebec Journal* (Augusta), the *Sun Journal* (Lewiston), the *Journal Tribune* (Biddeford), the *Times Record* (Brunswick), and the *Morning Sentinel* (Waterville). In addition, more than fifty weeklies cover communities from Caribou to Cutler, serving up local issues and news and offering a good taste of town politics and activities. "Obituaries are amazing to read," says Carole

Brand. "Often they are found on the second or third page of the newspaper, not 'buried' (sorry) in the back. They're like reading a life history, complete with hobbies, pets, favorite poems or quotes, and commentary from friends and family." There's no doubt that reading a good newspaper provides an excellent window into a particular community. Many also offer trial subscriptions with reduced rates. Appendix 3 lists addresses and phone numbers of all the Maine newspapers.

And what about the big city papers? Will moving to Maine mean sacrificing forever the *Wall Street Journal* or the *New York Times*?

While you can probably find your favorite paper on-line, stores in most Maine communities do sell major newspapers such as the *Wall Street Journal,* the *New York Times, USA Today* and the *Boston Globe.* Many local libraries subscribe to these papers as well. The only difference you may notice is that out-of-state papers tend to arrive at newsstands a tad later in the morning than in cities farther south.

Several magazines are published in Maine. Here are those that deal exclusively with the state:

- *Bangor Metro,* A new business, lifestyle, and opinion magazine serving central, coastal, eastern, and northern Maine. Published ten times per year. Call 207-941-1300, or visit www.bangormetro.com.
- *Down East,* "The Magazine of Maine." Published monthly. Call 800-747-7422 for information, or check www.downeast.com.
- *Maine Antique Digest,* "The World-wide Marketplace for Americana." Published monthly. Call 800-752-8521, or visit www.maineantiquedigest.com.
- *MaineBiz,* Maine's premier statewide business news publication. Published every other week. Call 207-761-8379, or visit www.mainebiz.biz.
- *Maine Boats, Homes and Harbors,* Published five times a year. Call 800-565-4951, or visit www.maineboats.com.
- *People, Places and Plants.* Published five times yearly. Call 207-428-4001, or visit www.peopleplacesplants.com.
- *Port City Life,* A new magazine that captures the flavor of Portland. Published bimonthly. Call 207-774-3775, or visit www.portcitylife.com.
- *Portland Monthly,* "Maine's City Magazine." Published monthly. Call

207-775-4339 or visit www.portlandmonthly.com.

⚑ *Travel Golf Maine.* Published bimonthly. Call 207-236-6716, or visit www.travelgolfmaine.com.

Shopping

In an era in which shopping is ranked one of America's favorite activities, it comes as no surprise that some newcomers cite lack of retail choice as one of the biggest challenges to living in Maine. Indoor malls are few: the Maine Mall in South Portland, the Bangor Mall, the Auburn Mall, and the Aroostook Mall in Presque Isle. While Freeport, with its village of stores, and Kittery, with dozens of outlet shops, are shopping destinations, in most communities smaller stores offering more personal service are the norm.

"I can get most anything I want in town," says Brad Rourke of Camden, "but there's not a great deal of choice. Catalogs help, but they can't supply everything you need."

"Shopping has been my biggest challenge," admits Lynda Chilton of Rockport. "Here in the midcoast we are at least an hour's drive from any mall or large department store. So trips for clothing, shoes, and specialty items that were only fifteen minutes away in Virginia have required some new strategies here. We have had to slow down our expectations, which is not necessarily a bad thing."

New residents have different ways of adapting to the dearth of large department stores. Some take shopping trips to busier areas once in a while. Others rely on catalogs or the Internet for purchases. After all, the growth of catalog and on-line retailing means miles don't matter—you can shop wherever and whenever. (UPS, Federal Express, and Airborne all make regular deliveries, and no extra time is required.) Some folks are pleasantly surprised to find they can live a little more simply in Maine, where consumerism is not a competitive sport. In other words, they buy less.

Of course, not everyone thinks the scarcity of sprawling malls is a hardship. Most people here—newcomers included—far prefer spruces to strip malls, not regretting the absence of the traffic, chain stores, noise, and bustle for which shopping areas have become known. "Readers considering relocation should know that there isn't a mall around the corner and that most of us love it that the stores are closed on holidays," says Ruth Anne Hohfeld.

And many come to cherish the kind of personal service smaller shops offer, service that is unavailable in busy big-box retailers. They appreciate the service from booksellers like Maine Coast Books in Damariscotta, for instance, where the owner knows just what type of mystery you enjoy. Or hardware stores like Rankins, in Camden, where second-generation owner Frank Rankin escorts you personally to find the right-size hinge. Service, attention, courtesy, and quality—these are the commonplace little things that make shopping a pleasure in Maine's small stores.

State Spirits

While many of us today are partial to a cup of coffee during the working day, Mainers of the early nineteenth century were far more likely to take "rum breaks." Back then, Maine was a major player in the seagoing "triangle trade" to the West Indies, with "demon rum" a profitable cargo in many a schooner's hold.

Despite (or perhaps because of) this fondness for rum, Maine was the first state to pass laws banning alcoholic beverages, earning it the title, "Birthplace of Prohibition." Temperance may have been popular with some, but others frequented their local bootlegger. More daring were smugglers who made clandestine trips to Canada, rum runners in their sloops, and bands of liquor pirates who raided them.

That exacting era ended with the repeal of Prohibition in the 1930s. Or did it? Some Maine communities rejected the return of legal spirits. To this day the towns of Linneus, Littleton, Monticello, and Blair, all in Aroostook County; Charleston and Corinth, west of Bangor; and the coastal towns of Cushing and Friendship remain"dry."

Outside of these communities, anyone over the age of twenty-one wishing to buy some bubbly can find it readily at privately owned "agency liquor stores." These establishments are located within larger supermarkets or convenience stores. Liquor prices are strictly regulated and are higher than in neighboring New Hampshire and Canada, which leads many people to stock up before crossing into Maine. To compete, the state-owned stores in Kittery and Calais offer discount prices—as much as 10 percent lower than the rest of the state.

No Butts

Unfortunately, Maine has a relatively high rate of smoking. With $60 million of its annual Medicaid budget spent on smoking-related illnesses, the state has targeted tobacco use as a high priority. A 1999 state law bans smoking in all restaurants and bars, and smoking is also banned in all hospitals and public buildings. Those under eighteen years of age are prohibited from purchasing tobacco, with stiff fines for vendors who sell to underage smokers.

The Partnership for a Tobacco-Free Maine (PTM) is the Maine State Tobacco Prevention and Control Program. Their website (www.tobac cofreemaine.org) can shed light on Maine's newest smoking rules and regulations. The PTM was originally developed as a result of the tobacco excise tax legislation passed in 1997 that doubled (to $.74 per pack) the tax. Maine is now one of five states that tax cigarettes at least two dollars a pack.

Although the fight to reduce Maine's dependence on tobacco is still underway, these efforts are not just smoke and mirrors. Since 1998, tobacco consumption in the state has dropped 16 percent, and Maine, which had the nation's highest teen smoking rate (39 percent) back in the 1990s, became in 2006 the first state to win a perfect score from the American Lung Association for its tobacco-fighting efforts. The association measures four categories: anti-tobacco program funding, smoke-free air, cigarette taxes, and youth access. Maine's grades contrasted sharply with those of the United States as a whole, which received mostly failing scores in the association's annual report card on anti-tobacco progress.

Maine Cuisine

Another tasty benefit of life in Maine is the freshness and variety of great things to eat. In many parts of the state, food ranges from the simple to the sophisticated, from nouveau cuisine to nostalgic favorites. Restaurants with creative chefs offer new twists on local ingredients like fiddlehead ferns or smoked mussels, as well as more traditional fare that changes with the seasons. Ethnic cuisine—once scarce in the state—is increasingly common, even in many small towns.

The state has its share of nationally recognized restaurants, too. Take Fore Street in Portland, for example. One of the city's best eateries, the restaurant's chef and co-owner, Sam Hayward, won a James Beard Foundation Award in 2004 as "best chef" in the Northeast.

Along with the old standbys such as diners, lobster shacks, and family eateries where generations of Maine residents and tourists have shared a meal, new restaurants are firing up their grills all the time. Nevertheless, some newcomers compare menus from large metropolitan areas and come up hungry.

"There are two extremes of restaurants in Maine, and very few in-betweeners," says Carole Brand. "The first is represented by Moody's Diner—a Maine tradition from the early 1900s where the menu has not changed since the opening (although the prices have), every item on the menu qualifies as "comfort food" (think macaroni and cheese and chocolate chiffon pie), and the concept of low carb must apply to your car engine and not your diet. The second is an astonishingly sophisticated high-end restaurant like Primo in Rockland, where reservations are required weeks in advance (months in the summer), presentation is as important as palate, and the menu contains items you are not comfortable pronouncing, let alone eating . . . but what you do eat is exquisite. Both varieties of restaurants have their passionate aficionados and long waiting lines."

Nancy Lawson moved to Maine in 2004 from California and says she finds "a lack of restaurants—especially Mexican restaurants—that offer good food at a good price." Ruth Anne Hohfeld, also an ex-Californian, thinks newcomers should know that "potlucks are better than most of the restaurants, and much more fun."

Ruth Anne has a point: casual dinners in which everyone brings a dish are popular in Maine, as is the famous big-clawed crustacean, *Homarus Americanus*.

To say that Maine is internationally known for lobster (more than 46 million pounds of them are harvested in a typical year) is an understatement. Maine is practically synonymous with the King of Seafood, and when you live here, you find yourself serving it to satisfied guests quite often. The Gulf of Maine is home to other equally delicious (though not as famous) gifts from the sea, such as mussels, clams, shrimp, scallops, and fish of all stripes. Some varieties you can catch yourself—others can be found at local supermarkets, fish markets, and fresh at the dock.

If seafood's not your style, markets and restaurants offer just about anything you crave—certified Black Angus beef, organically raised chickens, free-range turkeys, and spring lamb are just a few delicious possibilities. Small farms supply fresh eggs as well as a tempting array of cheeses, vegetables, and fruits. Farmer's markets display items like crunchy greens, fresh corn, and maple syrup, and supermarkets provide a wide variety of local (as well as imported) products and produce.

One item you may see on a Maine menu is the famous "Italian" (known outside the state as a sub, hoagie, or grinder,) a sandwich that combines ham, American cheese, and fresh veggies on a soft roll. The shop that brought the item to fame is Amato's, but you'll find the popular sandwich at pizza parlors and lunch counters throughout the state.

The changing seasons bring more of Maine's bounty: strawberries, raspberries, cranberries, and tangy little blueberries that thrive in our acidic soil. Come July, it's easy to see why the state produces 98 percent of the country's lowbush blueberries. Apples are another significant crop. Heirloom varieties like tart Northern Spies ripen alongside more common varieties such as McIntosh and Delicious at orchards large and small.

Living in Maine means savoring a whole pantry of delicious foods, including our famous red crustaceans, and hosting your share of potlucks. "I can eat a lobster roll for lunch," says Gloria Guiduli, who moved to the midcoast from Massachusetts in 2000. "Or sushi at the Japanese place, wonderful Italian food, and fresh croissants just out of the oven. Before I moved up, I wondered if finding ingredients for recipes here would be difficult, but I'm able to locate what I need at the local supermarkets and specialty stores."

Tips for selecting lobster from the Maine Lobster Promotion Council (www.mainelobsterpromo.com/index.html)

Color: Maine lobsters are usually greenish brown or black in color. Though they can also be blue, yellow, red, or even white, lobsters in these colors are so rare that they're not usually sold or eaten. The color of a lobster's shell does not affect its flavor or texture.

Activity: Look for lobsters that move around and hold their claws upward and their tails straight. Claws should never hang limply and the tails should never curl underneath its body.

Shells: Black marks or holes in the lobster's shell are the result of wear and tear and usually indicate an older lobster that hasn't recently shed its shell. Marks are not harmful in any way.

Hard-Shell Lobster: Hard-shell lobsters have been living in their shells for quite a while, and so they're usually fuller. However, it requires the use of utensils to gain access to the meat.

New-Shell Lobster: New-shell lobsters have recently molted and are growing into their new shells. Many people think new-shell lobster meat is sweeter and more tender than the meat of a hard-shell lobster, and it is significantly easier to remove from the shell.

PROFILE

"We thought we had a pretty clear understanding of what it would be like to finally live here, but we weren't prepared for how breathtakingly beautiful it is," says Maggy King. She and her husband Clay are licensed massage therapists who relocated in 2002. "The quality of life for all of us, the children in particular, is so superior to life in Atlanta, and I don't think we could have begun to comprehend how much we would all be affected." The Kings love the slower pace their new state encourages. "The biggest advantage is really slowing down and connecting with your family. When life is so frantic, as it was in Atlanta, you don't get the quality time that builds unshakeable relationships. You really discover what's genuinely important here. The only negative is how expensive it is. We thought it would be more affordable."

6 Weather and Wildlife

*"The coldest winter I ever spent was
a summer in Maine."*

—MARK TWAIN*

Summers in Maine are exquisite. Despite what Mr. Twain may have quipped, the state boasts one of the most comfortable summer climates in the continental United States, a prime reason why thousands of vacationers started "summering" here in the first place. And autumn is nothing short of glorious, with the crimsons and golds of the changing foliage enhanced by sunny, dry days in the sixties and low seventies.

And then there's winter. Most of the country harbors exaggerated notions about the severity of Maine's weather come December. Even southern New Englanders believe Old Man Winter saves the full force of his wrath for the Pine Tree State, relentlessly dumping foot after foot of the white stuff on uncomplaining Mainers. And springtime?

"Two words," says transplant Barry Hurtt, a midwesterner who moved to Cushing. "Mud season."

A Four-Season Climate

This part of the country has four distinct seasons, and that in itself can be a challenge for newcomers accustomed to the same weather no matter what the calendar reads. "I was concerned before moving about dealing with a truly seasonal climate," admits Gary Swanson, who moved with his family to Rockland in 1998. "Coming from California, we've found the weather associated with each of Maine's seasons to be quite dramatic. But if you're prepared, it's really a very livable climate."

----
*As appeared in *Portland Monthly* magazine, July 1999.

Carole Brand has spent only two winters, but says, "Frankly, I think the weather is an advantage. The summers are cool and the winters are manageable." Carole had wondered whether the winters would "live up to their reputation," but she says "good snow removal, road maintenance, weather reports, and a gas fireplace make winter not a problem."

There are many good-natured jokes about Maine's seasons, and in particular, their length and arrival dates. People quip that summer hits on the Fourth of July and winter sets in on July 5. Others maintain that "black fly season" comes with the melting snow, and that autumn is announced not by crisp, cool days, but by the onslaught of the fall tourists, or "leaf peepers."

My favorite definition of Maine's meteorological year is that it's

MAINE ANNUAL WEATHER FACTS

Precipitation: 43 inches.

Number of thunderstorms: 15 to 20.

Clear days—without fog or other precipitation: 120 days.

Average snowfall on the coast: 50 to 70 inches.

Average snowfall in southern interior section: 60 to 90 inches.

Average snowfall in northern interior section: 90 to 110 inches.

Days with one inch or more snowfall along the coast: 15 to 20 (although a "nor'easter" may occasionally drop ten or more inches in a single day).

Days with one inch or more snowfall in the northern interior: 30.

Snowiest month: January, with an average of 20 inches.

Month when hurricanes are most likely to occur: September.

Frequency of tornadoes: rare.

Number of sub-zero days along the coast: 10 to 20.

Number of sub-zero days in the northern interior: 40 to 60.

Average peak temperatures: 70° F throughout the state, usually in July, though during a very warm summer, temperatures may reach well above 90° F for as many as 25 days in the southern interior sections and for as long as a week along the coast.

Freezing temperatures encourage winter activities such as ice skating on smooth lakes and ponds. *Photo courtesy of the Camden Herald.*

"nine months of winter, and three months of mighty rough sleddin'."

But in reality, the climate is generally more moderate (especially along the coast) than in other northern states. Maine's size and its varied topography can make the weather very different in each corner of the state at any given time. Coastal areas receive cool breezes in the summer and warmer air in the winter. When it snows in the western mountains, it may rain Down East and be sunny on the south coast. Kids in Caribou do a great deal more sledding than do their counterparts in Kennebunkport.

WINTER

"Before I moved here, I wondered, 'What are the winters really like?'" says Barry Hurtt. "But after a decade in Chicago, Maine winters are no big deal."

Anyone accustomed to winters like those dished out in the Midwest can take Maine weather in stride. Contrary to popular belief, winter begins on the late side—some years not until mid-December. It's generally cold here, ranging between 21 degrees and 32 degrees in January, depending on where you are, but prolonged cold spells of several weeks are rare. Average snowfall ranges from 50 to 110 inches—again, depending on where you are when the flakes fly.

Folks who aren't used to chilly temperatures are often surprised that life goes on even when the mercury drops a little. "We've been amazed to see how active everyone is in the winter," says Thad Chilton of Rockport. "It's great to see families out walking, skiing, and having a good time together." And people who have spent several winters often grow to appreciate the profound beauty of the countryside under a blanket of white and the moody light and colors of the northern sky.

That's not to say a mean winter can't pack a punch or two, although old-timers claim that today's storms are considerably tamer than the legendary blizzards of yore. "Winter is our most variable season," says Gregory Zielinski, state climatologist and University of Maine professor. "Some are cold, some are warm." Zielinski says Maine winters have a tendency to run on 10- to 20-year cycles. "The 1950s to the '70s, we had more cold and snowy winters than not," he says. "In the late '70s, '80s, and part of the '90s, we had more warmer and less snowy winters."

This propensity is the result of the rapport between a low-pressure system near Iceland and a high-pressure system near the Azores, called the North Atlantic oscillation. Pressure differences in the Atlantic Ocean affect the form of the jet stream—fast-moving winds that blow west to east at high altitudes—which in turn influences much of Maine's weather.

Even in a mild year, the occasional nor'easter may drop several inches,

The ice storm of the twentieth century took place in January 1998. As many as 690,000 Mainers were left without electricity as the weight of a thick coat of ice snapped tree limbs, bringing down power lines all over the Northeast. *Photo courtesy of the* Camden Herald.

134

prompting television weathermen to put on their sweaters and predict doom and school superintendents to cancel classes. But there is not as much fanfare as you might think. Perhaps because Maine is a state adept at dealing with the white stuff, people often view winter storms more as an occasional treat than a frequent and daunting threat.

"While it snows more heavily and more often in Maine than in New Jersey, Maine snow has apparently acquired the ability to disappear within 24 hours after falling," says Carole Brand. "It is a mystery where it goes.....but the day after a snowstorm, not only are the roads and shoulders perfectly clear and dry, but the streets and sidewalks in town are also completely empty and passable. No enormous snowbanks to hurdle; no walking blocks to find a path shoveled through the snow; I'm not even sure why I bought a new pair of boots. I have a feeling there is a Maine Snow Depository, where the towns deposit the shoveled snow and those in the know can go skiing in August."

Many towns do have an ordinance that the streets must be clear within 24 hours of a snowfall. "I've been impressed with how well-maintained Maine roads are in the winter," notes Allie Lou Richardson of Islesboro. "Crews are at the ready to deal with storms right away."

Elizabeth Burrell of Rockland, a veteran of several Maine winters, agrees. "Don't worry about the weather," she advises. "Towns here are really very well adapted to dealing with whatever comes up."

Winter around the Country

State	Aver. Temperature (Deg.F)	Aver. Precipitation (Inches)
Connecticut	31.9	13.40
Delaware	39.6	14.08
Maine	17.9	8.78
Maryland	38.0	11.62
Massachusetts	31.1	12.19
New Hampshire	23.8	11.82
New Jersey	35.9	13.56
Pennsylvania	31.0	9.62
Rhode Island	35.0	13.66
Vermont	21.78	10.00
West Virginia	35.3	8.07

March's chilly winds and cool temperatures keep many schooners under wraps until April. *Photo courtesy of the* Camden Herald.

SPRING: APRIL IN PARIS (MAINE)

Another time of the year that makes many newcomers pause is the spring, including the interval known fondly in Maine as "mud season."

Unlike some states, Maine is not famous for showy springs. The season that follows winter Down East is a subtle, slow awakening, appreciated more for its quiet clues than boisterous displays. In some years the casual observer has a tough time finding any hint of spring's arrival throughout the chilly gray days of March and April. Because of this, Mainers watch eagerly for signs of the season, noting the first buds on the forsythia (bright-yellow-blossomed shrubs with a free-flowing form) and the robin's return. Towns hold annual ice-out contests, with participants guessing when area lakes will become free of winter's grip and open for navigation. Gardeners admire their daffodils, tulips, and jonquils as they break through the warming soil and bloom. And yes, everyone dons mud boots.

To newcomer Carole Brand, mud season means "it is impossible to keep your car clean for more than ten minutes at a time—and any car that

GEAR TO GET YOU THROUGH THE SEASONS

Based on a list of tongue-in-cheek suggestions from L.L. Bean's Dave Teufel.

SPRING

- *Bug-proof jacket, pants, and headnet.* These items won't stop the blackflies, but will hopefully confuse them long enough for you to make it back from the outhouse.
- *100% pure DEET insect repellent.* You'll need this to keep 'em off you while you're in the outhouse.
- *Traditional "Bean Boots" (the Famous Maine Hunting Shoe with rubber bottom and leather upper).* Height of the uppers depends on where in the state you are moving. In southern Maine, down around Kittery, the ten-inch style is fine, as you only occasionally step in mud. If you plan to spend mud season Down East, in the Lakes Region, or worse, in The County, then you'd best invest in the sixteen-inch version.
- *Rain gear.* Why? Because 50 percent of mud is water.

SUMMER

- You'll want a *canoe or kayak* to get the most out of the summer. But for the love of Pete don't put it off, Maine summers don't last but a few days!
- You'll need a *wetsuit* for going swimming. There's a week, usually late in August, where the ocean temperature soars into the upper 50s. With the right wetsuit, you can usually last a good five minutes before you have to head back to shore.
- A *fly-fishing outfit* is a must. Standing in a cold stream wearing rubber pants was stylish in Maine long before *A River Runs Through It...*
- You'll need a *cooler* to haul all the lobsters you're gonna need when every single flatlander you've ever known shows up at your door for their vacation.

continues →

is clean is immediately identified as being "from away," regardless of the fact that it has Maine license plates." Come spring, she tells herself, "Enjoy the mud . . . become one with the mud."

FALL
- Yes, the leaves are beautiful. But it's also mating season for the largest of the hoofed animals; the majestic moose. You will need a *mountain bike* for fast getaways from lovesick bulls on the loose.
- *Running shoes* will come in handy if you find yourself between a moose and a hard place.
- While you're out there, might as well bring your own *tent* and spend a few days camping. The leaf-peepers aren't leaving anytime soon, and there will probably be a few staying at your house.

WINTER
- You'll need *flashlights, candle lanterns, batteries, and camp stoves.* You can count on being out of power for at least four days—unless there is another ice storm like the one in '98, then triple it.
- Sell your fancy car and buy a *truck*. On the way home buy a baseball bat and let the truck have it. (You want to blend in, don't you?) Now, go buy an *auto tow strap, a come-along, and a packable shovel.* The fastest way to the heart of Mainers is to offer them roadside assistance when they are stuck in a snow bank.
- And remember, no matter if you have lived in Maine for sixty years, if you are originally from somewhere else, you will never be considered a Mainer by other Mainers. Just accept it and be proud of your birthplace! Even if you can't get there from here.

SUMMER

If there is one problem with a Maine summer, it's that leaving the state is difficult. Oh, physically, it's easy—the inconveniences that plague other vacation destinations, like crowded roads, high temperatures, and canceled flights are not all that commonplace in Maine, though certain spots (like Route 1 in Wiscasset) can become a tangle. Rather, leaving is hard because Maine summers are simply extraordinary. With temperatures in the seventies, cool nights, and clean air (the state averaged only one day of unhealthy air in 1999), why would anyone want to leave? More than one Mainer has come back from a summer vacation away and vowed never to depart again. Summers in Maine are a gift—the perfectly green landscape broken only by the colors of gardens, the gentle breezes—even more precious because of their brevity.

"The only downside we've found to living here is that our friends are mad at us for not wanting to leave Maine and go back to visit them!" says Jane Dahmen, who moved from Massachusetts in 2005. "We can't stand to drive south—and when we do we can't wait to get back to 'paradise'."

AUTUMN

The only thing that makes it bearable to part with summer is the beauty of autumn Down East. September, October, and November are months to treasure. September is often a sunny, crystal-clear month, perfect for hiking, camping, and enjoying the pleasures of summer without the crowds. October ushers in the crispness of fall, along with the glorious colors of the changing foliage. Occasional days of Indian summer can push temperatures into the high seventies, and prompt youngsters to wear shorts to school. November brings the tang of wood smoke to the air, frosted windowpanes, a peaceful landscape, and perhaps a few wispy tufts of snow.

Many residents, myself included, love autumn best of all. The air is invigorating, and the light takes on a painterly hue that is sometimes breathtaking. It's a beautiful string of russet-colored days, a time of harvest, of thankfulness, and of preparation for the colder weather to come. Tourists have discovered the pleasures of Maine's fall, yet those who come at this time seem more subdued than the boisterous crowds of August. And as each leaf falls, the state grows a little quieter.

"I think the most important thing when considering a move to Maine is to visit in all seasons," says Rockport's Lynda Chilton. "We've found that the weather here is perfect for all kinds of activities year-round."

Wildlife

Maine is home to a vast array of wildlife—one of the most varied populations in the eastern United States, in fact. White-tailed deer, bobcats, black bears, coyotes, loons, seals, ospreys, chipmunks, raccoons, beavers, lynx, muskrats, squirrels, otters, foxes, mink, weasels, skunks, and porcupines—the list goes on and on, including threatened species such as bald eagles, Blanding's turtles, and puffins—those colorful "sea parrots" that are making a comeback along the Maine coast. Most famous of all of the state's animals is probably its largest—the moose. "One advantage to moving here," quips Marlene Kinlin of Jonesport, "is watching moose stroll through my front yard."

It isn't every day that a moose comes to call, but living in Maine does make it possible. After all, there are more than thirty-thousand of the big beasts in the state. Their footprints are often visible on muddy hiking trails

Moose often wade into ponds and lakes to munch pondweed and water lily, two nutritious (and apparently delicious) aquatic plants.
Photo by Bill Silliker, Jr., from his book Uses for Mooses *(Down East Books).*

140

or dirt roads, and a bull's spreading antlers adorn many a fireplace mantel. Given a little luck and a kayak, you can paddle to a quiet cove on Moosehead Lake and spy one munching aquatic weeds—a favorite treat. On rare occasions, moose will even venture into busy downtown areas (we had one clip-clopping down our street one spring) or stroll across golf courses.

Rarer by far are sightings of wolves and mountain lions, two recent additions to Maine's endangered species list. Although state biologists have long questioned their existence here, both of these predators are found in Canada, and reports of their presence in Maine persist. In June 2000, a wolflike animal was captured west of Baxter State Park, but managed to escape before DNA testing could be done on it. A wolf was trapped in Aurora in 1996, and another one was shot in the Moosehead Lake area in 1993, yet wolf sightings are still extremely rare.

Maine is home to Canada lynx and bobcats, but a verifiable photograph or video of a mountain lion has yet to be taken. Nevertheless, hundreds of reports of cougars are recorded annually with the Department of Inland Fisheries and Wildlife, and several likely tracks have been found. In the hopes of seeing solid evidence of these secretive felines, wildlife biologists follow up reports in the field and conduct track surveys each winter.

Large predators notwithstanding, it's a relief to discover that Maine lacks many of the poisonous critters that plague other states. There are no poisonous snakes to contend with, no scorpions, and very few venomous insects. Instead, more than one hundred and fifty insects in the order *Odonata*, damselflies and dragonflies, flit on translucent wings over ponds, bogs, and fields. Nonpoisonous and colorful, they are a significant and conspicuous component of Maine's wildlife diversity.

Stewards of Wildlife

Marlene Kinlin isn't the only Mainer with an affinity for her neighborhood wildlife. Carole Brand will never forget the sight of two eagles surveying the harbor from the birch tree in back of her house, or the fox that scurried across her lawn. Living here often means a closer connection to animals of all types. According to a recent University of Maine study, 53 percent of Maine residents participate in wildlife watching, hunting, or fishing, which ranks the state fourth in the nation after Alaska, Montana, and Idaho. These

141

pastimes also mean tourism dollars for the state. Maine people (including hunters) recognize that wildlife, like any resource, must be responsibly managed, and, when necessary, protected.

A good example of this cooperation is the Maine Outdoor Heritage Fund, a partnership between the Sportsman's Alliance of Maine and the Maine Audubon Society. Created in 1994, the fund is a source of grants for projects that conserve the outdoors for Maine people and wildlife. In what may seem an unlikely alliance—the fishing and hunting crowd and the ardent environmentalists—the two groups started a referendum campaign to establish a scratch-off lottery ticket dedicated to conservation. So successful were their initial efforts that the legislature implemented the program on its own, bypassing the need for a referendum. Since Maine Outdoor Heritage tickets first went on sale in January 1996, more than 19 million have been sold, funding more than $5.14 million in grants to 185 projects. Tickets are available at most convenience stores, gas stations, and other outlets where Maine State Lottery tickets are sold.

Maine has more than sixty game sanctuaries and wildlife management areas. There are strong laws regulating treatment of wildlife, and wardens and deputy wardens make sure the laws are enforced. Even seemingly innocent acts that endanger wild animals, like the handling of seal pups, are punishable with stiff fines. (Seal pups are born in late spring and are often left on shore while their mothers find food. Never touch, or even approach, a seal pup—instead, call the Marine Animal Lifeline at 207-851-6625 should you find a stray, abandoned, or injured marine mammal.)

Birding

Maine's diversity of coastal and inland habitats offers birders the chance to add lots of feathered friends to their life list—more than 450 species have been identified in the state. In addition to the cheerful little black-capped chickadee, whose two-note song is such a harbinger of spring, there are robins and other thrushes, killdeer, blue jays, gray jays, starlings, crows, phoebes, kingfishers, common grackles, and warblers. Grosbeaks, crossbills, sparrows, and other finches commonly nest in Maine's woodlands, meadows, and swamps. Predatory birds found in Maine include owls and

Adult loons on a tranquil lake. Thanks to conservation efforts led by the Maine Audobon Society, loons are a common sight on some waterways. *Photo by Ken Bailey.*

A wild turkey hunts for food in the snow. *Photo by Ernie Rose.*

hawks, such as ospreys and red-tailed hawks, and bald eagles. Maine is the nesting and breeding ground for numerous migrant species of coastal and inland birds, and offers the opportunity to see rare and beautiful species like puffins and loons. In fact, Maine is fortunate to have the largest population of loons in all of New England, estimated at four thousand adults. Since 1977, The Maine Audubon Society has been working to protect the common loon in Maine, and thanks to their vigilance, the loon population now seems fairly stable.

For a checklist of Maine birds, contact the Audubon Society at 207-781-2330 or through its web site at www.maineaudubon.org. Another good web site for bird identification, sites, and trips is www.mainebirding.net.

Faces from the Past

Currently thirty-four species of fish and wildlife are listed as endangered or threatened under Maine's Endangered Species Act. Some are also listed on the federal government's list.

The state's Department of Inland Fisheries and Wildlife is working with concerned citizens and other groups to boost the dwindling numbers of animals such as piping plovers, box turtles, and twilight moths, and hopefully these efforts will succeed. Some species, like the peregrine falcon, have already shown great progress thanks in large part to protection of nesting sites. (Acadia National Park closes two popular hiking trails during peregrine nesting season.) Other success stories have been the reintroduction of the wild turkey and the Atlantic puffin.

PERSISTENCE PAYS OFF

A common sight (and source of dinner) during colonial days, the wild turkey, North America's largest upland game bird, disappeared from Maine in the early 1800s, largely due to hunting and loss of woodlands. Sportsmen tried reintroducing the birds in 1942, but to no avail. In 1977 and 1978, the Maine Department of Inland Fisheries and Wildlife obtained forty-one wild turkeys from Vermont and released them in the towns of York and Eliot. In the spring of 1982, thirty-three turkeys were trapped from the growing York County population and released in Waldo County. Two years later, more birds were relocated, this time to Hancock County, but poaching was believed to be their downfall. During the winters of 1987 and 1988, seventy wild turkeys were obtained from Connecticut to augment Maine's growing population. While some have succumbed to heavy snowfalls, the rest have prospered and multiplied. Today the state's flock has grown to more than eight thousand and spread well beyond its historic range. So large is the wild turkey population now that hunting the elusive birds is once again allowed.

PUFFIN PATROL

Maine is famous for a multi-colored sea bird, the common or Atlantic puffin. This bird spends most of its time in the North Atlantic, coming ashore only to breed and raise one chick in an underground burrow. A century ago, puffins were found on six Maine islands, but excessive hunting led to their near demise in Maine. By the 1900s, there was only one pair of puffins left south of the Canadian border. The lone couple lived on Matinicus Rock, a lonely spot twenty-two miles off the coast in Penobscot Bay. After Matinicus Rock's lighthouse keepers began protecting the puffins from hunters, their numbers began to increase. Today there are about a hundred and fifty nesting pairs on the rock.

In 1973, Stephen Kress, Ph.D., a summer resident of Bremen, began Project Puffin to re-introduce the birds to Eastern Egg Rock in Muscongus Bay. After eight years of trips to Newfoundland to find puffin chicks to "transplant," his efforts, with help from the National Audubon Society, paid off. Today, Maine has puffin colonies on at least four of the original six nesting islands: Eastern Egg Rock, Seal Island, Machias Seal Island, and Matinicus Rock. Several tour boats operate trips to the puffin colonies from different points along the coast in summer. The puffin-watching season begins around Memorial Day and goes until early to mid-August. For a list of tours, check out www.mainebirding.net or call the Maine Office of Tourism at 207-287-5710, or see their website at www.visitmaine.com.

Moose Watch

Like puffins and turkeys, moose were once in danger of disappearing in Maine. While explorers in the early 1600s found a plentiful supply of moose throughout New England, unrestricted hunting during the centuries that followed decimated the population. By the early 1900s, only two thousand or so moose were left.

Hunting the massive mammals was illegal from 1936 until 1980, and during those years, numbers of the animals slowly grew. In 1979, the moose population had grown so large that a bill allowing the state to issue up to seven hundred hunting permits to Maine resident hunters was signed into law. Since that time, the number of permits issued and the area open to moose hunting has increased. Non-residents are also allowed a percentage of the permits. In 1999, three thousand permits were issued, with five hundred of those earmarked specifically for "antlerless moose." Despite deaths from hunting and highway accidents, the Department of Inland Fisheries and Wildlife estimates that there are approximately thirty-thousand moose in Maine.

A white-tailed deer in winter. Maine's herd is estimated at more than 330,000. *Photo by Ken Bailey.*

MORE THAN YOU EVER THOUGHT YOU'D KNOW ABOUT MAINE MOOSE

- The Latin name for moose, *Alces,* means "elk," and in Europe moose are called elk. The animals are the largest members of the deer family.
- Of the four species of moose found in North America, it's the Eastern Moose that calls Maine home.
- Adult cows (females) weigh around eight hundred pounds. Bulls can weigh more than a thousand pounds.
- The total length of a moose is about nine feet. Height measured at the shoulder is about six feet.
- Both cows and bulls have "bells," or skin flaps on the underside of the neck. A cow's bell looks more like a tuft of hair, whereas a bull's bell is larger and rounder.
- The spread of a bull's antlers rarely exceeds sixty-five inches.
- Antlers on cows are extremely rare.

146

- Moose chomp away on "browse," the leaves and twigs of woody plants. Willow, aspen, birch, maple, pin cherry, and mountain ash are their favorites.
- Moose have no top front teeth.
- Balsam fir is a moose's winter junk food: tasty, but nutritionally lacking.
- Aquatic plants, such as pondweed and water lily, are an important part of a moose's diet.
- Moose begin breeding in late September.
- Cows may produce their first calf when they are two years old. Each May, cows give birth to one or two calves.
- Moose can see clearly only about 25 feet.
- Calves remain with their mother for one year and are driven off shortly before the next calf is born.
- Black bears, which are common in Maine, are potential predators of moose calves.
- The average life expectancy is eight years for a cow and seven years for a bull. Moose may live into their late teens, but rarely live past twenty.
- Moose are found statewide, but most happily thrive in northern Maine.(In the state's Moosehead Lake Region, moose outnumber people 3 to 1.)

Deer

According to wildlife biologist Gerry Lavigne, Maine is home to one of the largest subspecies of white-tailed deer, with some mature males, or bucks, weighing nearly three hundred pounds. While approximately 331,000 of these herbivores call Maine home, it's surprising to note that more deer per square mile (fifteen to twenty-five) live in central and southern sections than in the north, where only two to five deer per square mile can be found. In some particularly popular locales to the south, the Department of Inland Fisheries and Wildlife says there are populations of forty to one hundred deer per square mile.

Increasing numbers of deer (and moose, and even turkeys) mean automobile drivers must exercise caution on Maine roads, particularly at dawn and dusk. Take warning signs seriously—in deer or moose zones drive no faster than the speed limit, use your bright lights, and wear your seat belt.

Deer tend to travel in groups, so if you spot one, chances are that others are waiting in the woods. And if a deer or moose is standing in the middle of the road, your best course of action is to slow down, pull over, and exercise patience—honking won't always send them away.

Hunting Season

Avid sportsmen in Maine are in good company—the state has a strong tradition of hunting, fishing, and trapping. Generations of Maine families have hunted in the same quiet spots year after year, or tromped through the spring mud (despite the black flies) to wet a line and fish. Out-of-state hunters and fishermen have headed into the vast woods Down East for more than a century now, staying in remote lodges and employing local guides. Many return to the state each year in search of trophy deer, trout, ducks, or moose.

Fluorescent-orange hats, gun racks on pickups, and general stores transformed into game-tagging stations—all are part of the local scene

Entrepreneur and avid hunter Leon Leonwood Bean models his Hunting Safety Coat for an early L.L. Bean catalog. *Photo courtesy L.L. Bean, Inc.*

PROFILE

Gordon and Carol Doherty-Cox relocated to Maine after considering a move to the South. "We investigated various areas via the Internet, and we were impressed by the information we found about Maine. We knew where all the banks, theaters, cable companies, and the like were before we even moved," says Carol. "We've found friendly, helpful people here," she says, "and we love the more relaxed lifestyle. However, it's expensive to live here—it's not cheap to drive, heat your house, or cook your food. Variety in shopping is hard to come by, too." Carol and Gordon were surprised by the size of their new state. "We didn't realize how huge Maine is, and we're looking forward to exploring the whole state." The Coxes have some advice for those considering a move to Maine. "Leave your old lifestyle behind, and be prepared to be a part of Maine. If you're looking for a cheaper version of Connecticut, it won't work."

come fall. Many a new resident has been astonished to meet a camouflaged man with a rifle walking along a woods road, or see a dead deer in a pickup truck on an autumn afternoon. Whether or not you agree with the practice, hunting is a way of life in Maine. And yes, at times the crack of gunfire echoes through the woods.

Although November is the time of year most associated with hunting, seasons for various animals extend into other times of year. Deer season, for example, opens for archers in late September and continues through October. Deer hunting with firearms begins in November and lasts until early December. Hunting is not allowed anywhere in the state on Sunday, but it is always advisable to use caution and wear fluorescent-orange outerwear when walking in the woods during hunting season.

For more information on hunting regulations, contact your local town office or city hall, or the Maine Department of Inland Fisheries and Wildlife at 207-287-8000. Or check out the MDIFW's web site atwww.maine. gov/ifw.

SAFE HUNTING AND LAND ACCESS

Maine works hard to minimize problems during hunting season. Mike Sawyer, safety officer for the Department of Inland Fisheries and Wildlife, says the state is seeing a definite decrease in hunting accidents, due mainly to safety measures now practiced by many hunters, as well as stricter laws and better enforcement.

Respect for property is also an important focus. Maine has a long tradition of allowing reasonable access to unposted land. Given that approximately 94 percent of the land in Maine is privately owned, Maine's Inland Fisheries and Wildlife Landowner Relations Program urges hunters to respect landowners' rights to help ensure that access to and use of private property will continue in years to come. Landowners who do not wish hunting on their property may put up signs accordingly, and may orally or in writing tell others to stay off their property. Rules for posting land may be found at MDIFW's website at www.maine.gov/ifw or by calling the MDIFW landowner coordinator at 207-287-8091.

HUNTING LICENSES

Hunting licenses are available for deer, bear, moose, rabbits, bobcats, and foxes, as well as a variety of ducks and fowl. To obtain a hunting license for firearms or archery, present a previous year's license (from Maine or another state) to your local town office, or participating retail store. If you have never hunted, you must present a firearms safety course certificate to the local town office. The certificate is issued after the successful completion of a class on safe hunting given locally once or twice yearly. Archers must also pass a safety course before bow hunting.

You may also meet the requirements to purchase a hunting license online through the Department of Inland Fisheries and Wildlife at: www.maine.gov/ifw; under "Licenses and Registrations," go to MOSES (Maine Online Sportsman's Electronic System.)

Fishing

Given the abundance and accessibility* of Maine's inland and coastal water-

---

*For more information on both saltwater and freshwater shore access, see page 141.

ways, the relative simplicity of the gear involved, and the relaxing nature of the sport, it's no wonder fishing is a popular pastime. The images are many: picture a patient fisherman in his ice-fishing shack watching for a "tip-up"; a wader-clad soul casting in a rushing river in late spring; or a group of children jigging for mackerel on a wharf. It's a group of avid anglers around the table at a remote fishing camp, discussing the day's catch while dealing the next poker hand. It's fishing derbies, bait shops, sport-fishing charters, and hatcheries in which millions of trout, splake, and landlocked salmon are raised to stock ponds, lakes, and rivers.

FRESHWATER FISHING

Last year, anglers caught a variety of freshwater species: brook, lake, and brown trout; smallmouth and largemouth bass; white perch, chain pickerel, and landlocked salmon. Licenses are required for people sixteen and older. Most town offices as well as sporting-goods stores issue licenses, or they can be ordered on-line from the Inland Fisheries and Wildlife website at: www.maine.gov/ifw; under "Licenses and Registrations," go to MOSES (Maine Online Sportsman's Electronic System) or by mail from: Inland Fisheries and Wildlife, 284 State Street, 41 State House Station, Augusta, ME 04333-0041.

It's sad that Maine lakes, ponds, and rivers have not been spared from pollution by mercury. The mercury mostly blows in from out of state and settles into the waters, building up in the bodies of fish. According to the Inland Fisheries and Wildlife Department, fish that eat other fish show the highest mercury levels, and older fish have more mercury than young fish.

To prevent possible harm from consuming mercury, the Maine Center for Disease Control and Prevention has established safe eating guidelines for ocean and freshwater fish. Before you fry up that brook trout, check out their website at www.maine.gov/dhhs/eohp/fish or call 207-287-8141 for a copy.

Another health concern relates to water birds rather than humans. "Without a doubt, lead poisoning from lead sinkers and jig heads is the number-one killer of adult common loons," says Dr. Mark Pokras, Assistant Professor of Wildlife Medicine at Tufts University School of Veterinary Medicine. Loons, swans, cranes, and other water birds can die a slow and painful death from lead poisoning after swallowing lead fishing sinkers and jigs lost by anglers.

Fish-eating birds can also ingest the lead if a sinker or jig is still attached to the line or to an escaped fish. For the continued health of these birds, don't use equipment that contains lead.

In addition to the Inland Fisheries and Wildlife website, here are two good places for more information: www.fishing-in-maine.com and www.flyfishinginmaine.com.

SALTWATER FISHING

The Department of Marine Resources regulates fishing in coastal waters, where anglers hook a variety of ocean dwellers, including pollack, shad, bluefish, Atlantic cod, haddock, redfish, winter flounder, mackerel, bluefin tuna, and striped bass. While saltwater angling licenses are not required for recreational fishing, it's important to note the strict regulations concerning Atlantic salmon and sturgeon. Basically, it is against the law to "angle, take, or possess" these fish from all Maine waters (including coastal waters). Any Atlantic salmon or sturgeon incidentally caught must be released immediately, alive and uninjured, and at no time should the fish be removed from the water.

Special rules also govern fishing for bluefin tuna and striped bass. For current information, contact the Recreational Marine Fisheries Program, Maine Department of Marine Resources, P.O. Box 8, West Boothbay Harbor, ME 04575. Telephone: 207-633-9500. Specifics on size limitations, red tide contamination of shellfish, and other saltwater topics are available on their website at www.maine.gov/dmr. As in other parts of the country, many fishermen today release their fish in an effort to promote healthy stocks.

Harvesting Shellfish

Wondering whether you can dig your own clams or pick a bushel of mussels for dinner? Although the state allows anyone to dig up to a half bushel of clams without a license, most coastal communities have ordinances requiring some type of permit, so check with your town office before planning your clambake. Harvesting lobsters requires a recreational license from the state, which allows use of up to five traps. Harvesting snails, whelks, and scallops also requires a license. (See the Department of Marine Resources website for particulars: www.maine.gov/dmr, or call them at 207-633-9500.)

Anyone can pick up to two bushels of mussels without a mussel license; however, when harvesting any seafood, it's wise to check and make sure an area isn't closed due to pollution or red tide. The DMR's shellfish sanitation hotline is constantly updated and can be reached at 800-232-4733.

Wildlife Health Issues

RABIES

Most people find wildlife watching a rewarding experience. The thrill of spotting a deer, seeing a red-tailed hawk in flight, or glimpsing a porcupine as it shuffles off into the underbrush never seems to diminish. While observing wild animals from a distance is perfectly fine, feeding or petting them is never wise, particularly because of the threat of rabies, a dangerous and lethal disease.

Rabies is a virus that can infect any mammal. The highest number of cases came in 1998, with 248 confirmed. The number has been steadily declining since, with 61 confirmed cases in 2005. The southern counties have the highest share, although the disease is slowly creeping northward. The Maine Department of Inland Fisheries and Wildlife says that some animals—raccoons, skunks, woodchucks, and foxes—are particularly susceptible to the disease. The department notes that bats are also high-risk carriers, but rodents such as squirrels, rats, mice, and chipmunks very rarely have the disease. (In fact, you should always use extreme caution with bats, alive or dead.)

Thanks to vaccines, rabies is extremely rare among pets and farm animals. How can you tell if a wild animal is rabid? Diseased animals usually behave abnormally, but experts say signs can vary. Some rabid animals appear shy and fearful, while others become aggressive. Still others may simply stumble as though drunk or appear lame. If you believe an animal may be rabid, contact your town's animal control officer. Suspected animals who have come in contact with either a human or domestic animal are tested by the Health and Environmental Testing Laboratory in Augusta.

MAINE'S FAMOUS FLIES

Some Mainers jokingly refer to blackflies as the "state bird." The pesky insects are one of four particularly annoying pests in Maine, the other three being mosquitoes, large biting flies (deer, horse, and moose flies), and no-see-ums, or midges. Of these the blackfly probably wins the award for most irritating.

As anyone who has attempted a stroll through the woods in late May knows, black flies are at their hungriest in the spring. Their season lasts roughly from mid-May until the end of June, or as people like to say, "from Mother's Day to Father's Day." The bite of the blackfly is tiny, but vicious, causing open wounds and, in some people, noticeable swelling. Mainers cope with the arrival of blackflies in sensible ways, wearing light-colored clothing, long sleeves, and a little repellent. Breezes help, too, and early morning is often the best time to be outdoors during black fly season. But take heart: anecdotal evidence suggests that newcomers to black fly territory react most severely to the bites. After a couple of years many people find that their bodies do seem to adjust, and the bites are not so painful and itchy.

Mosquitoes and the larger biting flies can be kept at bay through the use of repellents. Not so for the tiny midges known as no-see-ums. They are most active at dusk and are unfazed by clothing color or most repellents. Their bite is like a tiny pinprick, irritating but not as severe as a blackfly's. One annoying characteristic of this tiny creature: its small size means it can sneak through window screens.

TICKS

Two kinds of ticks create headaches for Mainers: American dog—or wood—ticks and deer ticks. The University of Maine Cooperative Extension has a fact sheet with illustrations to help differentiate between the two species on their website at www.umext.maine.edu. (Click on Pests and Plant Disease Management, then Insect Fact Sheets.)

The tiny deer tick is a problem because it's capable of transmitting Lyme disease. Lyme disease is a serious condition, causing flu-like symptoms and, in severe cases, arthritis and damage to the nervous system and heart. Two factors to keep in mind are that not all deer ticks carry the

154

bacterium capable of spreading the disease, and a tick must remain attached to its host for at least 24 hours in order to cause infection.

It is too soon to know whether a new vaccine, recently approved by the federal Food and Drug Administration, will stop the spread of the disease. Researchers say the vaccine is 80 percent effective and requires three shots over a one-year period. So far, it has not been approved for children under age fifteen.

Another development may stop the spread of Lyme disease in the future by killing ticks on the deer themselves. A recent invention by researchers at the University of Rhode Island sprays a natural fungus on a deer's head, eliminating ticks without harming the host animal.

Without proven solutions, some island communities—most notably Monhegan and Peaks Island—have had to make tough decisions on whether to exterminate their rapidly growing deer populations in order to prevent the disease's spread. In both cases, islanders voted by a narrow margin to eliminate deer herds.

Wood ticks dwarf their smaller cousins and have a whitish shield on their backs. This tick readily attaches to humans (as well as our four-legged friends) and is common, particularly in southern Maine. At this writing, wood ticks are more annoying than dangerous, although some wood ticks outside of Maine can spread Rocky Mountain spotted fever, a serious disease that can be transmitted to humans. The symptoms of this malady are headache, fever, and aching muscles two to fourteen days after an encounter with a tick.

The brown dog tick is rarely found in Maine—thank goodness! When this type of tick is encountered here, it has hitchhiked from areas south of Massachusetts, most probably on pets and occasionally on clothes.

To prevent bites from ticks, wear hats, pants, and long-sleeved clothing when walking or hiking in the woods and fields. Use repellent and check yourself and your children or pets when you head in from the outdoors. If a deer tick bites you, check with your doctor for signs of Lyme disease, which is treatable, especially when caught early.

7 Vacationland

"In our first year here we have met people and become involved in the community in a way that we hadn't imagined. We have taken courses, attended concerts, volunteered, joined a health club, enjoyed hiking, kayaking, and the list goes on and on."

—KATHLEEN HIRSCH[*]

Maine's tourism industry began in the period following the Civil War. "Sports" from the Northeast were lured to the North Woods by tales of game and adventure, and wealthy families were attracted by cool coastal breezes. Railroad tracks for Maine Central crisscrossed the state, and steamships from Boston and ports south docked several times daily at coastal wharves. It wasn't long before impressive Victorian resorts began to spring up along the coast, as well as inland on large lakes like Moosehead and Sebago. Soon business was booming. Restaurants served lobster thermidor, yacht clubs held regattas, and dancing pavilions hosted orchestras that played to throngs of summer visitors.

From the beginning, Maine was a haven both for the moneyed and the masses. Summer colonies like those in Bar Harbor, Islesboro, and York Harbor attracted presidents, socialites, and the scions of America's wealthiest families, while nearby honky-tonk beach towns were frequented by working-class families who frolicked in the chilly surf. Religious groups held summer-long revivals here, the tang of the sea air lending a salty counterpoint to the sermons. For tourists then, as now, Maine represented clean air, relaxation, recreation, and nature.

Tourism Today

Not all of the state is a tourist mecca, but chances are, even the sleepiest of towns benefit from the state's popularity in some shape or form. Tax

----

[*]Kathleen Hircsh, resident of Owls Head since 2005.

revenues, for instance. In recent years, more than $300 million was brought in to Maine's General Fund to support education, social and natural resource programs, largely through taxes paid by tourists. Tourism is generally seen as a clean, nonpolluting industry that helps keep historic and cultural sites vibrant and alive, contributes to the protection and preservation of the state's natural resources, and creates cultural and recreational opportunities for Maine residents. Tourism creates economic opportunities as well, enabling many residents the independence of owning their own businesses.

What is it like to live in Vacationland? By far, the best benefit is the ability to enjoy year-round what others try to squeeze in during a brief few days. Fishing, hiking, sailing, skiing—the list is practically endless. Living in Maine means taking full advantage of the nearly limitless possibilities this great state provides.

PROFILE

Marlene Kinlin and her husband, Sarge, moved up from Wrentham, Massachusetts, in 1994 after building a retirement home on a point in Jonesport. The couple had always loved coastal Maine, and were attracted to Washington County by the breathtaking yet affordable property for sale. "I wondered whether I would become a part of the Jonesport community," says Marlene. "But I've met fascinating women through my book club, and I have wonderful, helpful neighbors." She drew on the strength of those friendships when Sarge unexpectedly died in 1995. "I would never have guessed I would stay here alone," she admits. "Sometimes I feel isolated, but I think that's my problem, not Maine's."

Like many folks who live in Vacationland, she hosts friends and family quite often during the warm months. "It's such a pleasure to entertain guests here," she says. "They can't help but love the incredible views." To those considering relocation in the state, Marlene Kinlin offers this advice: "Be sure you have inner resources. Maine will welcome you if you have strength of character. I'm still working on it."

Memories of Maine

Indeed, many new residents were once tourists or summer people. David Njaa, who relocated to Belfast from Chicago, has fond memories of the family cottage (Mainers tend to call them camps) on a small pond in Lincolnville. Marlene Kinlin and her husband, Sarge, moved to the state after years of family vacations on Damariscotta Lake. Thad Chilton of Rockport had vacationed only briefly in Maine, but had a feeling his wife would love it here.

"We like the mountains and skiing," Chilton explains. "We enjoy boating, swimming, and fishing. We like wide-open spaces, and small towns where you're not anonymous. I knew Lynda would love Maine, and sure enough, on her first trip here she was collecting real estate brochures."

Between the lighthouses, loons, schooner trips, and skiing trails, the hardest part of living in Maine is often deciding which activities to pursue. Despite the state's reputation for a slow pace of life, Mainers can be as busy as they want to be. The sites and activities described below are just a few of the many possibilities.

If you'd like even more options, two Maine tourism associations offer a wealth of ideas: The Maine Office of Tourism, the state's official tourism authority located in Augusta, www.visitmaine.com, and the Maine Tourism Association, a Hallowell-based organization formerly called the Maine Publicity Bureau, 207-623-0363; www.mainetourism.com. (For additional information on museums, refer to chapters 8 and 9.)

Hiking

The undulating landscape provides hikers with some of the best trekking terrain in the country, from relatively easy jaunts through nature preserves to more challenging climbs up steep mountains where unparalleled vistas await. "There's so much to explore in this state," say Michelle and Bill Davis, who moved from Atlanta in 2004. "The beauty of Maine stretches from one corner to another with vast, pristine, and often undisturbed wilderness and natural areas. It's wonderful to know we now have a lifetime here as residents to leisurely discover the environmental treasures."

Great hikes can be found in every corner of Maine—out almost everyone's back door. In addition, there are four world-class trail systems:

⚑*Acadia National Park.* Trails and carriage roads in Maine's only national park take day hikers up over coastal mountains, offering remarkable prospects of sea and shore. Acadia National Park, P.O. Box 177, Bar Harbor, ME 04609. 207-288-3338. www.nps.gov/acad/home.htm.

⚑*Appalachian Trail.* The famous hiking highway runs 276 miles through Maine, from the New Hampshire border to the AT's northern terminus at Mount Katahdin. Many who have hiked the whole trail call Maine's section the most beautiful. For information contact the Maine Appalachian Trail Club, P.O. Box 283, Augusta, ME 04332-0283. www.nps.gov.

⚑*Baxter State Park.* Home of Mount Katahdin, the "forever wild" backcountry park has more than fifty interconnecting trails that ramble for hundreds of miles, across peaks and to remote ponds. Some of the most beautiful scenery in Maine can be found within the bounds of the park. Reservations (required for overnight stays) are limited and in great demand. Contact Baxter State Park, 64 Balsam Drive, Millinocket, ME 04462. 207-723-5140. www.gorp.com/gorp/resource/statepark/me_baxte.htm.

⚑*White Mountain National Forest.* Many are surprised to learn that close to fifty-thousand acres of this national forest, normally associated with New Hampshire, are located along Maine's western border, allowing access to more than two hundred interconnecting trails.

For information on hikes in your area, contact your local chamber of commerce, the indispensable DeLorme *Maine Atlas and Gazetteer,* the Appalachian Mountain Club's excellent *Maine Mountain Guide,* or give the Maine Outdoor Adventure Club a call at 207-879-7490, or see their website at www.moac.org.

In Baxter State Park, the Knife Edge is a hair-raising trail that traverses outcrops and boulders to connect Mount Katahdin's Chimney Peak to Baxter Peak. *Photo by Susan Trenholm.*

THE TEN HIGHEST PEAKS IN MAINE

Name	County	Height above sea level	Relative Climb above base
Katahdin	Piscataquis	5,267	4,674
Sugarloaf	Franklin	4,237	2,931
Old Speck	Oxford	4,180	2,690
Crocker	Franklin	4,168	2,949
Bigelow	Somerset	4,150	3,028
North Brother	Piscataquis	4,143	1,323
Saddleback	Franklin	4,116	2,596
Abraham	Franklin	4,049	2,809
The Horn	Franklin	4,023	2,923
Spaulding	Franklin	3,988	2,748

State Parks

Maine is home to more than thirty state parks, which are enjoyed by residents all year long. Twelve state parks and the Allagash Wilderness

Waterway provide camping, and a number of sites require reservations. For more information about the reservation system, call 800-332-1501, or see the Bureau of Parks and Lands website at www.maine.gov/doc/parks. In addition to camping, state parks provide the dramatic backdrop for a range of day-use activities, from picnicking to ocean swimming. Here's a sampling, including some of the lesser-known gems.

- **Aroostook State Park.** Maine's first state park! On Echo Lake south of Presque Isle, this 577-acre park offers hiking on 1,213-foot Quaggy Joe Mountain and trout fishing on Echo Lake, as well as campsites, a bathhouse, and a beach with a lifeguard. Groomed cross-country ski trails are available when the snow flies. 207-768-8341.

- **Damariscotta Lake State Park.** A family favorite in Jefferson, this lakeside park is known for its sand beach, patrolled by lifeguards. It's also a popular place for picnics on summer evenings, with its group shelter and grills. 207-549-7600.

- **Grafton Notch State Park.** Some of Maine's better hiking crisscrosses this mountainous park north of Bethel—several trails extend through the Mahoosuc Range. But you don't have to be a trekker to enjoy the state park here. It also features several stunning roadside gorges. 207-824-2912.

- **Moose Point State Park.** On Route 1 between Belfast and Searsport, Moose Point is one of Maine's smaller and lesser-known state parks. Those in the know enjoy its picnic facilities, short but fun hiking trail, and exceptional views of Penobscot Bay. 207-548-2882.

- **Peaks–Kenney State Park.** Another of the state's less-busy parks, this beauty sits on lovely Sebec Lake just north of the picturesque community of Dover-Foxcroft. There's a swimming beach, camping facilities, and great upcountry vistas. 207-564-2003.

- **Roque Bluffs State Park.** Just south of Jonesboro, this Down East area has one of the few pebble beaches in Maine as well as a freshwater pond. Hardy swimmers take to the waters here, and picnickers enjoy the ocean breezes. 207-255-3475.

- **Swan Lake State Park.** North of Swanville, Maine's newest state park provides swimming and a playground. 207-525-4404.

⬥ *Wolfe's Neck Woods State Park.* What makes this park unique is its proximity to bustling downtown Freeport. Only 4.5 miles from L.L. Bean, Wolfe's Neck sits on more than two hundred acres and offers guided trails, picnic tables, and views of Casco Bay and the Harraseeket River. 207-865-4465.

Sea kayaking tours are a popular way to discover the quiet coves and inlets of the coast. *Photo courtesy of the* Camden Herald.

Canoeing the Saco and Great Ossipee rivers in Cornish. *Photo by Ernie Rose.*

On the Waters

SEA KAYAKING

Virtually everyone who tries this growing sport seems to become a fan. "Want to see how popular sea kayaking has become in Maine?" one outfitter asks. "Stand on the side of the Maine Turnpike in summer and count the skinny boats on the tops of cars." Indeed, the sport has exploded in the past decade, and Maine—with more than 3,500 miles of coast, as many islands, and innumerable bays and coves—is a paddler's paradise. Quite aside from the state's renowned natural beauty, it's also home to the Maine Island Trail, a network of islands along the length of the coast open to conscientious visitors. (Maine Island Trail Association, P.O. Box C, Rockland, ME 04841, 207-596-6456, www.mita.org.)

There are outfitters from Kittery to Calais now offering sales, rentals, and guided half-day and full-day trips, including equipment to keep you safe and dry. After a short clinic, you'll be ready to paddle off on a coastal adventure. The Office of Tourism website has loads of sea kayaking information. The site is www.visitmaine.com.

CANOEING

As Maine Guides and the natives before them knew, canoes are the perfect vessel for exploring lakes and ponds, allowing paddlers to get right up close and personal to the water. Maine's premier canoe company, Old Town, has an interesting website offering information on the heritage of the Maine canoe, plus loads of links to other sites—www.oldtowncanoe.com. One of the state's most popular canoeing destinations is the Allagash Wilderness Waterway, a world-famous chain of lakes and rivers stretching for close to one hundred miles in the northern part of Maine. The state has a wealth of canoe outfitters ready to send you paddling downriver or across a tranquil pond. Check out www.visitmaine.com for more ideas.

TEN LARGEST LAKES IN MAINE

Maine is dotted with more than twenty-five hundred lakes and ponds. Not all allow boats or personal watercraft, so check first with local authorities or the area chamber of commerce. Here are Maine's very biggest bodies of fresh water.

Name	Town	Square Miles
Moosehead	Little Squaw Township	117.02
Sebago	Sebago	44.95
Chesuncook	T3 R12 WELS	36.05
Flagstaff	Flagstaff Township	31.72
Pemadumcook	T1 R10 WELS	28.59

SHORELAND ACCESS

Most of Maine's shoreland, whether bordering the ocean or lakes and ponds, is privately owned. Until recently, the whole question of ownership was treated informally, with few proprietors caring if their stretch of beach was strolled upon. Thankfully, this attitude still prevails in some places, but in other spots, shorefront is posted to keep beachcombers off.

While many newcomers assume they can legally walk private shoreland below the high-tide line, unfortunately that's not the case. Maine's laws regarding shoreland access derive from the Colonial ordinance of 1642, which states that property owners own to the low-water mark. While the ordinance provides that others may use the flats (the land between the high- and low-water marks) for "navigation, fishing, or fowling," that does not include strolling or picnicking or swimming.

Many coastal towns maintain a town wharf or public boat-launching site. A tremendous benefit for Maine residents is the state's network of public shore-access sites. Marked on the DeLorme atlas as well as other maps, these areas provide everyone a way to get out on the water. Some, though not all, have vehicle-accessible boat ramps and parking space for cars.

Spednic	Vanceboro	26.90
Mooselookmeguntic	Richardson Township	25.47
Grand Lake (east)	Forest City Township	25.11
Grand Lake (west)	T5 ND BPP	22.41
Chamberlain	T7 R12 WELS	17.32

WHITEWATER RAFTING

Northern Maine offers exciting Class III to Class V whitewater from early May to early October on the Kennebec, Penobscot, and Dead rivers. Because of controlled dam releases from hydroelectric plants, Maine is the only state in the Northeast that can guarantee high water, along with unmatched scenery and wildlife. Two rivers, the Kennebec and the Dead, converge at

The Forks, headquarters for most of Maine's rafting companies. The West Branch of the Penobscot, largest of the three rivers, flows a few miles from towering Mt. Katahdin. For more information, call Raft Maine at 207-824-3694 or see their site at www.raftmaine.com.

SAILING

Some yachters have claimed that island-studded Penobscot Bay offers the best sailing this side of the Mediterranean. And that's only the start. For literally hundreds of years, the state's thirty-seven hundred miles of seacoast have been considered a sailor's dream. Deep harbors, quiet coves, good anchorages, and thousands of islands add up to memorable cruising trips, whether your vessel is a twenty-eight-foot sloop or fifty-foot yacht. If you don't (yet) own a boat, take a two-hour day sail on a historic vessel or spend several days aboard a Maine windjammer. You'll quickly see why many believe Maine offers the very best sailing in the world. (Maine Windjammer Association, P.O. Box 1144, Blue Hill, ME 04614. 207-374-2993. www.sail-mainecoast.com.)

In the Snow

CROSS-COUNTRY SKIING

No matter where you live in Maine, once the snowflakes fall you're not far from a place to cross-country ski. This winter sport has been part of Maine's heritage since 1870. Some say it was even introduced to the U.S. here, when the Swedish immigrants who founded the Aroostook County village of New Sweden brought with them their traditional ten-foot wooden skis with leather bindings. Today's Nordic skiers have more sophisticated equipment, but they enjoy the same beautiful countryside as did those early enthusiasts.

The state has several fancy cross-country ski centers where groomed trails and virtually unlimited backcountry skiing await. Favorite sites are Acadia National Park in Bar Harbor and the Bethel Inn Ski Touring Center in Bethel. The Maine Nordic Ski Council, 800-754-9263 or www.mnsc.com, has more information.

Native Americans made the first snowshoes using bent saplings with rawhide binding straps. Today's versions are strong and lightweight and offer a wonderful winter workout. *Photo by Victoria Doudera.*

SNOWMOBILING

Thousands of miles of signed, groomed snowmobile trails interconnect across Maine like mini-highways, circling frozen lakes, winding through snow-capped spruces, and meandering along country roads. Festivals, poker runs, organized rides, hill climbs, and radar runs keep scores of sledders and snowmobile clubs busy throughout the colder months. For more information on trails, you can contact the Maine Snowmobiling Association at 800-880-7669, or see their website at www.mesnow.com.

ALPINE SKIING AND SNOWBOARDING

"Maine is blessed with a wide variety of ski areas," says Greg Sweetser, executive director of the Ski Maine Association. "We've got everything from world-class resorts like Sunday River and Sugarloaf to classic community areas like the Camden Snow Bowl, where you can see the ocean from the top of Ragged Mountain. There are underdeveloped big mountains with unmatched scenery, like Saddleback and Big Squaw, and everything in between."

If you enjoy downhill skiing or snowboarding, a clear advantage to living in the state is proximity to the slopes. From Lonesome Pine Trails in Fort Kent to Shawnee Peak in Bridgton (northern New England's largest night-skiing mountain) most Mainers live within an easy drive of short lift lines, superior snow, and uncrowded trails. And unlike slopes in the west, several of Maine's ski areas are alongside beautiful lakes, making more activities available year-round. "There are a variety of programs for all ages,

167

A snowboarder catches some air at Sugarloaf USA in Carrabasset Valley. Snowboarding has taken off at mountains everywhere, and Maine's slopes offer winter parks as well as challenging natural terrain. *Photo by Victoria Doudera.*

too," adds Greg Sweetser. "Race leagues, learn-to-ski or -board clinics, women's programs—you name it."

Youngsters in Maine have the opportunity to learn downhill sports at an early age. "Many communities have really strong programs in place where kids four to twelve learn how to ski," notes Sweetser. "Even Portland and Bangor, which you wouldn't think of as ski towns, have school programs." The Maine Ski Association also sponsors the Fifth Grade Ski Pass, in which every fifth-grader in the state can enjoy free skiing and snowboarding at many Maine mountains.

For a complete list of ski areas, call the Maine Ski Association at 207-761-3774, or visit their website at www.skimaine.com.

Outdoor Education

Whether you want to learn to tie your own flies for fishing or master the J-stroke, a course at one of Maine's outdoor-education schools can show you the ropes. Take up a new sport, perfect one you already enjoy, or become a knowledgeable Registered Maine Guide. Outdoor courses are a great way to get to know Maine and Mainers fast.

⚴ ***Kittery Trading Post,*** Kittery. Maine's second-most-famous outfitter

Portland Head Light, one of Maine's best-known lighthouses. *Photo by Ted Panatayoff.*

offers instruction in kayaking, fly-fishing, fly-tying, and hunting. Call 207-439-2700 ext. 240 or 888-KTP-MAINE for more information.

⚑ *L.L. Bean Outdoor Discovery Program*, Freeport. The sporting-goods giant provides a wealth of resources and instruction year-round in everything from wingshooting to bicycling. Call 800-341-4341, ext. 6666 for more information.

⚑ *Maine Sport Outdoor School*, Rockport. Known for its kayaking courses and trips, Maine Sport also offers courses in becoming a Registered Maine Guide and wilderness medicine. Call 207-236-8797 for more information.

⚑ *Maine Bound*, Orono. An amazing resource based at the University of Maine, Maine Bound grew from an outing club to an outfitter to a provider of instruction. Rent everything from canoes to crampons at reasonable prices, sign up for a mountaineering course, or head out on an ice-climbing expedition. Call 207-581-1794 for more information.

⚑ *Maine Audubon Society*, Falmouth. From its nature centers in Falmouth and Holden (outside of Bangor), Maine Audubon offers a host of field trips and classes in subjects from bird watching to plant identification. Very reasonably priced, these seminars will help you quickly get to know your way around your Maine backyard. Call 207-781-2330 for more information.

▲ *The Nature Conservancy,* Brunswick. Workshops and outings have become a regular offering of this well-known conservation organization. See rare species up close or canoe a newly saved river. Call 207-729-5181 for details.

Lighthouses

Maine is justifiably famous for its lighthouses. Here's a partial list, beginning in York and proceeding Down East along the coast. Included are only those beacons where close-up views are possible. For a complete list, contact the Maine Tourism Association at www.mainetourism.com.

▲ *Cape Neddick,* York. A forty-one-foot white cast-iron conical tower, on the summit of Cape Neddick Nubble, this coastal sentinel was built in 1879.

▲ *Spring Point Ledge,* South Portland. A white brick and cast-iron cylindrical tower, the light at Spring Point illuminates the west side of the main channel of Portland Harbor. It was built in 1897.

▲ *Portland Head Light,* Cape Elizabeth. Maine's most famous and most recognizable light, this eighty-foot white fieldstone and brick tower was built in 1791 under the authorization of George Washington.

▲ *Pemaquid Point Light,* Pemaquid Point. The Pemaquid peninsula's thirty-two-foot, conical fieldstone tower was built in 1827 and is a popular place to watch crashing surf.

▲ *Monhegan Light,* Monhegan Island. Atop the enchanting midcoast island, the Monhegan Light was constructed in 1824 and looks out across Monhegan Harbor and nearby Manana Island.

▲ *Marshall Point Light,* Port Clyde (St. George). A twenty-five-foot white granite tower with an oft-photographed footbridge, Marshall Point Light was erected in 1832.

- *Rockland Breakwater Light,* Rockland. While it's a small lighthouse by Maine standards, the eighteen-foot square tower atop the Rockland Breakwater's fog signal house is among the most fun to visit because it sits at the end of a mile-long stone breakwater that juts clear into the middle of the harbor.
- *Owls Head Light,* Owls Head. Built in 1825, this is a twenty-foot white conical tower, constructed of brick.
- *Grindel Point Light,* Islesboro. Accessible by car ferry from Lincolnville. This tall island sentinel was built in 1851.
- *Bass Harbor Head Light,* Bass Harbor. Built in 1858, this twenty-six-foot cylindrical tower sits on a ledge on Mount Desert Island's "quiet side," and attracts some spillover tourist traffic from Acadia National Park.
- *West Quoddy Head Light,* Lubec. Set dramatically above soaring cliffs at the easternmost Maine point and looking out at the Bay of Fundy, this forty-nine-foot tower is the state's only red-and-white painted light. Great hiking trails wander along the shore and through the woods of the surrounding state park.

Covered Bridges

Once there were 120 covered bridges in the state of Maine, but most were lost to fire, flood, ice, and "progress." Here's a list of nine covered bridges, and the rivers they cross, from the Maine Office of Tourism. If you'd like more information, consult the Department of Transportation's website at: www.state.me.us/mdot/maint_op/covered/splash.htm.

- *Babb's Bridge.* Crossing the Presumpscot River, Babb's is Maine's oldest covered bridge, built in 1843. It is located off the River Road, between the towns of Gorham and Windham. Burned in 1973, it has since been rebuilt.
- *Hemlock Bridge.* Located off Route 302 in the town of Fryeburg, this old bridge spans a channel of the Saco River. Built in 1857, it is of Paddleford truss construction with supporting laminated wooden arches.

▲ *Low's Bridge.* Originally built in 1857, carried away when the Piscataquis River flooded in 1987, and rebuilt in 1990, this structure connects the upcountry villages of Sangerville and Guilford.

▲ *Sunday River Bridge.* Also known as "the Artists' Bridge," this span is the most painted and photographed bridge in the state. It was built in 1872 in Newry.

▲ *Porter Bridge.* Constructed as a joint project by the towns of Porter and Parsonsfield, Porter Bridge is a unique two-span structure, put in place above the Ossipee River in 1876.

▲ *Robyville Bridge.* Situated above Kenduskeag Stream, this Corinth span is the only completely shingled covered bridge in Maine.

▲ *Lovejoy Bridge.* At only seventy feet long, Lovejoy Bridge is the shortest covered bridge in Maine. It's perched above the Ellis River in the town of Andover.

▲ *Bennet Bridge.* Spanning the Magalloway River in Lincoln Plantation, this relatively young bridge was built in 1901.

▲ *Watson Settlement Bridge.* In the town of Littleton, the Watson Settlement Bridge has two distinctions: it is the newest covered bridge—built in 1911—and also the farthest north in Maine.

Exploring Waters and Sky

▲ *Maine State Aquarium* (207-633-9542). Located on the water in West Boothbay Harbor, the aquarium is operated by the Maine Department of Marine Resources and features many interactive exhibits and extraordinary lobsters of all sizes and colors, including Fritz, the 23-pound lobster with mammoth claws.

▲ *Mount Desert Oceanarium* (207-288-5005). This museum features a harbor seal exhibit, lobster museum, and salt-marsh trails.

▲ *Southwest Harbor Oceanarium* (207-244-7330). More than twenty tanks containing Maine sea life are located here.

▲ *Harbor Aquarium* (Boothbay Harbor, 207-633-9542). Coastal sea life is on display.

▲ *Maine Marine Fisheries Aquarium* (Boothbay, 207-633-5572). This new facility features displays of regional fish.

⚑ *Craig Brook Fish Hatchery* (Orland, 207-469-2803). Open seasonally.

⚑ *Bar Harbor Whale Museum* (Bar Harbor, 207-288-2339). Maine's gentle giants of the deep are celebrated here.

⚑ *University of Maine Planetarium* (Orono, 207-581-1341). This newly remodeled star-gazing facility is on the second floor of Wingate Hall.

⚑ *Southworth Planetarium* (Portland, 207-780-4249). This planetarium is part of the University of Southern Maine.

Golf

Mainers love their links, and the state offers close to forty eighteen-hole courses and more than sixty nine-hole courses scattered across the landscape. Many are challenging; virtually all are breathtakingly beautiful. Two are considered premier courses: Rockport's Samoset Golf Club, known as the "Pebble Beach of the East," and the Sugarloaf Golf Club located in Carrabassett Valley. A third course, the Belgrade Lakes Golf Club, was recently rated the fifth best "New Upscale" course in the country by *Golf Digest* magazine.

Portland is home to the Maine Golf Hall of Fame (P.O. Box 8142, Portland ME 04104-8142. Phone 207-799-0983.)

For a complete list of courses in Maine, try this website: www.travel golfmaine.com, or pick up a copy of *The Guide to Maine Golf Courses,* by Park Morrison (Down East Books, 2000).

Professional Sports Teams

In addition to NCAA champion university and college squads, Maine has two professional sports teams. Both are located in Portland. "This is a state where you don't have to take out a loan to take your family to a professional baseball or hockey game," say Michelle and Bill Davis. "The ticket costs are affordable and the games are fun without the heavy crowds and parking issues found in major cities. It's easy to be reminded that you're in Maine, however, when the contest of the night is 'who has the dirtiest car in the parking garage?'"

⚑ *Portland Sea Dogs.* A trip to cheer on Portland's Minor League AA

baseball team at Hadlock Field is fun for the whole family. The Sea
Dogs are an affiliate of the Boston Red Sox and have fast become
Portland's hometown team. Seats are close enough to see all the ac-
tion, tickets are cheap, and the players play for the love of the game.
Call 207-879-9500 for information, or see the team's website at
www.portlandseadogs.com.

⚓ *Portland Pirates.* Exciting AHL hockey is played at the Cumberland
County Civic Center each winter, where the crowd cheers on the
swashbuckling Pirates. Call 207-828-4665 for information, or check
the club's website at www.portlandpirates.com.

MAINE TOURISM FACTS

In a given year, there are . . .

9 million overnight trips

35 million day trips

Of overnight tourist trips . . .

56% occur in July, August & September

20% occur in April, May & June

14% occur in October, November & December

10% occur in January, February & March

Overnight visitors come to Maine to. . .

Tour the state (36%)

Enjoy Maine's superb outdoors (24%)

Take a beach vacation (12%)

Attend a special event (10%)

PROFILE

Ben and Vicki Corrington arrived in the Pine Tree State from the south in 2005. "My wife is a native," says Ben, "so we have visited Maine ever since we met. We were married here, and visited annually, and thought we'd end up here someday." When Vicki's sister became ill in the summer of '04, she came up from Georgia for weeks at a time to help with her recovery. "It came to a head one day in August, when the four of us were having lunch at the Waterfront restaurant on a perfect day. The sky was clear, the schooners were coming and going in the harbor, when I looked over at Vicki and she was crying. Not sad, but at the perfection of it all. I knew then we'd be moving here sooner rather than later, while I had one more practice startup left in me." Ben is a chiropractor, while Vicki is a personal coach. "After we made the decision, and considered what had to occur for it all to happen, everything fell into place freakishly easily at both ends. Makes you think it was meant to be."

8 Higher Education and Cultural Life

"The only way Maine is going to succeed in the transition from using our muscle to using our intellectual muscle is education, and the community colleges will allow us the low-cost point of entry for a quality education to get things started."

—HOUSE SPEAKER PATRICK COLWELL *

For centuries, Maine has been an inspiration for artists, musicians, and writers, yet one of the biggest fears of new residents is that a move to Maine means exile from the world of intellect and culture. "I questioned whether I could put myself in a rural situation and not miss the culture and hubbub of Boston," says Dottie Paradis of Cornish.

The longing for the bright lights of a big city prompted Dottie to take frequent pilgrimages back to the bustle. "I travel far and wide for cultural stimulation," says Dottie Paradis. "It's a lot of miles, but one trip to Portland will last me about a week. I travel to Boston about once a month."

Clearly, a rural or small-town lifestyle does not have all of the cultural perks of urban living; nor, of course, does it have the problems of urban living. But the question remains: Is culture lacking in the Pine Tree State, or is it a question of perception?

"We're happy and pleased that we made the move to Maine," says Carol Doherty-Cox of Port Clyde. "We investigated various areas on the Internet and were impressed with the information we found on the midcoast area in particular. But we've heard stories from others who've had difficulty adjusting to the lack of shopping or their (perceived) cultural isolation."

----

*House Speaker Patrick Colwell of Gardiner, quoted in the *Morning Sentinel*, article by Doug Harlow, July 2, 2003.

Most newcomers are pleasantly surprised to discover that Maine has much more to offer than lighthouses and loons. Ruth Anne and Wesley Hohfeld comment, "We are continually pleased with the varied and regular offerings of theater, creative arts, and culture. We'd expected to go to Boston and New York for stimulation." In fact, the state boasts a wealth of cultural and educational activities to keep most people happily enriched—museums of all kinds, theater in all settings, music of all varieties, and scores of festivals, workshops, and classes.

Some new residents find their new, less stressful lifestyles give them leave to participate in or try activities they couldn't find time for before. "I've started studying piano since we moved to Maine," says Lynda Chilton. "With my hectic lifestyle in Virginia, that just wasn't an option."

"For me, the biggest advantage to living in Maine is the small-town feeling with big city availability," says Barry Hurtt of Cushing. "From wonderful little book stores, to Maine PBS, to the variety of arts and music—there is actually too much available."

What also surprises new residents is the quality of activities available

PROFILE

Mary Griffin relocated to the Bangor region from Charleston, South Carolina, in 1996 so her husband could attend graduate school at the University of Maine. "I was concerned about the move," she admits. "I'd only been to Maine once, and that was a day trip to L.L. Bean from Cape Cod." Griffin's biggest worry was whether she'd find a decent job. "I landed one of the most challenging and rewarding positions I've ever had. I love Bangor, and the people are just fantastic."

Now that her husband has earned his M.B.A., Griffin hopes they will remain in Maine. "We're having a difficult time finding a job that will justify his degree," she explains. "Unfortunately, we may have to look at other states or regions, but we eventually will come back. It's definitely the best thing we've ever done. I would wholeheartedly, unreservedly, recommend a move to Maine. It truly is 'The way life should be.'"

away from the state's larger cities. "There are excellent concerts and theater programs in Down East Maine," says Marlene Kinlin of Jonesport. "And I've audited courses at the University of Maine in Machias that were terrific."

Only in Maine can you learn to build a Friendship sloop, hear a Bach cantata performed by the country's oldest symphony orchestra, and rub elbows with the founder of a multinational computer company at a cutting-edge technological conference. Maine offers its residents diverse opportunities that aren't usually found in a rural state: the chance to study Russian with a native, for example, or play the harp at a world-renowned harp colony, or take in an exhibit of Andrew Wyeth's paintings in a highly regarded museum not far from where they were painted.

You can tour a Shaker village, visit Revolutionary War General Henry Knox's mansion, or hitch a ride on an antique steam train. Not only that, but you can see just about any world-class performance you'd like at many of the state's auditoriums and theaters. As more than one newcomer has discovered, there's a heck of a lot to do here.

Higher Education

UNIVERSITIES

One source of cultural activities is the University of Maine System (www.maine.edu), a group of seven distinct institutions located across the state. A common board of trustees and a chancellor oversee the schools, but each university has its own president, faculty, and administration.

The system's flagship school is located in Orono, twelve miles from Bangor, and is called simply the University of Maine, or "UMaine" (www.umaine.edu). It is a four-year residential university with five colleges—Business, Public Policy and Health; Education and Human Development; Engineering; Liberal Arts and Science; and Natural Sciences, Forestry, and Agriculture. It's particularly well known for its forestry and engineering departments, although the past two decades have seen a big expansion of its biotechnological research facilities and programs, which now include numerous research and teaching laboratories. By all accounts, UMaine is thriving. The class that hit the books in the fall of 1999 was 15 percent larger than the one that started in 1998 and 42 percent larger than the one that started in 1997.

Residents enjoy many benefits due to the university's presence. World-class performances at the Maine Center for the Arts, three on-campus museums, and Division I sports teams (including the 1999 NCAA champion men's hockey team) are just a few examples.

The second-largest institution in the University of Maine System, the University of Southern Maine (USM), offers graduate degrees in law, business, computer science, manufacturing management, and many other fields. USM (www.usm.maine.edu) is a major force in southern Maine's business community, offering special courses, training programs, computer learning centers, technical assistance, and research services. The university is also a cultural power, sponsoring performances of all kinds and offering adult-ed classes and free lectures to the public.

The other University of Maine campuses also contribute much to their surrounding communities: drama, dance, and music performances; art exhibits and museums; sporting events; access to services such as libraries and athletic facilities; and, of course, the opportunity for lifelong learning. As proof of the public support for the University System, Maine voters approved a $20 million research and development bond referendum in 1998.

Another institution that is making more and more contributions to the culture of southern Maine is the University of New England, an independent, coeducational school whose charter dates back to 1831. The university (www.une.edu) has two distinct campuses—the main campus is located on a beautiful oceanside site in Biddeford, while the Westbrook College Campus is in Portland.

The University of New England offers graduate and undergraduate degree programs focused on the health and life sciences, human services, management, education, and the liberal arts. It also is home to Maine's only medical school, the University of New England College of Osteopathic Medicine, which emphasizes the education of primary-care physicians.

COLLEGES

Maine is also home to many fine colleges. Three—Bates, located in Lewiston, Bowdoin, in the heart of Brunswick, and Colby, overlooking Waterville—are listed among the top twenty-five liberal arts colleges in the nation. Others, such as the College of the Atlantic in Bar Harbor, Husson College in Bangor, and Maine College of Art in Portland, bring inquisitive learners to the state and offer residents a wealth of activities to enjoy. From free lectures on wellness to performances of *Macbeth*, from jazz ensembles

MAINE'S HIGHER EDUCATION INSTITUTIONS

UNIVERSITIES:
University of Maine at Augusta
University of Maine at Farmington
University of Maine at Fort Kent
University of Maine at Machias
University of Maine (Orono) (www.umaine.edu)
University of Maine at Presque Isle
University of New England
University of Southern Maine

COLLEGES:
Bates College, Lewiston
Bowdoin College, Brunswick
Colby College, Waterville
College of the Atlantic, Bar Harbor
Maine Maritime Academy, Castine
St. Joseph's College, Standish
Thomas College, Waterville
Unity College, Unity

COMMUNITY COLLEGES:
Andover College, Portland
Central Maine Community College, Auburn
Eastern Maine Community College, Bangor
Kennebec Valley Community College, Fairfield
Northern Maine CommunityCollege, Presque Isle
Southern Maine Community College, South Portland
Washington County Community College, Calais
York County Community College, Wells

to modern dance performances, these small colleges alone have enough cultural and educational activities to keep anyone happily stimulated most of the year. Some—such as Bowdoin College—even allow area seniors to audit courses at no charge.

A new era of higher education began in 2003 with the transition of Maine's technical colleges to the new community college system. Established by Governor John Baldacci, the switch is more than just a change in name. Maine's seven community colleges offer more classes than ever, with courses in high-growth areas such as telecommunications, computers, and electronics, as well as traditional trades, along with free, customized pre-employment training for qualified businesses. Since the transition, enrollment at Maine's community colleges has grown 58 percent, to 10,188 students. Maine joins 45 other states that have community college systems in place to prepare students for the workplace with a two-year course of studies or for four-year degree programs at state and private colleges and universities. For residents of Wells, South Portland, Calais, Auburn, Bangor, Fairfield, and Presque Isle, where the colleges are located, these schools offer opportunities for community enrichment in such areas as continuing education and exhibits.

BANGOR THEOLOGICAL SEMINARY

Built in the 1800s, Bangor Theological Seminary (www.bts.edu) is an ecumenically based institution affiliated with the United Church of Christ that prepares men and women for the ministry. Headquartered in Bangor, but with an additional campus in Portland, the school offers academic programs leading to degrees of Master of Divinity, Master of Theological Studies, and Doctor of Ministry.

In keeping with the school's larger vision to be a place where inquiry about the critical issues of society can evolve, the school offers workshops, symposia, and public forums. Bangor Theological Seminary is the only accredited theological institution in northern New England.

DISTANCE LEARNING

Years ago, people living in isolated villages had little access to higher education. Beginning in the 1980s, the University of Maine System introduced a distance-learning network using television programming that connected

182

Mainers from Kittery to Fort Kent with dozens of college courses and degrees. Today, people throughout the state pursue professional training or follow lifelong dreams through challenging distance-education courses and supportive university centers.

High school students from across the state can connect with one another and with their teacher by high-speed Internet and video screens as well, thanks to the Maine Distance Learning Project (www.mainedistance learningproject.org). Created in 1996 as part of a $15 million telecommunications bond for distance learning, the project continues to link schools as a way to provide students in rural areas with classes they wouldn't otherwise have access to.

ADULT EDUCATION

An incredible array of courses is available through local high schools and community centers. From stargazing to massage therapy, conversational Italian to Public Speaking 101, Maine residents can brush up on subjects or become immersed in entirely new fields of study—and at a very reasonable cost. Look in the phone book under school districts for adult education offerings in your area.

Maine Public Broadcasting

The Maine Public Broadcasting Network (www.mpbn.org) takes its mission to engage the minds and enrich the lives of Mainers seriously. Available to all Maine people every day, MPBN was previously known as Maine Public Broadcasting Corporation. It was created in 1992 with the merger of Maine's two public broadcasting systems (WCBB, founded by Colby, Bates, and Bowdoin colleges in 1961; and the educational radio and television stations, founded by the University of Maine System).

The Maine Public Broadcasting Network broadcasts award-winning television (Maine PBS) and radio programming, creates special programs for Maine's schools and businesses, and has an excellent website. A recent statewide vote—passed by nearly 65 percent of those who voted—earmarked funds for the network's transition from analog to digital. The new service was launched statewide on May 21, 2002. Two digital channels are offered: one is a medley of national PBS high-definition programming, and one is the regular Maine Public Broadcasting Network schedule—complete with local shows.

Maine Public Television broadcasts about nineteen hours a day on Channel 10 in central Maine, Channel 26 in southern Maine, Channel 12 in northern Maine, and Channel 13 in eastern Maine. Its broadcast area covers the entire state, even venturing into New Hampshire and New Brunswick, and is available in 'podcast' formats. All in all, Maine PBS covers an area of approximately five hundred thousand households.

In addition to carrying the popular PBS programs such as *Nova* and *Masterpiece Theatre,* Maine Public Television produces a substantial amount of original programming on local people and local issues. Among the local productions Mainers tune in to are: *Made in Maine, MaineWatch, True North,*

The Raymond H. Fogler Library at the University of Maine (Orono) is the largest in the state, with nearly eight hundred thousand books and bound journals, more than 1.5 million government documents, and subscriptions to nearly seven thousand periodicals. *Photo by David McLean, Dept. of Marketing, courtesy of University of Maine.*

Capitol Connection, RFD Maine, Quest: Investigating the World We Call Maine, as well as the station's annual ten-day fundraising auction, now in its thirty-sixth year, an April extravaganza featuring goods and services from around the state.

One surprise for newcomers who tune into Maine Public Television occurs in February, during the high school basketball playoffs, when the network airs both the boys' and girls' championship games. "It's the only place I have ever been where *The NewsHour with Jim Lehrer* is preempted by local high school basketball," says Carole Brand. The explanation for this annual disruption may lie in something former Celtics point guard Bob Cousy once mused: "Indiana gets credit for having the most rabid basketball fans in the union, but Maine is a very, very active basketball state."

Maine Public Radio hit the airwaves in 1970. It broadcasts on seven FM stations throughout the state: WMED Calais 89.7; WMEA Portland 90.1; WMEP Camden 90.5; WMEH Bangor 90.9; WMEW Waterville 91.3; WMEM Presque Isle 106.1; and WMEF Fort Kent 106.5.

More than one hundred and twenty thousand listeners each week enjoy comprehensive local news coverage, classical music, and programming from National Public Radio and Public Radio International. Many Mainers are devoted listeners, and MPR is a frequent winner of broadcasting awards.

Libraries

Maine's libraries are precious pearls scattered throughout the state. Many are housed in historic buildings that speak volumes about the state's history with their presence alone. All are linked through technology in a high-tech Internet necklace of information that makes researching and learning a snap. Maine's librarians just may be the most knowledgeable in the country, or perhaps it is their willingness to be helpful and pleasant that makes consulting them such a productive joy.

In addition to books, Maine's libraries big and small provide online assistance, access to periodicals, including magazines and newspapers, and they sponsor a host of public meetings and activities.

For a comprehensive list of the state's public, school, academic, state agency, and special libraries, check out www.mainelibraries.com. Many local libraries have their own web pages, so you can see what's going on in specific institutions around the state.

Cultural Activities

Below is a sampling of cultural offerings available throughout the state. While this list is by no means complete, it gives a good idea of the variety of opportunities available at all times of the year. Phone numbers are provided so you can check on particulars.

THEATER

Since the days of nineteenth-century summer theater, Mainers have enjoyed all kinds of theatrical performances, from Shakespeare under the stars to old time vaudeville to modern one-acts. There are professional companies, festivals with touring productions, and civic theaters, where the local chief of police may have the starring role. Venues include historic old opera houses, converted churches and train stations, as well as more conventional auditoriums and theaters. Here's a sampling of what you might find:

The Belfast Maskers Theatre, Belfast. This group performs in a converted station house on the old Belfast/Moosehead railroad along the Belfast waterfront. Luminaries who have appeared with the Maskers over their twelve-year history include Liv Ullman and Ali Magraw. 207-338-9668; www.belfast maskers.com.

A scene from a murder-mystery opera, *La Pizza Con Funghi,* presented by Opera Maine under the artistic directorship of David Katz, with the Chamber Orchestra of Maine. *Photo by Michael York, courtesy of Opera Maine.*

▲ *Camden Civic Theatre,* Camden. This talented ensemble of local actors performs year-round in the restored Camden Opera House, an elegant setting for entertainment of all types. Recent productions have included *Oliver!* and *Music Man.* 207-236-2281: www.camdencivic theater.com.

▲ *Chamber Theatre of Maine,* Damariscotta. Once called "the best-kept entertainment secret on the coast of Maine," the Chamber Theatre performs a variety of shows at the Round Top Center for the Arts. 207-354-8807.

▲ *Deertrees Theatre and Cultural Center,* Harrison. Nestled in the woods of western Maine, Deertrees is listed on both Maine's Register of Historic Landmarks and the National Register of Historic Places. The building was the dream of an opera coach from the New York Metropolitan Opera Company and was constructed in 1933 on the site of a former deer run. It was restored in 1984 through the efforts of a community group and hosts a variety of theatrical performances. 207-583-6747; www.lakesregionofmaine.gen.me.us/deertrees/

▲ *Figures of Speech Theatre,* Freeport. Figures of Speech is a seventeen-year-old, nationally known touring company whose actors are accompanied by live music and a cast of imaginative puppets. 207-865-6355.

▲ *Lakewood Theatre,* Skowhegan.The theater company at Lakewood has been performing for a century on tranquil Lake Wesserunsett, in a glen surrounded by a grove of towering birches. Productions include seven regular season plays, plus reprises, children's shows, and a theater camp for kids ages six to sixteen years old. 207-474-7176. www.lakewoodtheater.org.

▲ *Mad Horse Theatre,* Portland. One of the state's premier drama troupes, Mad Horse often performs in collaboration with local playwrights and USM students. 207-828-1270; www.madhorse.com.

▲ *Maine State Music Theater,* Brunswick. Maine's only professional music theater has been playing to sell-out crowds for more than forty years. The group performs favorite musicals in the newly renovated Pickard Theatre on the campus of Bowdoin College. 207-725-8769; www.msmt.org.

▲ *Ogunquit Playhouse,* Ogunquit. "America's Foremost Summer Theatre" offers ten weeks of productions in a 750-seat restored, converted barn. Since opening in 1933, the cast of performers in the outstanding productions at the Playhouse has included Lee Remick, Basil Rathbone, Art Carney, and scores of others. 207-646-5511; www.oqunquitplayhouse.org.

▲ *Penobscot Theatre Company,* Bangor. In 1997, the Penobscot Theatre acquired the historic Bangor Opera House, a beautiful locale built in 1888. Performances are held there, as well as outside on the bank of the Penobscot River during the warmer months. 207-942-3333; http://maineguide.com.

▲ *The Theater at Monmouth,* Monmouth. Designated by the state legislature in 1975 as "The Shakespearean Theatre of Maine," this company presents the work of the old bard in the century-old Cumston's Hall. It's an intimate setting (275 seats) in which plays are performed in rotating repertory. 207-933-9999; www.theatreatmonmouth.

ART

Over the last century, Maine has become synonymous with fine art, having inspired generations of internationally recognized artists such as Rockwell Kent, Winslow Homer, Marsden Hartley, Louise Nevelson, and the Wyeth family. It also is home to a handful of world-famous art colonies, like those at Ogunquit and Monhegan. Works by famous artists are in many collections across Maine, and there are also a dozen or so fine galleries along the length of the coast where you might find as yet unknown masterpieces. Here are a few of the outstanding museums that make up the state's newly formed Maine Art Trail, as well as a handful of more unusual offerings.

▲ *Bates College Museum of Art.* The prints, drawings, and paintings of Marsden Hartley, a Lewiston native, are featured in this collection, along with a variety of works by other well-known artists, including Alex Katz, Alan Bray, and Ann Lofquist. 75 Russell Street, Bates College, Lewiston. 207-786-6158; abacus.bates.edu/acad/museum.

▲ *Bowdoin College Museum of Art.* Here you'll find one of the earliest collegiate collections in America, with art from ancient Greece, Rome, and Asia, as well as European and American works representing a broad time period. Walker Art Building, Bowdoin College, Brunswick.

188

207-725-3275; www.bowdoin.edu/cwis/resources/museums.html.

▲ *Colby College Museum of Art.* Twentieth-century American artists including John Marin, Fairfield Porter, and George Bellows are showcased here, along with a large collection of works by Alex Katz. The museum also features early portraiture by John Singleton Copley, Gilbert Stuart, and Charles Wilson. 5600 Mayflower Hill, Colby College, Waterville. 207-872-3228; www.colby.edu/museum.

▲ *Farnsworth Art Museum.* A focus on art created in or inspired by Maine has earned the Farnsworth recognition as one of the finest regional art museums in the country. Works by Fitz Henry Lane, Rockwell Kent, and Louise Nevelson are part of the permanent collection, but the biggest attraction is the museum's new Wyeth Center, which boasts the world's largest collection of art by N.C., Andrew, and Jamie Wyeth. 356 Main Street, Rockland. 207-596-6457; www.farnsworthmuseum.org.

▲ *Jones Museum of Glass and Ceramics.* A unique and very respected museum in the world of glass, the Jones Museum features more than seven thousand works in the permanent collection, plus a research library and gallery shop. 35 Douglas Mountain Road, Sebago. 207-787-3370.

▲ *Museum of African Tribal Art.* More than one thousand years of African history are represented in this world-class collection of tribal masks and artifacts. 122 Spring Street, Portland; www.africantribalartmuseum.org.

The Bangor Symphony Orchestra, under the direction of Christopher Zimmerman, Music Director and Conductor. *Photo courtesy of Bangor Symphony Orchestra.*

⚑ *Nowetah's American Indian Museum.* Genuine American Indian art from all parts of the U.S., Canada, and South America, plus a collection of more than three hundred old Maine Indian sweetgrass/brown-ash split baskets. New Portland. 207-628-4981.

⚑ *Ogunquit Museum of American Art.* More than thirteen hundred paintings, sculptures, drawings, and prints by Marsden Hartley, Edward Hopper, Walter Kuhn, and other twentieth-century American artists are shown here in a delightful setting with beautiful grounds. The many painters of the famous Ogunquit art colony are, of course, well represented. 183 Shore Road, Ogunquit. 207-646-4909.

⚑ *Portland Museum of Art.* The state's best-known museum has gained world renown with the gift of the Joan Whitney Payson Collection of Impressionist and Post-Impressionist works by Renoir, Degas, Monet, Picasso, and other masters. The heart of the museum is the State of Maine Collection, which features the work of such Maine artists as Winslow Homer, Edward Hopper, Rockwell Kent, John Marin, Maurice Prendergast, and Andrew Wyeth. Special exhibits and programs include a collection of fine and decorative arts dating from the nineteenth century to the present. The museum also hosts traveling exhibitions. 7 Congress Square, Portland. 207-775-6148; www.portlandmuseum.org.

⚑ *University of Maine Museum of Art.* Highlights include works by Winslow Homer, Francisco Goya, and Pablo Picasso, as well as works on paper by David Hockney, Roy Lichtenstein, and Elizabeth Murray. 5712 Carnegie Hall, UMaine, Orono. 207-581-3255; www.umma.umaine.edu.

MUSIC

The music scene in Maine is as lively a mix as can be found anywhere: chamber and choral groups, chanty singers, blues artists, fiddle players, rock bands, several orchestras, and a bevy of music festivals. This incredible diversity has prompted the Maine Arts Commission to award a $25,000 grant to the Maine Performing Arts Network to launch a statewide network of musicians similar to the successful Maine Art Trail.

The Maine Music Trail program aims to increase the awareness and appreciation of Maine's rich music heritage, as well as current music offerings.

190

Its wonderful website (www.mainemusic.org) can help anyone get in tune with the Maine music scene.

"Maine is incredibly vibrant musically," says Kathy Hammond of the Portland Symphony Orchestra. "There's a lot to do here, and a great variety of types of music, including folk, ethnic, and classical. Maine offers ways for music lovers to observe, and ample opportunities for musicians to play."

ORCHESTRAS

Maine has a number of orchestras, based in Augusta, the midcoast, southern Maine, and at university campuses around the state. And there are two professional symphonies: the Bangor Symphony Orchestra and the Portland Symphony Orchestra.

The Bangor Symphony Orchestra's first performance was in November 1896, making the group the oldest continuously performing community orchestra in the United States. Today's performances are held at the Hutchins Concert Hall at the Maine Center for the Performing Arts in Orono, a venue with remarkable acoustics and not a bad seat in the house. The symphony is currently composed of ninety members, most of whom live within the state and have full or part-time jobs in addition to their musical careers. (One is a lobsterman.) The BSO's conductor is Xiao-Lu Li. Favorite performances by the orchestra include Beethoven's Ninth Symphony, accompanied by a two hundred-voice chorus. For more information call 207-942-5555 or visit their website, www.bangorsymphony.com.

Not quite as old, but just as beloved, the seventy-six-year-old Portland Symphony Orchestra performs at Merrill Auditorium, home of the famous Kotzschmar Organ, one of the largest pipe organs in the world. The PSO is a $2.6 million orchestra, offering fifty-six full concerts each year under the direction of sensational guest conductors as their search for a new music director continues. In addition, the group performs more than one hundred other programs, including Mozart & More, informal concerts celebrating the genius of Mozart. For lighter fare, the orchestra's pops concerts present offerings as diverse as swing dance music, Broadway hits, Hollywood favorites, and the familiar music of Rodgers and Hammerstein. For more information call 207-842-0800 or visit the PSO's website at www.port landsymphony.com.

MORE MUSIC

⚑ *Bay Chamber Concerts.* A series of classical music concerts have been held in the Rockport Opera House, winter and summer, in the midcoast community since 1961. Rockport. 207-236-2823; www.baychamber concerts.org.

⚑ *Cormorant Chamber Players of Maine.* A small but lively combo based in Boothbay Harbor. 207-633-3936.

⚑ *Center for the Arts at the The Chocolate Church.* An eclectic mix of music (including folk) and theater is offered at this Bath landmark year-round. 207-442-8455.

⚑ *Machias Bay Chamber Concerts.* Ensemble performances are held each summer in the historic Centre Street Congregational Church. Machias. 207-255-3889.

⚑ *Maine Music Society.* The Society presents the Androscoggin Chorale and Maine Chamber Ensemble in a series of choral and orchestral performances throughout the year. They also offer the Summer Chamber Music Series with educational outreach programs in the Lewiston/Auburn area. 207-782-1403; www.mainemusicsociety.org

⚑ *Round Top Center for the Arts.* Damariscotta. 207-563-1507.

OPERA

⚑ *The Gilbert & Sullivan Society of Hancock County.* Each year the society produces a Gilbert and Sullivan comic opera, with both winter and summer shows. The cast, crew, and orchestra are all volunteers. Ellsworth. 207-667-9500; http://ellsworthme/org/gsshc.

⚑ *Portland Opera Repertory Theatre.* PORT performs in the newly refurbished Merrill Auditorium to sell-out crowds of opera fans. The past season's production was an elaborate performance of Puccini's *La Boheme.* Portland. 207-767-0773; www.portopera.org.

⚑ *Opera Maine.* Unlikely though it may seem, Maine's professional opera company is based about as far from a city as it could be—in the tiny Down East village of Steuben. But it's recognized for exceptional performances of opera, chamber music, recitals, and educational programs. Directed by noted professionals and featuring international, award-winning casts, Opera Maine is one of the fastest-growing arts organizations in the state. Steuben. 207-546-4495.

DANCE

Many Mainers enjoy dancing, both as performers and as spectators. Grange halls host foot-stomping contradances, folk dances, and square dances, and studios for jazz, ballet, tap, swing, ballroom, and African dancing are found around the state. Here are just a few of the many performance offerings.

- *Maine State Ballet.* Established in 1986, the Maine State Ballet has quickly become the leading professional dance company in the state. In cooperation with the Maine State School for the Performing Arts, the Maine State Ballet educates, entertains, and enriches the community through varied dance programs, including full-length ballets and one-act productions. The company is accompanied by the Maine State Ballet Orchestra. Portland. 207-842-0800; www.mainestateballet.org.

- *Ram Island Dance Company.* One of the state's best-known modern troupes, Ram Island offers performances at venues around the state. Portland. 207-773-2562.

- *Robinson Ballet.* Headquartered in Bangor's River City Dance Center, the Robinson company has been delighting audiences for more than twenty years, including popular annual Christmas performances of the *Nutcracker*. Bangor. 207-942-1990.

Schools and Workshops

Want to try your hand at a new art form? Build a dory or a highboy? Maine is home to many quality programs for everything from language study to ceramics. Here are a few ideas.

- *Atlantic Challenge.* Here's where you'll find highly respected boat-building courses along the shore of Penobscot Bay. Rockland. 207-596-0884; www.apprenticeshop.com.

- *Center for Furniture Craftsmanship.* Founded in 1993, the Center provides programs for novice, intermediate, and advanced woodworkers to hone their craft in a supportive environment. Rockport. 207-594-5611; www.woodschool.org.

- *Haystack Mountain School of Crafts.* A nationally known school offering two- and three-week workshops in visual arts and craft media.

Atlantic Challenge in Rockland teaches the fine art of boatbuilding. *Photo courtesy of the* Camden Herald.

Faculty work is on display periodically. Deer Isle. 207-348-2306; www.haystack-mtn.org.

▲ *The Landing School of Boatbuilding and Design.* A full-time vocational school, this southern Maine facility offers courses in yacht design and boatbuilding. Arundel. 207-985-7976; www.landingschool.org.

▲ *Maine College of Art.* Right in the center of downtown, the Maine College of Art invigorates Portland's "Arts District" with young and enthusiastic artists and a well-regarded faculty. Portland. 207-775-3052; www/meca.edu.

▲ *Penobscot School.* The Penobscot School was founded in 1986 as a nonprofit language school and center for international exchange, and it has attracted people from around the world to the small city of Rockland. Programs include summer English immersion for adults from away, foreign language immersion weekends for Mainers and visitors, and weekly classes—from beginner to advanced—in many languages. Rockland. 207-594-1084; www.languagelearning.org.

▲ *Rockport College/Maine Photographic Workshops.* Now in their thirty-fourth year, the Maine Photographic Workshops have an international reputation for courses in both photography and film. Top Hollywood players often pick up tricks of the trade right here in the little village of Rockport. 207-236-8581; www.theworkshops.com.

⚑ *Skowhegan School of Painting and Sculpture.* A famous arts institution for serious students. Skowhegan. 207-474-9345; www.skowhegan art.org.

⚑ *WoodenBoat School.* The WoodenBoat School is an offshoot of the authoritative *WoodenBoat* magazine, and it's where serious aficionados go to build their dream vessel. Brooklin. 207-359-4651; www.wooden boat.com.

History Museums

Maine loves its rich history, as the number of history museums and historic buildings scattered across the state attest. These venerable institutions run the gamut from historic houses offering a well-preserved glimpse into the past to respected professional facilities with full-time staffs and research facilities. Some are open seasonally, so be sure to call before museum-hopping your way through the state. Here is a partial listing; for a complete list, check Maine Archives and Museums at www.mainemuseums.org or call them at 207-623-8428.

⚑ *Abbe Museum.* Located within Acadia National Park at Sieur de Monts Spring, this award-winning museum celebrates Maine's Native American heritage. Discover ten thousand years of culture, history, art, and archaeology through changing exhibits and workshops taught by Native American artists. Bar Harbor. 207-288-3519; www.abbemuseum.org.

⚑ *Brick Store Museum.* A history and art museum focusing on southern Maine with changing exhibitions and a semipermanent exhibition on Kennebunk and the Federal period. Kennebunk. 207-985-4802; www.brickstoremuseum.org.

⚑ *Burnham Tavern Museum.* The tavern, built in 1770, features Revolutionary War information and artifacts. It was the staging point for the first naval battle of the war. Machias. 207-255-4432.

⚑ *Center for Maine History.* Part of the Maine Historical Society campus on Congress Street in Portland, the center features more than eight thousand items and hosts large-scale annual exhibitions. Portland. 207-774-1822; www.mainehistory.com.

⚑ *College of the Atlantic Natural History Museum.* The nature museum at this highly regarded ecology school features dioramas of animals and plants of Mount Desert Island, from foxes to finbacks. Bar Harbor. 207-288-5015; www.coa.edu.

⚑ *Colonel Black Mansion.* One of the few buildings in Maine that can rightly be called a mansion, this richly furnished Georgian-period home is known for its gracious gardens. Ellsworth. 207-667-8671; www.ellsworthme.org/cbmm/index.html.

⚑ *Colonial Pemaquid.* A unique collection from the Colonial era, Colonial Pemaquid is a sort of in-the-field archaeological museum situated as it is alongside on-going excavations. Pemaquid. 207-677-2423; www. state.me.us/doc/prkslands./prkslnds.htm.

⚑ *Hudson Museum.* On the campus of the University of Maine, this unusual museum—an anthropology collection featuring pre-Columbian artifacts—wraps around the Maine Center for the Arts. UMaine, Orono. 207-581-1901; www.ume.maine.edu/~hudsonm/.

⚑ *The Kittery Historical and Naval Museum.* The building of naval vessels in Kittery began during the Revolutionary War with the construction of John Paul Jones's sloop *Ranger* in 1777. The museum showcases a model of that vessel, plus artifacts galore depicting shipbuilding in the southernmost town in the state. Kittery. 207-439-3080.

⚑ *Maine Folklife Center.* An up-and-comer on Maine's museum scene, the Folklife Center showcases the folklore and oral history of the state. UMaine, Orono. 207-581-1891; www.umaine.edu/folklife/.

⚑ *Maine Forest and Logging Museum.* Just outside of Bangor, this is a living-history museum, a 265-acre property on which a late eighteenth-century logging operation is recreated. Orono. 207-581-2871.

⚑ *Maine State Museum.* Located in the Capitol Complex in Augusta, the Maine State Museum features very detailed exhibits on all aspects of the state's history and culture from its earliest days. Many states have state museums—this one has a reputation as being among the best. Open daily, year-round. State Street, Augusta. 207-287-2301; http://janus.state.me.us/museum/.

⚑ ***Moosehead Marine Museum.*** The centerpiece of this upcountry, lakeside museum is the restored steamer *Katahdin,* which offers cruises on the state's largest lake every summer. Greenville. 207-695-2716.

⚑ ***Museum of Vintage Fashion.*** A highly regarded collection of antique clothing in The County, open seasonally. Island Falls. 207-862-3797.

⚑ ***Norlands Living History Center.*** Rural Maine life in the 1800s is relived on this 430-acre farm. Try the ninety-minute guided tour. Livermore. 207-897-4366; www.norlands.org.

⚑ ***Patten Lumberman's Museum.*** An outstanding collection of artifacts of the lumbering era in the Maine woods, this museum includes more than 3,000 artifacts displayed in nine buildings. Patten. 207-528-2650; www.lumbermensmuseum.org.

⚑ ***Peary-MacMillan Arctic Museum.*** This museum is filled with the photographs, diaries, and personal records of Admiral Robert Peary, the first man to reach the North Pole, and his assistant, Donald MacMillan. Bowdoin College. Brunswick. 207-725-3062; www.bowdoin.edu/dept/arctic.

⚑ ***Pownalborough Courthouse.*** Not far from Wiscasset, this is the oldest pre-Revolutionary hall of justice in Maine. Dresden. 207-882-6817.

⚑ ***Shaker Museum.*** Maine is home to the only remaining colony of Shakers, and this small museum—right at their homestead—offers an excellent overview of life in a Shaker village. New Gloucester. 207-926-4597; www.shaker.lib.me.us/.

⚑ ***Thompson's Ice House.*** Back when ice was an industry, Thompson's was a player. Now you can see ice cut the old-fashioned way at a site on the National Register of Historic Places. South Bristol. 207-729-1956.

Maritime Museums

Few places have as rich a seafaring legacy as does Maine, and the state displays its salty heritage proudly at a handful of institutions.

⚑ ***Maine Maritime Academy.*** While not exactly a museum, Maine Maritime Academy's training ship *State of Maine* is living history. Tour it and the school, too. Castine. 207-326-4311; www.mainemaritime.edu.

⚓ *Maine Maritime Museum.* With its collections and exhibitions, Maine Maritime Museum interprets the role of Maine ships and sailors in national and international maritime affairs since 1607. The museum's centerpiece is the Maritime History Building, where an extensive collection of artifacts, ship models, portraits, photographs, and memorabilia is displayed. The thirty-thousand-square-foot building is adjacent to the restored Percy & Small Shipyard, which may be the only wooden shipbuilding yard from the nineteenth-century still in existence in the U.S. At one time, majestic four-, five-, and six-masted schooners were built here, and today wooden boats are still crafted in the yard. The museum's excursion boat *Summertime* makes several cruises along the adjacent Kennebec River, adding a nice dimension to

Maritime museums highlight the history of seafaring vessels such as these, tied up at a Portland wharf in 1882. *Photo courtesy of the Island Institute.*

an entertaining and educational visit. Open year-round. Bath. 207-443-1316; www.bathmaine.com.

⚓ *Penobscot Marine Museum.* Much of the seafaring activity that built this nation's early economy began in the Penobscot Bay region. This museum, right on Route 1 in Searsport, features a pristine collection of marine paintings, small craft, and artifacts that trace the history of boat building in the area. The collections and exhibits are housed in eight historic structures, including the newly renovated Captain Jeremiah Merithew House (1816), home to a fine collection of twenty-five marine paintings by noted artists James and Thomas Buttersworth. Both children and adults will enjoy the Fowler-True-Ross House, a nineteenth-century sea-captain's home reflecting family life and the treasures brought back from many voyages. In the Nichols-Colcord-Duncan Barn, the museum's collection of recreational small craft and local fishing vessels are showcased. Searsport. 207-548-2529; www.penobscotmarinemuseum.org.

⚓ *Maine Lighthouse Museum.* The state's largest collection of lighthouse and Coast Guard artifacts are at this unique museum, formerly displayed at the Shore Village Museum until its closing in October 2004. Items include rare lighthouse lenses, working lights, buoys, fog horns, bells, and lifesaving and lighthouse equipment. The museum also has lighthouse and ship models, a permanent exhibit of Civil War uniforms and weapons, and a Liewella Mills doll collection complete with costumes, from circa 1399 to 1890. Rockland. 207-594-3301; www.mainelighthousemuseum.com.

Transportation Museums

See an antique biplane zoom overhead, take a bumpy ride in a Model T, or feel the wind in your hair as a steam train chugs through the countryside. Maine has an extensive collection of transportation museums, with everything but lunar modules on display.

⚓ *Boothbay Railway Village.* A summer favorite in the Boothbay area, this museum is a miniature village and includes a fine collection of antique cars and a narrow-gauge railroad. Boothbay Harbor. 207-

633-4727; www.railwayvillage.org.

▲ *Cole Land Transportation Museum.* If it is an industrial vehicle that was once put to work in Maine, it can be found in this Bangor museum. A fine collection of antique trucks and accessories. Bangor. 207-990-3600; www.classicar.com/museums/coleland/cole.htm.

▲ *Maine Narrow Gauge Railroad.* Narrow-gauge trains once crisscrossed Maine. The two-footers operated from rural areas, hauling slate, wood, and farm products to standard-gauge trains for shipment to markets around the world. The Trust for the Preservation of Maine Industrial History and Technology brought some of these vehicles back to Maine from the Edaville Railroad Museum in Massachusetts in 1993. Inside the museum are a 1913 locomotive, seven passenger cars, and much more. Portland. 207-828-0814; http://mngrr.rails.net/.

▲ *Maine Watercraft Museum.* One of the best-kept secrets in the mid-coast area, this museum houses watercraft built prior to 1960. There are more than one hundred antique and classic craft on display, including Old Town canoes. Open seasonally. Thomaston. 207-354-0444; www.midcoast.com/~oldboats.

▲ *Owls Head Transportation Museum.* An institution on the midcoast, this museum boasts one of the finest collections of landmark aircraft and pre-1930 vehicles to be found anywhere. Pioneer engines, automobiles, carriages, bicycles, and motorcycles are maintained in operating condition and demonstrated during weekend special events and airshows, attracting visitors from all around the Northeast. (Hundreds bring their own pre-1970 vehicles to exhibit.) Highlights include World War I fighter planes, the Red Baron's Fokker Triplane, and a full-scale replica of the Wright Brothers' famous 1903 flyer. Road machines include a 1914 Rolls-Royce Ghost limousine and a restored Model T bus ready for riders. Open all year. Owls Head. 207-594-4418; www.ohtm.org.

▲ *Seal Cove Auto Museum.* This often-overlooked collection features more than one hundred antique autos, including Edsels. Seal Cove. 207-244-9242.

▲ *Seashore Trolley Museum.* More than 200 transit vehicles, many operational, including MBTA trolleys, wooden cars from Europe, old New England horse-drawn cars, and much more are featured at this

Vintage vehicles such as this classic are just some of the attractions at the Owls Head Transportation Museum. *Photo courtesy of the Maine Office of Tourism.*

south-coast institution. Kennebunkport. 207-967-2800; www.trolley museum.org.

⚓ ***Stanley Museum.*** This small museum features famous Stanley Steamer cars, invented by the twin Stanley brothers from right here in Kingfield. Also displayed are fascinating antique photographs by the Stanleys' sister, Chansonetta Stanley Emmons, a pioneering shutterbug. Kingfield. 207-265-2729; www.stanleymuseum.org.

⚓ ***Wells Auto Museum.*** Some eighty restored autos, many of them built before 1915, including a large display of "Brass Era" antique cars are housed here. (After 1915, manufacturers turned from polished brass to painted headlamps, radiators, and trim.) Wells. 207-646-9064; www.classicar.com/museums/wells/wells.htm.

Festivals and Fairs

Maine is home to scores of wonderful celebrations. Some spotlight talented musicians, artists, and dancers, while others highlight the state's seafaring or agricultural heritage. Still others celebrate Maine's variety of cultures.

Whatever the reason, if you're a fan of festivals or fairs, you're sure to find something to your liking. Here's a selection of offerings, For more information, see the Maine Tourism Association's calendar of events at www.maine tourism.com, or call them at 207-623-0363.

- **Acadian Festival.** Way up in The County, this annual June gathering celebrates the local French-Acadian culture through music. St. John Valley. 207-728-7000; www.madawaska.net.
- **Annual Maine Indian Basket Makers Sale and Demonstration.** This December event takes place at the Hudson Museum on the University of Maine campus. It features Maliseet, Micmac, Passamaquoddy, and Penobscot craftspeople who sell their handmade, one-of-a-kind, ash-splint and sweet-grass basketry. Work baskets, such as creels, pack and potato baskets, and curly bowls may be found, along with quill jewelry, wood carvings, and birch-bark work. Traditional foods served up by the Indian Island Cafe, storytelling and flute music, and demonstrations of brown-ash pounding are also presented. Orono. 207-581-1901.
- **Common Ground Fair.** The Common Ground Fair is held each fall in late September to celebrate rural living. Sponsored by the Maine Organic Farmers and Gardener's Association, the fair is three days of music, farm displays, children's activities, and wonderfully tasty organic food. The sheep-dog demonstrations are always popular. Unity. 207-623-5155; www.mofga.org.
- **La Kermesse Festival.** A four-day Franco-American festival held in late June, La Kermesse features a parade, block party, and loads of entertainment. Biddeford. 207-286-3247.
- **Maine Festival.** Produced by Maine Arts, Inc., this is a four-day, multifaceted art and cultural festival, founded twenty years ago by the late Maine storyteller Marshall Dodge. Held annually in early August, there are workshops, demonstrations, music, food, and entertainment galore. The festival grounds are handicapped accessible. Thomas Point Beach, Brunswick. 207-772-9012; www.mainearts.org/festhome.html.
- **Maine Lobster Festival.** A three-day extravaganza the first weekend in August, featuring Maine's most famous crustacean. Highlights include a lively parade, big-name music acts, exhibits, and—you guessed it—

pot after pot of steaming lobsters. Rockland. 207-596-0376; www.mainelobsterfestival.com.

⚑ *Maine Potato Blossom Festival.* Hooray for Maine's spuds! This July event includes the crowning of the Potato Blossom Queen, a pageant, mashed-potato wrestling, fireworks, and the thrilling 'Roostook River Raft Race. Fort Fairfield. 207-472-3802.

⚑ *The Moxie Festival.* A wacky and fun festival featuring crafts, a parade, entertainment, and carnival rides, this July staple honors Maine's indigenous soft drink with the distinctive flavor. Lisbon. www.moxiefestival.com

⚑ *North Atlantic Blues Festival.* Rockland gets rocking for a few days in July when nationally known blues artists show up and play. Rockland. 207-596-0876; www.northatlanticbluesfestival.com.

⚑ *Thomas Point Beach Bluegrass Festival.* This shindig has enjoyed great popularity in recent years. It's held in early September and draws bluegrass fans from around the state (and many from away, too). Thomas Point Beach, Brunswick. 207-725-6009.

⚑ *Topsham Fair.* One of Maine's largest agricultural fairs, this great festival is held annually in August. Thousands show up for farm-related displays, harness racing, crafts, and home cooking. Topsham. 207-725-2735.

⚑ *Yarmouth Clam Festival.* Bivalves get their day during mid-July, celebrated with a midway, parades, races, good eatin', and more. Yarmouth. 207-846-3984.

⚑ *Union Fair and Blueberry Festival.* An old-fashioned agricultural fair with harness racing, pig scrambles, and a farm museum, plus a tasty festival celebrating Maine's tangy wild blueberry takes over the Union Fairgrounds every August. Union. 207-594-5563.

Conferences

Maine is the site of several exciting annual conferences. The state's universities and colleges sponsor conferences on every imaginable topic, such as the annual Women in Leadership Conference—featuring Maine's most dynamic leaders from business, politics, and education—held at Thomas College in Waterville.

Maine is also the kind of place where a group of people can organize a series of seminars and start something really exciting. For example, in 1989 a small group of people interested in world affairs—many of them because they were once deeply involved in such things—decided to organize a conference in the midcoast area. The event drew residents as well as government officials from around the globe who came together to hear lectures and participate in discussions. So successful was The Camden Conference (www.camdenconference.org) that it has continued every February for more than twenty years.

Family Life

"I like this state's politics, which put families first."
—Lynda Chilton*

Best Place to Raise Kids

Before he became Governor, John Baldacci served for eight years in the U.S. House of Representatives, living and working in the nation's capital. The rest of his family stayed in Maine, because, as he has said in public statements, "frankly, this was the best place to raise children." The Governor's assertion has been seconded numerous times by children's advocacy groups who applaud Maine's kid-friendly policies, safe streets and cities, clean air, and old-fashioned sense of community. "In Maine, my nine- and six-year-old girls can be comfortable being kids," says Lynda Chilton, who moved to the state in 1998. "Having fun can mean chasing frogs all afternoon, or going to the corner shop with friends for ice cream. They can walk home from school or go to the library without parental supervision," she explains. "In Virginia, children were becoming mini grown-ups, with stresses and peer pressures that I didn't face when I was little."

Shortly after his election in 1994, Governor Baldacci's predecessor, Angus S. King, Jr., established the Children's Cabinet. Made up of the commissioners of the five state agencies most closely involved with children and families, the group has worked since 1994 to organize the best services for Maine children, families, and communities.

One 1997 initiative of the Cabinet, Communities for Children, has had a measurable impact. More than two hundred municipalities around the state participated by developing local councils that tapped into state resources to create prevention programs for problems such as substance abuse, youth violence, and teen pregnancy. The program also helped communities in the

---

*Lynda Chilton, resident of Rockport.

THE TOP TEN PLACES TO RAISE A CHILD

1. Maine	6. North Dakota
2. Massachusetts	7. Maryland
3. Connecticut	8. Kansas
4. Vermont	9. Wisconsin
5. New Hampshire	10. Iowa

Source: 1999 annual report of the Children's Rights Council, Washington, D.C. The organization considered a variety of factors, including child immunization rates, the percentage of juvenile arrests, the number of mothers receiving pre-natal care in the first trimester, divorce rates, and instances of child abuse and neglect. Maine has never placed lower than twelfth in the study, and in 1998 the state's ranking was eighth. Maine garnered the top spot in 1999, say officials, in part because of a series of initiatives for children established by Governor King's administration.

state connect and share information through a website, publications, local training events, and statewide gatherings.

The success of Communities for Children and the Children's Cabinet has garnered Maine national recognition, from Vice President Al Gore's Partnership for Reinventing Government, the National Governor's Conference, and a designation in 1999 by the Children's Rights Council. However, the best proof that these programs are working is in critical statistics such as the following:

In recent years, Maine has been able to claim:

- The lowest infant mortality rate in the nation.
- The highest immunization rate in the nation.
- The fifth-lowest teen birth rate in the nation.
- The greatest decline (30 percent) in teen birth rates in the nation from 1991 to 1996.
- The highest rate (90 percent) of women receiving prenatal care in the nation.

206

⬥ The lowest number of families currently on public assistance since 1970.

These important baselines help ensure that every Maine child has a healthy start.

More serious concerns aside, there is something magical about Maine and children. Think back to your childhood. Can you remember what mattered most to you? I have always loved roaming beaches, tromping through the woods, and spying on wildlife while canoeing on a quiet lake—fragments of time spent with family members in special, unhurried places. Maine is made for family recreation, for fun times that don't need to wait for a vacation.

Another special quality of life in Maine is the small-town atmosphere. Children are enriched by the community connections—the very real knowledge that grown-ups other than their parents know them, care about them, and will tell on them if they don't look when crossing the street. "Children have more freedom here," says Ruth Anne Hohfeld. "But if they act up, someone they know will call their parents."

And snow. What child doesn't find the phenomenon of snowflakes swirling down to earth a marvelous, miraculous event? (Not to mention the chance to miss school.) "Jason and I moved to Maine because of family ties, but also because we wanted to raise our kids in a place that was safe, normal, beautiful, and full of good folks," says Kristy Scher. Maine is that place.

Kids and Safety

According to Maine law, all passengers in a moving car must be buckled up. As far as adults are concerned, the seatbelt law is a secondary law, which means a vehicle cannot be stopped just because a police office suspects the driver isn't wearing a seatbelt. Where children are involved, however, the law is tougher. All kids under eighteen years of age must be strapped into their safety belts, and since this law is mandatory, drivers can be pulled over for it.

In 2003, Maine's Child Safety Seat Law got tougher. The new regulations state that children 4 years of age and under must be in an approved child safety seat. A child who weighs less than 40 pounds and who is under the age of 4 must ride in a Child Safety Seat. A child who weighs at least 40 pounds but less than 80 pounds and who is under 8 years of age must ride in a federally approved child restraint system, such as a booster seat or a EZ-On Harness/Vest. A child under age 12 and weighing less than 100 pounds must be properly secured. Whenever possible, children should ride in the back seat of the vehicle. As to bicycles, kids sixteen and under must wear helmets when riding their bikes.

Health Care

State-of-the-art birthing centers are found in Maine's hospitals, with certified nurse midwives and doula services becoming increasingly common. For serious pediatric concerns, The Barbara Bush Children's Hospital at Maine Medical Center in Portland offers a comprehensive array of services for children, including the inpatient unit and other services throughout the hospital and beyond. Other facilities around the state have pediatric wings, such as Eastern Maine Medical Center in Bangor, which boasts a brand-new twenty-four bed children's wing.

The Barbara Bush Children's Hospital at Maine Medical Center offers all aspects of pediatric medicine for infants, young children, and teens. *Photo courtesy of Maine Medical Center.*

Adoption

Maine Adoption Placement Services (MAPS) is a full-service non-profit international and domestic adoption agency that has placed more than 4,000 children since 1977. Through its State Agency Adoption Program, MAPS works to place as many infants and children living in state-run foster care as possible. Visit the website at www.mapsadopt.org. You might also visit the "Maine's Waiting Children" site (www.adoptuskids.org/states/me/). There you'll find profiles of Maine children awaiting adoptions as well as a database search of eligible children, plus a link to the National Adoption Center. All Maine children looking for adoptive parents will eventually be listed on the site.

Schools

Education is among any parent's top concerns when relocating to a new

QUALITY SCHOOLS

Just where does Maine figure in terms of educational quality? Here are some facts from the Department of Education:

- Maine's fourth and eighth graders scored among the highest in the nation in math, reading, and science assessment tests.
- Maine's education system is ranked second in the United States in the "school climate" category according to *Education Week* in 1999.
- All of Maine's schools and libraries, nearly twelve hundred sites, are linked via Frame Relay Service, allowing Internet access.
- Maine exceeds the national average in education investment— the state is twelfth in the nation in education spending.
- Maine is ranked thirteenth in the nation for high school graduation rate.
- Maine was one of only eight states to receive a five-year, $12-million grant to launch a model education reform agenda.
- Maine ranks second, along with Utah, in the percent of education dollars that are spent directly to support instruction, a remarkable achievement given Maine's high cost for transportation and facilities due to its rural geography.

community. "We were really concerned about schools for Alex," says Jan Njaa of Belfast. "After talking with a school administrator and some parents, we felt that Belfast would be a great place for her. We've been told there is a lack of activities for older kids, but we'll tackle that as it comes."

Maine has a progressive education system that is ranked among the top ten in the country. In fact, the K–12 system may very well be the best in the country. In recent years, the National Educational Goals Panel recognized Maine as the state with the highest performance in the nation in improving public education. Among the strengths of Maine's schools are small class size (the average is fourteen students per teacher), high student engagement, and high parental involvement. Communities tend to be concerned about—and involved in—what goes on within the school's doors.

"Just after we moved here from Chicago, our daughter's elementary school was threatened with consolidation," says Jan Njaa. "The community voiced concern and we were impressed with how much the parents and neighbors valued having the school in the neighborhood. The building was renovated instead. There's a real sense of community in Maine, and we feel like the quality of the education Alex will get will be high."

A 1997 study by *Forbes* magazine revealed that, in a nationwide comparison, Maine gets the biggest bang for its education buck. Per-pupil spending is near the national average, even though Maine students have the highest composite scores on the National Assessment of Educational Progress (NAEP). As the Maine Department of Education itself notes, "Average investment and top performance—not a bad scorecard!"

In 2002, Maine could boast that 100 percent of public schools were "wired"—that is, linked to the Internet, and, in 2003, Maine was the first state in the country to provide all seventh and eighth grade students and teachers with portable, wireless computers. (See Chapter 11, Virtual Maine, for more information.)

Maine consistently outperforms other states—and often, countries—in reading, mathematics, and science studies. In 2006, Maine was in the top tier in the nation with the designation of "highly qualified" teachers—educators who had at least a Bachelor's degree, state license, and proven competency in every subject they teach. Here are some facts provided by the

Maine Department of Education, but for even more information, see its website at www.maine.gov/education/index.shtml.

- ▲ Maine boasts a school completion rate that is higher than the national average, at 87.22 percent (2005).
- ▲ Only students in Singapore outperformed Maine eighth graders in science in comparisons with the 41 countries participating in the Third International Mathematics and Science Study (1998).
- ▲ Maine eighth graders came in eighth in mathematics in comparisons with the 41 countries participating in the Third International Mathematics and Science Study (1998).
- ▲ Maine eighth graders placed first in the nation in reading, and Maine fourth graders placed fourth in the nation in reading on the 1998 National Assessment of Educational Progress.
- ▲ Maine eighth graders placed first in the nation in science on the 1996 National Assessment of Educational Progress.
- ▲ Maine fourth graders placed first in the nation, along with Minnesota and Connecticut, in mathematics on the 1996 National Assessment of Educational Progress (NAEP).
- ▲ Maine eighth graders also placed first in the nation in math, along with North Dakota, Minnesota, Wisconsin, Montana, and Iowa on the 1996 test.

Educational Assessment

When Maine educators and parents want to improve learning, define teacher training needs, update classroom curriculum, or measure who's mastering the metric system, they turn to a set of standards adopted in 1996 called Maine's Learning Results. The Learning Results work in tandem with a test called the Maine Educational Assessment (MEA), which is given to kids in grades 4, 8, and 11. Individual student scores are reported in English language arts (once referred to as reading and writing), mathematics, and science.

So comprehensive are the Maine Learning Results that they address even non-academic subjects such as gym. To help fight rising obesity rates among children, the Department of Education developed several innovative initiatives to help schools create a healthy nutrition and physical activity environment. One of the first steps has been to create the Learning Results Standards for Physical Education—a blueprint for assessing the physical well-being of Maine students.

School Organization

Schools in Maine are under local control. Some towns and cities supervise their own schools individually, others combine and pool educational resources in school administrative districts (S.A.D.s) or community school districts (C.S.D.s). "Kids do not seem to socialize with friends from school as much as I expected," says Betsy Biemann, who moved from New York City in 2005. "Here, social networks seem to be focused more on neighbors and other networks. But that is an artifact in part of how Brunswick schools are organized—each of the four elementary schools draws kids from different parts of town, so not all of their classmates live nearby."

Most Maine schools are supervised by a school board or committee, which administers education through a superintendent of schools. See the Department of Education's website for a complete list of school districts.

State Funded Schools

Three schools in Maine are directly funded by the state: the Governor Baxter School for the Deaf in Falmouth, the Maine School of Science and Mathematics in Limestone (Maine's only charter school), and the Arthur R. Gould School in South Portland.

Private Schools

There are more than 100 approved private schools in Maine, everything from Montessori schools to Waldorf to parochial schools. A few of these—like Lincoln Academy in the Damariscotta-Newcastle area—serve as public schools for local towns, which pay tuition for students. Size of student body varies: the Hilltop School in Bangor has only eighteen students, while Fryeburg Academy provides education for 530.

Arts in the Schools

L/A Arts, an outfit that brings world-class talent to the twin cities of Lewiston and Auburn, sponsors an innovative program that puts performers and artists into the schools on a regular basis. So popular is the program that it has been copied in communities around Maine and has served as a model for similar programs in other states.

Betsy Biemann has found "wonderful, and very inexpensive programs for kids in art, swimming, and other after-school and weekend activities," in the midcoast area as well.

Challenges Still to Be Met

There are family issues in Maine that need work, problems that the state and local communities are working hard to solve. "We've found so many plusses to living here," say Gordon and Carol Doherty-Cox of Port Clyde. "On the negative side, we were astonished at the amount of domestic abuse." Another newcomer, Gary Swanson, makes this observation: "Maine seems to have its share of dysfunctional individuals and families."

Maine has looked the problem of domestic abuse squarely in the eye and is taking steps to deal with it. In 2006, Governor Baldacci signed the first law in the country that gives judges the authority to protect pets when domestic-abuse victims seek a protection order. "Maine is once again leading the nation by putting its people first," the Governor said. The landmark law not only gives judges the power to include Spot and Fluffy on a protection from abuse order, but also gives them authority to impose penalties if the order is violated.

Children in Maine, like everywhere, are affected by poor parenting practices. While the number of children living in poverty in Maine is well below the national average, it is still a cause for concern. Maine isn't perfect—no place is—and there are challenges to be met within the state's homes and schools.

For instance, although Maine students score at or near the top of the nation in mathematics, reading, and science, the Department of Education feels that one out of four students here has not acquired a level of literacy that is acceptable by most standards. Maine children may outperform the other states, but they are not performing up to their full potential as outlined in Maine's Learning Results standards.

Maine's schools are already on the honor roll, but Education Commissioner Susan Gendron wants the marks to keep improving. "As *Education Week*'s 'Quality Counts' assessment of America's schools indicated, Maine could rest on its laurels," she says. "After all, the achievement of our students in mathematics, science, and reading puts Maine at the top of the nation. But our state has chosen to set high expectations for its public school system. Indeed, we are committed to continuous improvement."

Kid-Friendly Activities

"My girls can do all of the activities they did in Virginia and more," says Lynda Chilton. The Chilton family relocated to the midcoast in April 1998 after lots of research and years of looking for the best place to raise their two daughters. "I wanted to make sure my family would not sacrifice anything from changing locations," explains Lynda. "I researched housing costs, available activities such as horseback riding and ballet, public and private schools, and business technology such as Internet access, multiple phone lines, and delivery services."

With information in hand, Lynda and her husband, Thad, realized they had no major concerns about relocating. "From visits here, we knew we loved the beauty and people of Maine," says Lynda. "We love the outdoors, and we enjoy real winters. The hard part became leaving my parents in Virginia who lived only a few minutes away." Fortunately, Lynda's parents have visited often and even bought a second home in Maine themselves. "People should think about what they really like to do, and see if they can keep doing those things in Maine," suggests Lynda. "Most of Maine is small-town living, and that has a character all its own."

Dance classes, music lessons, art workshops, Kindermusik—Maine has it all, in a setting that is conducive to quality family time. In addition to the offerings listed in Chapter 8, here are a few more activities specifically for the young and young-at-heart.

Children in Maine have the natural world in their backyards. Shells and crabs are among the interesting items to find at Warren Island State Park on Islesboro. *Photo by Victoria Doudera.*

THEATER

Theater for children ranges from the many puppetry groups to several troupes in which kids are cast in starring roles. Best known of these is the Children's Theatre of Maine, headquartered in Portland, which features year-round productions, plus a comedy troupe and improvisational classes. For more information call 207-878-2774.

MUSEUMS

Maine is home to several museums that offer children insight into the state's rich history, art, and culture. Some are listed in Chapter 8, but here are three specifically geared to the younger set.

- *The Children's Museum of Maine.* Three floors of interactive exhibits aimed at kids one through fourteen, right in downtown Portland. The lobster boat, mini space shuttle, and camera obscura are big hits. Portland. 207-828-1234; www.childrensmuseumofme.org.
- *Children's Discovery Museum.* This relatively new museum presents hands-on opportunities for children through grade five. Augusta. 207-622-2209.
- *Maine Discovery Museum.* Located in a landmark Bangor building—the former Freese's Department Store—this museum is the largest kid-friendly space north of Boston. Bangor. 207-262-7200; www.mainediscoverymuseum.org.

▲ *Western Maine Children's Museum.* A family learning center providing exhibits that encourage child/adult interaction. Carrabassett Valley. 207-235-2211.

MUSIC

Gifted musicians abound in Maine, ready to instruct your child in his or her instrument of choice. In addition to lessons, though, there are remarkable concert series designed just for children. Here are a few options:

▲ *Kinderkonzerts.* These concerts by members of the Portland Symphony Orchestra bring live chamber music to preschool kids in Maine and New Hampshire. The children are introduced to the different families of orchestral instruments and the elements of music through audience participation, exciting demonstrations, and narration. Portland. 207-773-6128; www.portlandsymphony.com.

▲ *Portland Youth Concerts.* Held at Merrill Auditorium, these Portland Symphony Orchestra concerts introduce children ages seven through thirteen to the full symphony orchestra. 207-773-6128.

▲ *Bangor Youth Concerts.* The magic of live orchestral music—courtesy of the Bangor Symphony—is brought to more than four thousand school children from across the state. A highlight of each concert is a solo performance by the winner of the Bangor Symphony Orchestra's Maine High School Concerto Competition. Bangor. 207-989-2104; www.bangorsymphony.com.

▲ *The Bangor Symphony Youth Orchestra and Ensemble.* The BSO Youth Orchestra provides an opportunity for student musicians to play orchestral music of a quality unmatched by school programs and private instruction. The orchestra inspires the musicians' confidence, challenges their music abilities, and brings together peers who enjoy playing orchestral compositions. Bangor. 207-989-2104.

▲ *New England Music Camp.* A family-run music camp begun in 1937, New England Music Camp offers quality and intensive musical education with popular sports and recreational activities. A sort of summer camp with horns. Sidney. 207-465-3025.

SCOUTING AND 4-H

Scouting for boys and girls is popular in the Pine Tree State, probably because of the many prime areas for top-notch outdoor activities. Hiking, tenting, canoeing, and swimming are all within a stone's throw for most scouts, and beautiful camping areas—some owned by the scouting councils—abound. The Pine Tree Council BSA oversees boy scouting in Maine. To contact the council, try its website at www.pinetreebsa.org or call 207-797-5252. For Girl Scout information, contact the Kennebec Valley Girl Scout Council at 800-660-1072.

Maine is also home to an active 4-H community, in which youngsters do such projects as raise livestock, make clothing, or grow vegetables. They then exhibit their efforts at fairs around the state. In Maine, 4-H is the youth development program of the University of Maine cooperative extension. For more information, call 207-581-3877 or see the website at www.umext.maine.edu/topics/4handyouth.htm.

SUMMER CAMPS

Thousands of children from across the country come to camp in Maine every summer. They roast marshmallows, learn the breaststroke, and laugh and sing in their platform tents until they absolutely cannot keep their eyes open. They make friendships that may last for years, and learn skills that stand them in good stead into adulthood.

Many of the nation's first summer camps were founded in Maine, and some are still run by second- and third-generation camp directors. Dr. Luther H. Gulick, one of the founders of the Camp Fire Girls, started several of Maine's first camps, and championed the idea that summer camps should provide both educational and recreational activities. For more information on children's summer camps, see the website of the Maine Youth Camping Association at www.mainecamps.org or call them at 207-581-1350 and request their free directory.

FORTS

What kid doesn't love a fort? Fortunately, Maine's got plenty. Here are a few to explore, but for more ideas, see the Maine Department of Conservation's listing at www.maine.gov/doc/parks/programs/db_search/index.html.

- **▲ Fort Edgecomb.** This octagonal blockhouse has beautiful picnicking grounds overlooking the Sheepscot River. Edgecomb. 207-882-7777.
- **▲ Fort Halifax.** This fort's blockhouse was built in 1754 and is the oldest in the United States. Winslow.
- **▲ Fort Kent.** This blockhouse was erected in 1839 as part of military preparations for what looked like an impending war against Canada. Fort Kent. 207-941-4014.
- **▲ Fort Knox Historic Site.** Perhaps the midcoast's best-known fort, Fort Knox was built in 1844 to protect citizens from the British, and it has underground passages that never fail to intrigue children. Prospect. 207-469-7719.
- **▲ Old Fort Western Museum.** A restored sixteen-room garrison house from 1755, Old Fort Western is listed as a National Historic Landmark and hosts many educational programs. Augusta. 207-626-2385.
- **▲ Fort William Henry.** Fort William Henry is a replica of a colonial fort

A cannon at Fort Knox State Historic Site in Prospect, the first granite fort built in Maine. *Photo courtesy of Maine Bureau of Parks and Lands, Maine Department of Conservation.*

with fantastic views across Pemaquid Harbor. Bristol. 207-677-2423.

⚑*Fort Williams.* A very popular park in Greater Portland, Fort Williams has extensive grounds as well as some ruins that are fun to explore.

ANIMALS

⚑*Acadia Zoo.* A small zoo with one hundred and fifty animals plus a rainforest exhibit and petting area. Bar Harbor. 207-667-3244.

⚑*The Maine Wildlife Park.* This park, managed by the Department of Inland Fisheries and Wildlife, is home to injured or orphaned animals such as bear, deer, lynx, and even a mountain lion. The park is located in Gray. Call 207-657-4977 for more information, or see their website at http://janus.state.me.us/ifw/education/wildlifepark.htm.

The nostalgic clip-clop of hooves is often the only sound on a hayride. *Photo by Ken Bailey.*

MAINE FOODS AND FARMS

One of the benefits of life in a rural state is the opportunity to visit working farms and orchards. Below are just a few places around the state where you can pick just about anything from blueberries to bush beans. More than one hundred pick-your-own farms open themselves to visitors, so for a complete list, check out the Maine Department of Agriculture's website at www.mainefoodandfarms.com or call 207-287-9072.

⚑*Alheri Gardens.* Create bouquets from this Greater Portland farm's lovely gardens. Daffodils, tulips, peonies, and summer annuals are all available. Gray. 207-657-4358.

▲ **Simons Hancock Farm.** Pick-your-own peas, beans, and pumpkins. Come fall, the farm offers hay rides to the pumpkin field, a big pumpkin smash, pumpkin weight guessing, and other games and amusements. Hancock. 207-667-1359.

▲ **Dot Rupert's Strawberry Farm.** Tasty home of strawberries, raspberries, and highbush blueberries in the foothills of the western mountains. Hebron. 207-966-2721.

▲ **Boutilier's Vegetables.** Pick-your-own vegetables way up in The County, including peas, beans, corn, tomatoes, carrots, beets, beet greens, and cucumbers. Island Falls. 207-757-8312.

APPLE ORCHARDS

Of the forty orchards listed with the Maine Department of Agriculture, thirty-two are classified as pick-your-own. Some even offer kids the chance to visit farm animals, see a cider press, or take a hayride. Here is a sampling:

▲ **The Apple Farm.** Pumpkins, squash, cider, and apples ripe for the picking are the attraction here. Fairfield. 207-453-7656.

▲ **Apple Ridge Farms.** One of Maine's largest orchards, this farm offers hayrides and farm animals. Auburn. 207-225-3455.

▲ **County Fair Farm.** This Lincoln County farm has a full farm stand, a baby-animal barn, and weekend hayrides. Jefferson. 207-549-3536.

▲ **Lemieux's Orchards.** Cider is made right here at the orchard, and you'll find loads of apple varieties. North Vassalboro. 207-923-3518.

▲ **Merrill Apple Farms.** Look for the cider press and other produce in addition to all the apples. Ellsworth. 207-667-5121.

▲ **Spiller Farm.** Lots of varieties of apples await at this southern Maine farm, plus hayrides and garden veggies. Wells. 207-985-2575.

MAINE MAPLE SUNDAY

Every March the state celebrates one of spring's sweetest rites—the making of maple syrup. Sugar makers open the doors of their sugarhouses to demonstrate just how maple sap is turned into everyone's favorite pancake-topper. Many offer a variety of other treats and activities, including syrup on pancakes or ice cream, sugarbush tours, sleigh or wagon rides, and lots more. Maine Maple Sunday is always the fourth Sunday in March. For a list of participating sugarhouses, contact the Department of Agriculture at 207-287-9072 or visit the agency's website at www.mainefoodandfarms.com.

PROFILE

The Price family—Bob, Laurie, and their two daughters—moved to Maine in 1996 from Washington, D.C. "We'd wanted to relocate here for a long time," explains Bob, who is originally from Houston, Texas. "My wife is from Connecticut, but she has family in Eagle Lake. I'm active-duty military, and we were very pleased to be stationed in Caribou. From the first, we liked it up here. It's a laid-back, easygoing lifestyle, and this is a great community that really welcomes people. There's no 'keeping up with the Joneses,' and the school system is very strong." Bob is actively trying to make Maine's educational system even better through his efforts with the State PTA Board. "Maine is the number-one place to raise kids," Bob Price says, "and if we focus on the future we can make Maine's schools unbeatable. We've got a clean environment, low crime, caring people, and real respect for each other in Maine. It's a great place to live."

10 Joining the Community

"People don't use their front doors, and being allowed to visit in the kitchen means you are part of the community."
—RUTH ANNE HOHFELD*

How can you nourish your soul in Maine? Besides spending time enjoying nature, new residents find there are all kinds of community organizations that need and welcome participation. "There's plenty of opportunity for 'volunteer' employment," says Allie Lou Richardson of Islesboro. "I had worried that I was leaving all my friends, my church, and my community activities behind, but there's plenty to do, and welcoming, friendly people to do it with."

Many new residents find they enjoy giving back to their adopted communities through donating their time at service organizations, churches, and nonprofit groups. Still others train to become volunteer firefighters, docents at local museums, or directors on the board of the community YMCA. There are opportunities to mentor youth, maintain hiking trails, and care for wildlife. Once you've settled in a bit, town committees are another option for interested residents who want to see the inner workings of town politics.

Perhaps you enjoy ornamental or vegetable gardening. Each year, it seems, more and more Mainers spend their spare time enriching the soil and cultivating beautiful blooms. "I was told people don't garden much in Maine," says Jan Njaa of Belfast. "But now that I live here, I see that's clearly not the case." In spite of (or perhaps because of) a short growing season, Mainers love their gardens and enjoy ready access to a variety of services that support green thumbs. In addition, an ever-increasing number of farmers' markets have sprouted in all corners of the state, providing high-quality, delicious produce as well as inspiration.

----

*Ruth Anne Hohfeld, resident of Rockland.

Spiritual Life

"I'm surprised we've become so involved in church since moving to Maine," says Lynda Chilton. "We attended services in Virginia, but were never really a part of it. Here, it seems the churches are more integrated into the community. I think that's why there is such a good overall spirit here, and why kids seem to grow up more wholesome. Church is really a support to the family, and I like that."

Maine is a place of many faiths, too numerous to list completely. There are Presbyterian, Methodist, Congregational, Episcopalian, and Catholic churches along with Quaker Meeting Houses and Jewish synagogues. Many communities have Baptist and Unitarian-Universalist churches. And Eastern religions, while in the minority, are slowly growing. Most Maine congregations—regardless of faith—are small by city standards.

The Maine Council of Churches has a new 150-page directory that includes many of Maine's religious institutions, including synagogues, sorted

For more information on religious denominations in Maine, try these organizations:

American Baptist Churches of Maine, 207-622-6291
Assemblies of God, 207-878-2777
Church of the Nazarene, 207-623-4255
Congregational Christian Churches, 207-797-2487
Episcopal Diocese of Maine, 207-772-1953
Evangelical Lutheran Church, 508-791-1530
Jewish Federation of Maine, 207-773-7254
Maine Conference of the United Church of Christ,
    207-846-5118
Presbyterian Church U.S.A., 603-629-9900
Religious Society of Friends, 207-359-8090
Roman Catholic Diocese, 207-773-6471
United Methodist Church, 207-773-4375
Unitarian-Universalist Church, 207-797-3246

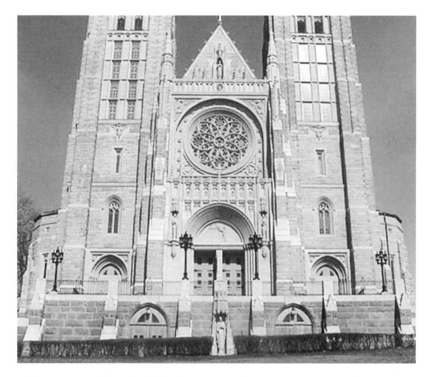

Saints Peter and Paul Basilica in Lewiston boasts twin spires and a majestic rose window reminiscent of Notre Dame. Construction of the magnificent building took thirty-two years—from 1906 until 1938—with mill workers scraping money together even during the Depression. *Photo by William Karz, courtesy of Androscoggin County Chamber of Commerce.*

by county and town. Call them for more information at 207-772-1918. Here are profiles of some of Maine's larger religious groups.

Maine's Roman Catholic population grew rapidly with the influx of Irish immigrants in the early 1800s, and again, following the Civil War, with the large numbers of French Canadians who came to work in the mills. Today about one-quarter of Maine's people are Roman Catholic, worshipping in 191 churches ranging from large cathedrals such as Lewiston's stunning Saints Peter and Paul Church, to tiny missions whose visiting parish priests travel by ferry.

Congregationalism, a Protestant denomination, goes back a long way in

225

Maine. Many of the state's most historic buildings are United Church of Christ churches, built a century or so ago for town meeting halls as well as places of worship. There are approximately 175 active Congregational Churches in Maine today, including the First Parish Congregational in Brunswick, where Martin Luther King, Jr. once preached and Harriet Beecher Stowe regularly worshipped.

The Episcopal Diocese of Maine estimates there are seventeen thousand Episcopalians in the state, worshipping in sixty-eight congregations. Maine's Episcopalians are presided over by Bishop Chilton Knudsen, one of only eleven female bishops (out of six hundred) in the world. Seventeen summer chapels, most of which are found on the coast and islands, are also open for worship in the warmer months.

Maine's Jewish community is small but active. There are approximately twenty synagogues in the state, with more than five hundred families at Portland's Temple Beth El alone. Beth El, located on Deering Avenue, also has a Hebrew school with more than 140 pupils.

The VolunteerMaine Partnership

Here's another example of how Mainers break new ground with innovative thinking. Established in 2003, the VolunteerMaine Partnership is a collaborative effort between state, non-profit, public, and private agencies to promote volunteerism. Run by the State Planning Office, the program links volunteers with organizations, both locally and out-of-state, seeking help through a statewide web-based volunteer database—the first of its kind in the nation. Recent listings seek volunteers to rake leaves for seniors, winterize homes for low-income residents, and to drive to Boston to retrieve dogs displaced by Hurricane Katrina. Check out their website at www.volunteermaine.org to see which organizations need you!

Service Organizations

Maine men and women can get involved in a wide range of service organizations, from Rotary International to the American Association of University Women. Here is what's available, for example, in Hancock County alone:

American Legion	Daughters of the
Rotary International	American Revolution
Elks Club	League of Women Voters
Kiwanis Club	Lioness Club
Lions Club	Women's Literary Club
Peace, International	Zonta Club

To research which groups can be found in individual communities, contact area chambers of commerce listed in Appendix 4.

Nonprofit Organizations

In addition to service clubs, scores of nonprofit groups assist causes ranging from protecting Maine's islands to helping victims of AIDS. Maine has branches of national organizations such as Habitat for Humanity and the Make-A-Wish Foundation, as well as nonprofits that are specific to the state.

For example, Maine Island Trail Association volunteers manage recreational use of about eighty public and private islands along more than three hundred miles of coast. Based in Rockland and Portland, the organization was set up to encourage thoughtful, low-impact use of Maine islands. The association depends on volunteers, as do so many worthwhile groups. Again, your local chamber of commerce will know what groups are in your area. (If you'd like more information on the Maine Island Trail Association, contact them at 207-761-8225, or see their web site at www.mita.org.)

Retired Senior Volunteer Program (RSVP)

The RSVP program matches volunteers aged sixty and older with community service jobs such as delivering meals, providing companionship to homebound individuals, and teaching in literacy programs. RSVP volunteers also serve at the Maine State Museum, in local schools, libraries, nursing homes, and hospitals. For more information contact:

⚑ *Aroostook RSVP*
P.O. Box 1288
Presque Isle, ME 04769
207-764-3396

⚑ *Mid-Maine RSVP*
8 Highwood Street
Waterville, ME 04901
207-873-1127 or 207-626-3430

⚑ *Mid-Coast RSVP*
P.O. Box 808 (43 Park Street)
Rockland, ME 04841
207-596-0361

⚑ *Southern Maine RSVP*
P.O. Box 10480
(307 Cumberland Avenue)
Portland, ME 04104
207-775-6503

⚑ *RSVP of Eastern Maine*
304 Hancock St. Suite 2E
Bangor, ME 04401
207-941-2803

Service Corps of Retired Executives (SCORE)

This organization of volunteers, which is supported by the U.S. Small Business Administration (SBA), recruits retired executives who are interested in utilizing their past experience to counsel people who are starting up small businesses. Volunteers receive travel expenses. For more information contact:

⚑ *Augusta SCORE*
SBA—Federal Building
40 Western Avenue
Augusta, ME 04330
207-622-8509

⚑ *Bangor SCORE*
Husson College
Peabody Hall, Room 229
Bangor, ME 04401
207-941-9707

⚑ *Central and Northern Aroostook SCORE*
c/o Chamber of Commerce
P.O. Box 357
Caribou, ME 04736
207-498-6156

⚑ *Lewiston-Auburn SCORE*
Androscoggin County
Chamber of Commerce
P.O. Box 59
(179 Lisbon Street)
Lewiston, ME 04243-0059
207-782-3708

⚑ *Oxford Hills SCORE*
215 Main Street
Norway, ME 04268
207-743-0499

⚑ *Portland SCORE*
66 Pearl Street, Room 210
Portland, ME 04101
207-772-1147

Maine Senior Games

Held in Portland and Bangor, the Maine Senior Games are the state's largest organized competitive event for the fifty-plus members of the population. For information about how you can have fun (and stay fit) by competing in the games, call the Southern Maine Area Agency on Aging at 1-800-427-7411.

Gardening

Nourishing the soil is another way to nourish one's soul. "If you can garden in Maine, you can garden anywhere," was the old slogan of *People, Places and Plants,* a gardening magazine established in 1996 in Gray that now covers all of New England and New York. Maine's four growing zones, a frost-free season of—in some years—only one hundred days, and its notoriously rocky soil, might lead people from outside the state to doubt that anything can grow here. What's going to bloom in a place with chilly springs and short—albeit glorious—summers?

"The reality is that Maine has, per capita, the most dynamic horticultural scene in New England," says Paul Tukey, editor and publisher of *People, Places, and Plants.* "Ornamentally, there's extraordinary first-rate gardening going on here, and organic vegetable production is exploding."

The secret to gardening successfully, say veterans, is picking the right

plants. "There are so many incredible varieties that are hardy in Maine," says Paul Tukey. "And we have the University of Maine's Horticultural Department, which is possibly the best in New England, plus Johnny's Selected Seeds, in Albion, with the most extensive trial gardens anywhere. Those two insti-

Members of the Camden Garden Club spruce up the Village Green for spring. *Photo courtesy of the Camden Herald.*

229

tutions take great pains to identify through extensive testing and research what plants will work well here."

Other resources available to gardeners include the University of Maine Cooperative Extension Service, part of an amazing federal network that exists to impart free or low-cost agricultural information to the public (call 207-581-3188 or 1-800-287-0274 to find the office nearest you). And then there are your neighbors, who invariably seem to know the answers to gardening questions.

The length of the growing season depends on several factors. Location is one determinant. Depending on where in the state you garden, you may

POPULAR PLANTINGS

Want to know what Mainers plant? Here are the most popular varieties ordered from Johnny's Selected Seeds in Albion.

ANNUALS
- Dwarf sunflower, *Helianthus annuus*
- Cosmos, *Cosmos bipinnatus*
- Nasturtium, *Tropaeolum majus*
- Sunflower, multi-branching, *Helianthus annuus*
- Painted tongue, *Salpiglossis sinuata*

PERENNIALS
- Lupine, *Lupinus polyphyllus*
- Shasta daisy, *Leucanthemum X superbum*
- Yarrow, *Achillea millefolium*
- Wild Indigo, *Baptisia australis*
- Delphinium hybrid, *Delphinium X belladonna*

VEGETABLES
- Bright lights Swiss chard
- Stringless bush bean
- Stiffneck garlic
- Mild Mesclun mix
- Early Nantes carrot

Harvesting flowers at Johnny's Selected Seeds, in Albion. *Photo courtesy of Johnny's Selected Seeds.*

have a slightly longer growing season and warmer temperatures. Luck is another factor. Killing frosts don't always arrive when the calendar says autumn. "Some years, we've had gardens blooming from May 1 until mid-October without a frost," says Paul Tukey. "In my book, that's really not a short growing season."

Gardening in Maine has its distinct advantages. For one thing, blooms are more brilliant, due to the cooler temperatures and intensity of the growing period. Another bonus is that many pests that plague gardeners in warmer climes can't survive the chilly winters. The cool summer nights are a boon to many plant varieties, and pleasant daytime temperatures and usually reliable rains mean spare time isn't spent watering. Probably the biggest advantage to gardening here, though, is the anticipation of and excitement during the growing season.

"Perhaps because the time is short, Mainers throw themselves into gardening," says Paul Tukey. "I am continually amazed at the quality, quantity, and sheer beauty of Maine's gardens and the incredible talent and dedication of Maine's many gardeners."

Farmer's Markets

The one hundred or so farmer's markets in Maine forge a direct link between consumers and farmers, which means unparalleled freshness. Markets are located throughout the state, and each offers a unique blend of personalities and products.

Johnny's main trial fields, where everything from astilbe to zucchini is carefully grown. *Photo courtesy of Johnny's Selected Seeds.*

Here are two examples—to find the market nearest you, check out the Department of Agriculture's website at www.mainefoodandfarms.com.

- ⬆ ***Belfast Farmer's Market.*** Located at the junction of Routes 1 and 3 in Reny's Plaza, the market features the Bread Box Bakery, Maine-ly Poultry, and Field of Greens, in addition to other farmers and vendors. Open May through October, Tuesday 2:30 to 5:30 pm, and Friday and Saturday 9 am to 1 pm. Contact www.appletoncreamery.com for more information.
- ⬆ ***Orono Farmer's Market.*** Located between College Avenue and the Stillwater River, less than a mile from downtown Orono, at the University Steam Plant Parking Lot, the Orono market features local produce, maple syrup, jams and jellies, and local crafts. Open every Saturday morning and Tuesday afternoon, May through October, rain or shine.

Public Gardens

Mainers show their enthusiasm for growing things at the more than fifty public gardens maintained by garden clubs and other organizations. Here they are, courtesy of *People, Places and Plants*, listed in roughly geographical order running from south to north.

- *Hamilton House Gardens.* Maine's best example of a Victorian-era garden, this display was recently renovated. South Berwick. 207-384-5269 or 603-436-3205.
- *Laudholm Farm.* The buildings and grounds at this classic saltwater farm offer a glimpse into past seaside farm life, with natural tidal-zone plantings. Wells. 207-646-1555.
- *Grounds and Gardens of St. Anthony's Monastery.* One of the more unusual places to stay in the Kennebunks, St. Anthony's Monastery has gardens with intriguing pathways and peak rhododendron viewing in June. Kennebunkport. 207-967-2011.

PROFILE

Howard Lupovitch came to Maine in 1998 from Detroit, Michigan, to become the Assistant Professor of Jewish Studies at Colby College. "I'd camped in Acadia a few times as a teenager," he says. "And that was the extent of my time in the state. But both my wife and I grew up in four-season climates, so we were used to winter."

The Lupovitchs are enjoying the hearty lifestyle Maine affords, and like living in Waterville. "We're a young couple, just starting out, and we bought a great first house. Plus the people are friendly, the city is clean, and we hardly ever lock a car door," he notes. "We do miss our families, but I like working at Colby very much."

At first, the couple wondered why the state won such high praise. "We enjoyed the summer, but it was in the fall that the magic of Maine really hit us. Our neighbor's tree turned this incredible mixture of yellow and orange, and we looked at each other, and said, 'Ah, Maine—now we get it.'"

Garden at Marrett House. The restored Victorian gardens here feature an excellent iris collection. Standish. 207-642-3032.

Deering Oaks Rose Circle. The peak bloom of the hybrid tea roses here is during July and early August, when more than 600 species are exhibited. Portland. 207-874-8300.

Longfellow Garden. A Colonial Revival garden featuring shade plants and color, this lovely spot is on the Congress Street grounds of the Maine Historical Society. Portland. 207-879-0427 or 207-774-1822.

Harraseeket Inn Gardens. One of Freeport's nicest inns, the Harraseeket has an old-fashioned courtyard appearance, and it's ideal for gatherings. Freeport. 207-865-9377.

Gardens at Harrington House. The gardens here include plants from the 1860s, including a 150-year-old lavender. Freeport. 207-865-3170.

Heather Garden. This seaside estate near a neat working farm has well-maintained gardens. Wolfe's Neck, Freeport. 207-865-3428.

Heather Garden at Walker Art Building. Many hardy heaths and heathers surround Bowdoin's classic art museum. Bowdoin College, Brunswick. 207-725-3000 ext. 3311.

Coastal Maine Botanical Garden, Inc. This evolving 128-acre site is the result of an aggressive effort by local citizens to build a premier garden. Barter Island Road, Boothbay. 207-633-4333.

Christina's Garden at the Olson House. Maintained by the Farnsworth Museum in honor of the Wyeth family, this garden is named after the subject of the classic American painting, *Christina's World.* Cushing. 207-354-0102.

Camden Amphitheater. Escape summer crowds in this classically designed garden by Fletcher Steele. 207-236-3440.

Camden Children's Garden. A Camden favorite, the children's garden was built in 1996 at the Camden Public Library to honor authors of children's books. Camden. 207-236-3440.

Conway Homestead and Museum. Known for its historical authenticity, this relatively unknown garden is hidden away in the middle of the tourist mecca. Camden. 207-236-2257.

Merryspring. An excellent public reference resource, with improving public grounds, this Camden favorite is a nice place to stroll. Rockport-Camden town line. 207-236-2239.

Gardens of the Castine Inn. These classic formal gardens sit in a picturesque seaside setting. Castine. 207-326-4365.

Amen Farm Gardens. Pretty gardens at the home of the late Roy Barrette, garden writer and essayist. Features a newly planted arboretum with 150 uncommon trees. Brooklin. 207-359-8982.

Leighton Sculpture Garden. The garden at Leighton Gallery is a favorite of many Mainers. Blue Hill. 207-374-5001.

Abby A. Rockefeller Garden. Dazzling interplay of flower beds and sculpture at this private garden, appointment needed. Seal Harbor. 207-276-3330.

Asticou Azalea Garden. Maine's finest Japanese-style garden, with ties to legendary gardener Beatrix Farrand. Northeast Harbor. 207-276-5130.

Beatrix Farrand Garden at College of the Atlantic. One of Acadia's last examples of Farrand's work. Bar Harbor. 207-288-5015.

Thuya Garden. Thuya is noted for its excellent reference library and massive perennial collection. Northeast Harbor. 207-276-5130.

Wild Gardens of Acadia. Twelve different plant habitats at the state's only national park display Maine's native plants. Acadia National Park. 207-288-3338.

Bernard McLaughlin Garden. Famous for its lilacs, the McLaughlin Garden was voted the favorite public garden in Maine by the readers of *People, Places and Plants.* South Paris. 207-743-7620.

Featuring sculpted shrubbery and perennial borders, The Thuya Garden in Northeast Harbor is a great example of the magic of the Acadia National Park region. *Photo courtesy of the Maine Office of Tourism.*

235

⚑ *Gardens of the Blaine House.* Originally designed in 1920, the gardens at the Governor's mansion were completed during the 1990s. Augusta. 207-662-6363.

⚑ *Kennebec Valley Garden Club Park.* This Augusta garden is impeccably maintained by one of Maine's most vital garden clubs. Augusta Civic Center, Augusta. 207-622-1124 or 207-622-5227.

⚑ *Pine Tree State Arboretum.* Ornamental trees, an extensive well-labeled hosta collection, and acres of forests distinguish the state's arboretum. Augusta. 207-621-0031.

⚑ *Johnny's Selected Seeds.* Johnny's is home to America's most extensive trial gardens for vegetable seedlings, and it also has herbs and flowers. Albion. 207-437-9294.

⚑ *Fay Hyland Botanical Plantation.* Affiliated with the University of Maine, this botanic collection features hardy plants native to Maine. Orono. 207-581-2978.

⚑ *Gardens of Brewster Inn.* Designed by architect John Calvin Stevens in the 1930s for a former Maine governor, these beds have been updated by local innkeepers. Dexter. 207-924-3130.

PROFILE: Moving Out of Maine

Polly and Bob Knapp, originally from Tennessee, sold their ocean-view home in Rockport in 2006. It was a difficult decision to make. "With a new grandbaby on the way and all our children in the south, we have sadly chosen to move to North Carolina to be closer to family," says Polly. "We have made friends with so many wonderful Mainers along the way that have openly accepted our southern conservative ways and our funny accent. This is what we will miss the most." The Knapps insist, however, that they are not gone for good. "We leave knowing that we will certainly return to Maine one day to breathe the cool crisp air, admire the perfectly shaped pine trees, and the late afternoon light that defines the landscape into an artist's dream."

11 Virtual Maine

"I could do what I'm doing elsewhere, but I want to live here, because of the lifestyle, outdoor activities, and community."
—Steve Hand*

Libraries linked to the Internet. High-bandwidth ATM. The Maine Technology Institute. If your image of Maine is limited to lighthouses, loons, and lobster, it's time to expand that cozy vision to include cutting-edge technology. Although it may come as a surprise to those who hold the "vacationland" image dear, the state is definitely in the race—and sometimes even in the lead—when it comes to the technology marathon. Beginning in the late 1990s, when Maine became the first state to connect every school and library to the Internet, the state has demonstrated not only a commitment to the information age, but a willingness to become a tech-savvy leader.

Infrastructure

A key component in today's increasingly connected world is a reliable telecommunications backbone that supports ever-evolving equipment. Wireless, cable, and fiber optic technologies are available throughout Maine, allowing businesses, schools, and someone sitting at a computer in their living room the freedom to connect anywhere in the state. As MESDA, the statewide trade association for Maine's software and information technology industry, puts it, "Maine has DSL, ISDN, ATM, Frame Relay, T1, T3, OC48… the whole alphabet soup of cutting-edge voice, data, and video services." The state's primary telephone provider, Verizon, has deployed SONET ring technology, which provides redundancy and reliability throughout the state,

----

*Steve Hand, founder of Know Technology, LLC, in Camden.

237

even the most rural areas. Maine has a high-bandwidth ATM (asynchronous transfer mode) network throughout the state, enabling users to simultaneously transfer voice, data, and video at very high speeds. And Maine's telecommunications backbone is 100% digitally switched, with long-distance POP (point-of-presence) locations strategically placed throughout the state.

Government Online

Look no farther than the state's unbelievable websites for a snapshot of technology at work. In fact, Maine's online government services are some of the very best in the country, according to an annual e-government analysis conducted by researchers at Brown University.

Researchers evaluated websites for the presence of various electronic features, such as online publications, online databases, audio clips, video clips, foreign language or language translation, advertisements, premium fees, user payments or fees. They also evaluated sites with regard to disability access, privacy policy, security policy, online services, digital signatures, credit card payments, e-mail addresses, comment forms, automatic e-mail updates, website personalization, PDA accessibility, quality control, and readability. When all the votes were in, Maine came in second, beaten only by Utah. The next highest ranking New England state was Massachusetts, coming in 8th place.

A good example of why Brown's researchers loved Maine's websites is Access Maine.org (www.accessmaine.org). Developed to assist Mainers with disabilities, their families, and providers, the website has loads of information, plus a search engine, useful links, short "tip sheets" offering helpful hints, and toolkits on various topics. It is updated continuously by webmasters who welcome suggestions from users through a handy feedback button.

When you navigate the waters of Maine.gov, the state's official website, you'll find an astonishing amount of information on-line, plus handy services you can access with a click of your mouse, such as burn permits, vanity-plate checks, Blaine House press releases, recipes using Maine ingredients, and more. There's even a section called "How do I plan my move to Maine?" (www.maine.gov/portal/family/moving.html).

Virtual Library

Here's a real gem that I discovered while updating this book -- MARVEL!, Maine's Virtual Library (www.maine.gov/marvel). Like the comic book publisher of the same name, this place is a superhuman powerhouse. Instead of the Incredible Hulk, you'll find something even more valuable: access to a collection of full text and abstracts from magazines, newspapers, and reference books. *U.S. News & World Report,* Encyclopedia Britannica, national copyright laws . . . MARVEL! doesn't stop there. Students, business people, public library patrons, and educators also have the powerful ability to search a number of resources at one time for needed information—information that is reliable and reputable. The estimated print value of the resources provided in these databases is in excess of $500,000 per library, a feat even the Incredible Hulk would admire.

MARVEL! exists thanks to a collaboration between the Maine State Library, University of Maine, the State Legislature, and the Maine Telecommunications Educational Access Fund, or MTEAF. This collaboration makes state-wide licensing of MARVEL! resources extremely cost efficient, providing them for every school, library, and resident of Maine.

The Maine Technology Institute (MTI)

The Maine Technology Institute (www.mainetechnology.org) was created by the Legislature in 1999 to jumpstart research and development activity in the state, with the goals of new products, new services, and more jobs for Mainers. The Institute's programs are designed to enhance advanced technologies in seven targeted fields: Forestry & Agriculture, Aquaculture, Biotechnology, Composite Materials, Environmental Technology, Information Technology, and Precision Manufacturing. The idea is that with some funding and assistance, one or more of these areas will thrive and create new jobs.

MTI can make a real difference for new Maine start-ups in terms of early stage capital. To fund first-rate ideas with sound business plans, the Institutes' board of directors approves seed grants to technology companies across Maine. Ranging from $1,000 to $10,000 per project, the grants are offered on a competitive basis to support product development, commercialization, or business planning and development. A company may be awarded a maximum $25,000 in seed grants for a specific project, and each grant requires a 1:1 match consisting of actual cash, salaries, staff time, or equipment directly attributable to the proposed project.

"These grants are a great source of early stage capital for entrepreneurs," says Betsy Biemann, MTI president. "They help Maine companies transform their good ideas into new products and services for the market." The work of the Maine Technology Institute is great news for all Mainers, and has already paid off. MTI programs have been very successful in a short time in supporting substantial innovative activity. Studies have shown that companies funded by MTI create jobs faster and with higher wages than the average Maine company.

Research and Development

MTI isn't the only Maine organization encouraging technological growth in the state. Maine has developed an innovative system for funding and assisting research and development (R&D) companies through MTI and the work of groups such as the Maine Patent Program, the Applied Technology Development Centers, and the Maine Office of Innovation. Part of the Department of Economic and Community Development, the Office of Innovation (www.maineinnovation.com) was established to coordinate R&D activities and foster collaboration among the state's higher educational and nonprofit research institutions and the business community.

The effort is paying off. Maine has increased its investment in R&D thirty-fold in the last ten years, says a North Carolina research team hired by the state in 2006 to study Maine's five-year investment in research and development. Maine's technology initiatives boost the state's economy, benefiting more than just new age sectors such as biotechnology. Traditional core industries, such as paper products and boat building, can be greatly enhanced through new and better ways to do business. Innovative products, better processes, and increased efficiency can help any business to add value and create more jobs.

For instance, workers at Tex Tech in North Monmouth now make fireproof fabric for Europe's giant Airbus in the same facility where former employees made woolen baseball uniforms. This kind of transformation in a traditional industry is exactly how Maine can hit economic home runs through technology.

Maine needs to maintain its forward economic momentum by continuing to invest and by increasing its efforts, say the researchers. Suggestions included focusing on areas in which the state already has a competitive advantage, such as wood-based composites or marine industries. Investments should be made in a sustained way, so that businesses know Maine's commitment to R&D is solid. Above all, Maine can't rest on the accomplishments of the past decade alone.

Their findings support a plan forwarded in 2005 by the Office of Innovation, calling for R&D activity to double statewide in the coming years. A $1 billion annual spending goal is projected for 2010, with major increases hailing from private and public organizations. Also targeted for 2010: Governor Baldacci's proposal to "Connect Maine." This initiative aims to serve 100 percent of Maine communities with cell phone coverage by 2008, and 90 percent of Maine homes and businesses with broadband by 2010. So far, the plan is ahead of schedule, with the broadband goal expected to be completed by 2007.

Maine Learning Technology Initiative

Maine can't compete in the brave new world of technology unless Mainers themselves jump on the information superhighway. Toward that end, the state has a goal to make its students "the most technologically literate in the world." That effort got off to a great start in September 2002, when middle schools in Maine started an incredible journey by providing every seventh grade student with his or her own laptop. The Maine Learning Technology Initiative (www.mainelearns.org) fosters a new learning environment in which students develop 21st-century learning skills by using Apple iBook computers. They and their teachers have learned to use technology as critical tools for learning, research, collaboration, communication, and creative self-expression.

Since 2002, more than 36,000 iBook computers have been placed in the eager hands of every 7th and 8th grade teacher and student in Maine's public middle schools. Since the introduction of the laptops, student engagement and motivation are up, absenteeism and disciplinary incidents are down, and students are taking a more active role in their education. Seventh graders create PowerPoint presentations on Harriet Beecher Stowe; eighth graders make mini-movies in Spanish. Simply put, technology has enabled them to achieve at higher levels than ever before. The results have motivated other states—Massachusetts is one—to emulate the program.

Celluloid Maine

Speaking of movies, no "virtual" chapter would be complete without mention of Maine's starring role on the silver screen. One of the most recent pictures to spotlight the state was the award-winning film *Empire Falls,* based on the Pulitzer-prize-winning novel of the same name by Richard Russo. Filmed in Skowhegan and Waterville, the film not only brought luminaries such as Paul Newman and Joanne Woodward to the Pine Tree State, but added $34 million to the state's economy.

In recent years, films shot in Maine have included *Man Without a Face,* starring Mel Gibson; *In the Bedroom,* with Sissy Spacek; *Casper;* and several Stephen King thrillers. If the state has its way, even more casts and crews will roll into Maine's towns for action. In 2006, the Legislature approved and Governor John Baldacci signed "The Maine Attraction Film Incentive Plan," an innovative financial package designed to encourage more film, television, and other media in the state. Already up and rolling is a new venture in Camden called VisionMill. The brainchild of cinematographer Rob Draper, whose work includes dozens of hits including *The Spitfire Grill* and *Cagney and Lacey,* the new production company is off to a good start with six shows in development.

PopTech Conference

Ten years ago, a group of the world's most interesting minds met in Camden's restored 19th century opera house to discuss and debate new ideas in technology. Since then, the three-day PopTech conference has grown in popularity and price (tickets top $2000 apiece) to become a not-to-be-missed fall event among the very tech-savvy. Participants discuss and debate new ideas such as neuroscience and human emotion, or the use of "green" technologies around the globe. For more information, visit the group's website at www.poptech.com.

The Challenge for Maine

Maine is at an exciting juncture. With the investment in our telecommunications infrastructure, great work ethic, and appeal as a safe, clean place to live and work, the state can continue to transform its economy through technology, attracting innovative businesses and strengthening old ones. Such a transformation benefits everyone. Not only do cutting-edge businesses expand the economy, but also the products developed can help us all in practical ways. (Think healthier fish, or new prescription medicines.) The key at this point is for all Maine residents—new and established—to understand and voice support for research and development funding and other activities that help foster high-tech investment here.

MAINE TELECOMMUNICATIONS AT A GLANCE

(Courtesy of MESDA: Maine's Software & Information Technology Industry Association, www.mesda.com)

- With more than 110,000 miles of fiber optic cable and 100 percent digital phone-switching technology in place, Maine leads the country with its telecommunications infrastructure.
- Maine is highly "nexus-friendly"—a safe haven in which call centers and their clients can avoid collecting and remitting sales tax.
- Maine was the first state to have a statewide ATM (Asynchronous Transfer Mode) fiber-optic-based network, allowing efficient digital transmission of voice, data, and full-motion video.
- Maine was the first state to link every school and library (nearly 1,200 sites in all) via Frame Relay Service. This allows Internet access at every site, and positions Maine to take advantage of new distance-learning opportunities.

- One hundred percent of Maine's telecommunications network is switched using digital technology, making it one of the first states in the nation with this distinction. Digital networks support advanced, higher-bandwidth technologies at higher speeds.
- Maine's telecommunications system is one of the most reliable in the country. Based on FCC service-quality data, Maine service and reliability ratings are among the best in the country.
- Public telecommunications policies in Maine are among the country's most supportive of economic development.
- Maine telecom companies offer the most advanced services available. Services include Integrated Services Digital Network (ISDN), Frame Relay Service, Voice Messaging Services, 25 Megabit Service (MBPS), Infopath Packet Switching Service, Switchway Switched 56 Kilobit (KB) service, Superpath 1.544 Megabit Service (MBPS), Flexpath Digital PBX Service, Digital Centrex Service, Digital Data Services 2.4 KB 56 KB, Caller Identification, and Call Trace.

Internet Access Providers in Maine

The nature and extent of the services offered by these Maine-based ISPs vary, as do the communities that lie within their local dial-up service areas. For details, contact the provider directly. This list is maintained by the Maine State Library for the benefit of the library community and the general public. Corrections and changes should be directed to the compiler, beiser@maine.edu

- *207ME.COM.* Box 301, Mars Hill, ME 04758, 888-229-2411, support@207me.com, www.207me.com.
- *Aroostook Internet.* 51 North Street, Presque Isle, ME 04469, tel 769-2691 or 800-752-4330, fax 764-7125, ericw@ainop.com; Houlton tel 532-9576, office@ainop.com., http://www.ainop.com.
- *BWSnet.net.* 40 Joseph Street, Medford, MA 02155, Portland Office # 207-618-5734, www.bostonwebspace.com.

⚓ *CC-Net.* 846 State Road, West Bath, ME04530, tel 442-7709, fax 442-0611, email webmaster@clinic.net, web http://www.clinic.net

⚓ *Coastal Telco Services.* POB 179, Nobleboro, ME 04555, tel 563-9929, fax 563-9936, email info@tidewater.net, web http://www.tidewater.net

⚓ *DialMaine.* The Center, 93 Main Street, Waterville, ME 04901, tel. (800) 624-6380, web http://www.dialmaine.com/contact/contact.html

⚓ *Downeast Net,* Downeast.net, P.O.Box 5093, Ellsworth, Me. 04605, tel 667-7414, email merlin@downeast.net, web http://downeast.net

⚓ *Dream Link Online.* 76 Webster St., Suite 6, Lewiston, ME 04240, tel: (207) 786-3207, email sales@dlois.com, web http://www.dlois.com

⚓ *FKGlobal.com.* 70A West Main Street, Fort Kent, ME 04743, tel (877) 243-4731, email webmaster@fkglobal.com, web http://www.fk-global.com

⚓ *Great Works Internet.* 8 Pomerleau Street, Biddeford, ME 04101, tel 207-286-2054 / 800-201-1476 fax 207-756-8773 email sales@gwi.net (human), info@gwi.net (auto-responder) web http://www.gwi.net/

⚓ *HyperMedia Communications.* P.O. Box 299, Brooklin, Maine 04616, tel 359-6573, email hypermedia@hypernet.com, web http://www.hy-pernet.com

⚓ *InterRamp (PSI Net).* 510 Huntmar Park Drive Herndon, VA 22070, tel 703-0709-0300 or 800-psi-3031, fax 703-904-1207, email info@psi.com, web http://www.psi.com

⚓ *JavaNet.* 37 Exchange St., Portland, ME 04101, tel 800-528-2638, email info@javanet.com, web http://www.javanet.com

⚓ *Katahdin Area Internet.* PO Box 3, Lincoln, ME 04457, tel 794-3059, fax 794-3059, email info@kai.net, web http://www.kai.net

⚓ *The Kobayashi Alternative.* 5 Roak St., Auburn, ME 04210, tel 784-9582, email info@tka.com, web http://www.tka.com

⚓ *KyND Internet Services.* PO Box 175, Guilford, ME 04443, tel 876-2736, 888 876-2736, fax 876-4664, email kynd@kynd.net, web http://www.kynd.net

⚓ *Lightship Telcom.* 190 Riverside Drive, Suite 6A, Portland, ME 04103, tel 877-548-7447, email customercare@lightship.net , web http://www.lightship.net

⚓ *Log On America.* 108 Lafayette Center, Kennebunk, ME 04043, tel

985-3668, fax 985-8259, email sales@cybertours.com, web http://www.cybertours.com. http://www.cybertours.com.

▲*Maineline.net Internet Services.* 76 Main Street, Machias, ME 04654, tel 255-3825, toll free 1-866-708-7998, email office@maineline.net or support@maineline.net, web http://www.maineline.net

▲*Megalink.* 945 Center Street, Auburn, ME 04210, 511 Congress Street, Portland, Route 117, Buckfield, ME 04220-0071, tel 786-2300, 336-2300, 800-520-9911, email info@megalink.net, web http://www.megalink.net

▲*MFaXcess.* 422 Main St., Presque Isle, ME 04769, tel 764-4024 fax 764-4601, email mfx@mfx.net, web http://www.mfaxcess.com

▲*Midcoast Internet Solutions.* PO Box 669, Rockland, ME 04841, tel 594-8277, fax 596-7248, email help@midcoast.com, web http://www.midcoast.com

▲*Mid-Maine Communications.* 44 Broadway, Bangor, ME 04401, tel 826-9911, 800-835-5453, email jason@midmaine.com, web http://www.mid-maine.com

▲*Moosehead Online.* P.O. Box 772, Greenville, ME 04441, tel 695-4676, fax 695-4675, email mol@moosehead.net, web http://www.moose-head.net

▲*Northern Lights BBS.* PO Box 1961, Portland, ME 04103, modem 761-4431, bbs 761-4782, email jkilday@nlbbs.com, web http://www.nlbbs.com

▲*Onperfect.com.* 53 Main Street, Lincoln, ME 04457, tel. (207) 794-9065, email alan@onperfect.com, web http://www.onperfect.com

▲*Panax.* 25 Pine Street, Ellsworth, ME 04605, tel 207-667-2768, email clyon@panax.com, web http://www.panax.com.

▲*Pctech.Net (Pctech, Inc.)* Route 1, The Triangle, Store #3, Ellsworth, ME 04605, tel 207-667-4146, fax 207-664-0209, email lyndon@pctech.net, web http://www.pctech.net

▲*Pine Tree Networks.* 92 Oak Street Portland, Maine 04101 Tel 207 699-2105 Fax 207 699-2103 john.beatrice@pinetreenetworks.com

▲*Pioneer Wireless.* 29 North Street, Houlton, Maine 04730, tel 532-1254, fax 532-4474, email info@pioneerwireless.net, web http://www.pioneerwireless.net

⚑ **Pivot.NetUtilities, Inc.** POB 1480, Standish, ME 04084, tel 642-9911, 888-667-4868, fax 642-3095, email info@pivot.net, web http://www.pivot.net

⚑ **Points South.** Midtown Mall, Sanford, ME 04073, 207-490-4949, email connect@psouth.net, web http://www.psouth.net

⚑ **Portalsmith, LLC** 14 Main Street, Suite 100, Brunswick, ME 04011, tel 207-373-1541, fax 207-373-1542, email: info@portalsmith.net, web http://www.portalsmith.com

⚑ **Prexar.** 40 Summer Street, Bangor, ME 04401, tel (207) 974-4300, fax (207) 974-4378, email: sales@prexar.com , http://www.prexar.com

⚑ **Road Runner (Time Warner Cable of Maine)** 118 Johnson Road, Portland, ME 04102, tel 775-3431 or 800-833-2253, email info@twmaine.com, web http://www.timewarnercable.com/

⚑ **Route 1 Internet Service.** Bradford House, Wiscasset, Maine, 04578, tel 882-4488, email srafter@wiscasset.net, web http://www.wiscasset.net

⚑ **Solar Eclipse Information Services.** tel 775-3841, email cbigelow@seis.com, web http://www.seis.com.

⚑ **St. John Valley Communications.** 26 Market Street, Fort Kent, ME 04743, tel 834-3312, web http://www.sjv.com.

⚑ **Suscom.** 336 Bath Road, Brunswick, ME 04011, tel 729-6663, email info@SuscomMaine.net, web http://www.blazenetme.net

⚑ **USA Internet (Cybertours)** 5 Bragdon Lane Suite 200, Kennebunk, ME 04043, tel 1-877-USA-2800 ext. 200 (sales) or 207-467-9030 ext. 140 (Beverly Staples), fax (207) 467-8008, email sales@link2usa.com; Web site http://www.link2usa.com

⚑ **Uninet.** 25 Main Street, Unity, Maine 04988, tel 948-6387, email info@uninet.net, web http://www.uninet.net

⚑ **Watchic Link Internet.** 780 Boundary Road, Steep Falls, Maine 04085, email info@watchic.net web: http://www.watchic.net

⚑ **Waterville Online Internet Services.** 76 Main Street, Waterville, ME 04901, tel 861-8800, email info@wtvl.net, web http://www.wtvl.net

⚑ **XpressAmerica.** 7 Green Street, Biddeford, ME , tel 286-9477, fax (253) 595-9497, email support@xpressamerica.net, web http://www.xpressamerica.net

Here are two sites with lists of more Maine Internet service providers:

Mecklermedia, publisher of *Internet World*, maintains a list that includes both national and local firms active in Maine, but leaves out some of the providers included in the NetMaine list. It can be found at http://thelist. iworld.com/areacode/207.html.

The Internet Access Providers Meta-List collects a variety of lists of Maine providers. It is located at http://www.herbison.com/herbison/iap _meta_list_us_me.html.

Of course, national online services like CompuServe, America Online and Prodigy, are also worth looking into.

PROFILE: Back to Maine

"Leaving Maine after getting married was always viewed as a temporary thing," says Michael White, Director of Business Development for Know Technology, LLC, in Camden. The company provides networking, hosting, and development services for businesses throughout Maine and New England. "My wife wanted to get her Masters Degree in New Hampshire and so we went . . . ten years later, with a family, we've come back."

"Other than wanting our kids to be closer to their grandparents (something neither one of us had growing up), Suzanne and I really wanted to be back in the Midcoast area. We're not natives, but we both went to high school here and have fond memories and strong ties to the area. These ties came in handy and provided a wealth of contacts when we decided to make the move and started looking for jobs, homes, etc. We looked at boat building, IT, startups, one job, two jobs, one and a half jobs . . . we really saw a lot of different options available. The increasingly better cell coverage, broadband access and really the departure of credit card giant MBNA seems to have made the Midcoast area rich in talented people getting a great amount of work accomplished. This continues to be encouraging."

"Perhaps because we've made the drive in and out of the state so many times, Camden no longer "feels" as isolated as it did when we were younger. Some things we'd like to see change: the cost of living, which seems higher than when we were in southern New Hampshire. Food, clothing, gas, dining, etc, seem to cost more. Also, we seem to struggle internally with the missing "big box" stores. Sometimes we wish they were closer, sometimes we're glad they're not here—yet."

"The draw of the outdoors is also a very powerful one. Here we have the Camden Snow Bowl, Penobscot Bay, and Camden Hills State Park. We think we've found the best spot for who we are, and what we do."

Acknowledgments

I send out a heartfelt thank you to all those who shared their Maine experiences with me during the writing of this book. I appreciate the help of all the great folks around the state who have assisted with my research, or graciously allowed me to include their photographs. The folks at Down East books are always terrific to work with and I thank all of them for their expertise. I wish to acknowledge the support of Camden Real Estate Company, and in particular, Scott Horty, for his help and advice with this new edition. And finally, thanks to my family, Ed, Matt, Nate, and Lexi. Maine wouldn't be my favorite place without you.

APPENDIX 1:
Maine at a Glance

Data provided by *Down East* magazine.

County	Androscoggin	Aroostook	Cumberland	Franklin
Population 2004*	107,022	73,390	273,505	29,736
Population 1990	105,259	86,936	243,135	29,008
Population 1980	99,509	91,344	215,789	27,447
Largest Town (2000 pop.)	Lewiston 35,690	Presque Isle 9,511	Portland 64,249	Farmington 7,410
People per square mile	220.8	11.1	317.7	17.4
High School Graduates	79.8%	76.9%	90.1%	85.2%
College / Adv. Degree	12.6%	12.5%	27.6%	17.7%
Median Household Income	$35,793	$28,837	$44,048	$31459
Aver. Temp. Range, °F	Lewiston	Caribou	Portland	Farmington
January	29.2 to 11.1	19.4 to −1.6	30.3 to 11.4	25.8 to .5
April	53.1 to 34.2	46.7 to 29	52.3 to 34.1	51 to 28.5
July	80.7 to 60.7	76.5 to 54.5	78.8 to 58.3	79 to 53.4
October	59 to 40.5	52 to 34	58.7 to 38.3	57.4 to 32.3
Crime Rate per Thousand (2000)	35.79	20.61	30.23	31.81

* Most recent census estimate.

Maine At A Glance, continued

County	Hancock	Kennebec	Knox	Lincoln
Population 2004*	53,556	120,645	41,008	35,236
Population 1990	46,948	115,904	36,310	30,357
Population 1980	41,781	109,889	32,941	25,691
Largest Town (2000 pop.)	Ellsworth 6,456	Augusta 18,560	Rockland 7,609	Waldoboro 4,916
People per square mile	32.6	134.9	108.2	73.7
High School Graduates	87.8%	85.2%	87.5%	87.9%
College / Adv. Degree	27.1%	20.7%	26.2%	26.6%
Median Household Income	$35,811	$36,498	$36,774	$38,686
Aver. Temp. Range, °F	Ellsworth	Augusta	Rockland	Wiscasset**
January	30.1 to 10.5	27.6 to 10.4	32 to 10.2	30.1 to 10.4
April	51.7 to 32.3	52.1 to 34.4	50.3 to 33.6	52.4 to 34.2
July	77.9 to 57	79 to 60.1	79.9 to 57.1	77.9 to 59.3
October	57.8 to 39.3	57.5 to 39.8	56.2 to 39.6	58.4 to 39.4
Crime Rate per Thousand (2000)	23.78	23.72	19.07	15.41

* Most recent census estimate.
** Based on the average temperatures at Brunswick, the nearest National Weather Service station.

Maine At A Glance, continued

County	Oxford	Penobscot	Piscataquis	Sagadahoc
Population 2004*	56,614	148,196	17,525	36,927
Population 1990	52,606	146,601	18,653	33,535
Population 1980	49,043	137,015	17,634	28,795
Largest Town (2000 pop.)	Rumford 6,472	Bangor 31,473	Dover-Foxcroft 4,211	Bath 9,266
People per square mile	26.3	42.7	4.3	138.6
High School Graduates	82.4%	85.7%	80.3%	88%
College / Adv. Degree	15.7%	20.3%	13.3%	25%
Median Household Income	$33,435	$34,274	$28,250	$41,908
Aver. Temp. Range, °F	Rumford	Bangor	Dover-Foxcroft	Bath**
January	27.2 to 5.8	26.7 to 8.2	24.2 to 2.4	30.1 to 10.4
April	52.3 to 31.2	50.9 to 32.8	49.5 to 28.8	52.4 to 34.2
July	79.6 to 56.4	78.1 to 58.3	78.6 to 54.5	77.9 to 59.3
October	57.5 to 36.6	56.9 to 38.7	55.6 to 33.6	58.4 to 39.4
Crime Rate per Thousand (2000)	21.89	29.02	26.15	23.9

* Most recent census estimate.
** Based on the average temperatures at Brunswick, the nearest National Weather Service station.

Maine At A Glance, continued

County	Somerset	Waldo	Washington	York
Population 2004*	51,584	38,392	33,558	200,359
Population 1990	49,767	33,018	35,308	164,587
Population 1980	45,049	28,414	34,963	139,739
Largest Town (2000 pop.)	Skowhegan 8,824	Belfast 6,381	Calais 3,447	Sanford 20,942
People per square mile	13	49.7	13.2	188.4
High School Graduates	80.8%	84.6%	79.9%	86.5%
College / Adv. Degree	11.8%	22.3%	14.7%	22.9%
Median Household Income	$30,731	$33,986	$25,869	$43,630
Aver. Temp. Range, °F	Madison	Belfast	Eastport	Sanford
January	26.8 to 2.1	32 to 10.7	29.7 to 13.9	32.5 to 10.4
April	51.2 to 30.1	53.9 to 32.3	48.5 to 32.8	57.3 to 32
July	79.1 to 55.6	79.9 to 57.1	72.9 to 53	83.2 to 57.1
October	57.2 to 34.7	59.9 to 38.9	55.7 t0 40.8	62.5 to 37.1
Crime Rate per Thousand (2000)	28.74	8.48	22.57	25.67

* Most recent census estimate.
** Based on the average temperatures at Brunswick, the nearest National Weather Service station.

APPENDIX 2:
Quality Medical Care—Maine Hospitals

Data provided by *Down East* magazine.

Note: Numbers in parentheses following hospital names indicate number of acute care beds in that facility.

Augusta

Maine General Medical Center *(287)*
6 East Chestnut St., Augusta, ME 04330
207-626-1000

Bangor

Acadia Hospital *(100)*
268 Stillwater Ave., Bangor,
ME 04402-0422 207-973-6100

Eastern Maine Medical Center *(411)*
489 State St., P.O. Box 404,
Bangor, ME 04402-0404
207-973-7000

St. Joseph Hospital *(82)*
360 Broadway, Bangor, ME 04401
207-262-1000

Bar Harbor

Mount Desert Island Hospital *(25)*
10 Wayman Lane, P.O. Box 8, Bar Harbor,
ME 04609-0008 207-288-5081

Belfast

Waldo County General Hospital *(25)*
118 Northport Ave., P.O. Box 287,
Belfast, ME 04915 207-338-2500

Blue Hill

Blue Hill Memorial Hospital *(25)*
Water St., Blue Hill, ME 04614
207-374-2836

Biddeford

Southern Maine Medical Center *(150)*
1 Medical Center Drive, P.O. Box 626,
Biddeford, ME 04005 207-283-7000

Boothbay Harbor

St. Andrews Hospital *(20)*
6 St. Andrews Dr., P.O. Box 417,
Boothbay Harbor, ME 04538
207-633-2121

Bridgton

Northern Cumberland Memorial
Hospital *(25)*
10 Hospital Dr. (off South High St.),
P.O. Box 230, Bridgton, ME 04009
207-647-6000

Brunswick

Mid-Coast Hospital *(73)*
123 Medical Center Dr., Brunswick, ME
04011 207-729-0181

Parkview Hospital *(55)*
329 Maine St., Brunswick, ME 04011
207-373-2000

Calais

Calais Regional Hospital *(25)*
22 Hospital Lane, Calais, ME 04619
207-454-7521

Quality Medical Care—Maine Hospitals, continued

Caribou

Cary Medical Center *(23)*
163 Van Buren Rd., Caribou, ME 04736
207-498-3111

Damariscotta

Miles Memorial Hospital *(35)*
35 Miles St., Damariscotta, ME 04543
207-563-1234

Dover-Foxcroft

Mayo Regional Hospital *(25)*
897 West Main St.,
Dover-Foxcroft, ME 04426
207-564-4342

Ellsworth

Maine Coast Memorial Hospital *(64)*
50 Union St., Ellsworth, ME 04605
207-667-5311

Farmington

Franklin Memorial Hospital *(70)*
1 Hospital Dr., Farmington, ME 04938
207-778-6031

Fort Kent

Northern Maine Medical Center *(48)*
194 East Main St., Fort Kent, ME 04743
207-834-3155

Greenville

C.A. Dean Memorial Hospital *(14)*
Pritham Ave., P.O. Box 1129, Greenville,
ME 04441   207-695-5200

Houlton

Houlton Regional Hospital *(25)*
20 Hartford St., Houlton, ME 04730
207-532-2900

Lewiston

Central Maine Medical Center *(250)*
300 Main St., Lewiston, ME 04240
207-795-0111

St. Mary's Regional Medical
Center *(233)*
P.O. Box 291,
Lewiston, ME 04243-0291
207-777-8100

Lincoln

Penobscot Valley Hospital *(25)*
7 Transalpine Rd., Box 368,
Lincoln, ME 04457-0368
207-794-3321

Machias

Down East Community Hospital *(25)*
RR 1, Box 11, Machias, ME 04654
207-255-3356

Millinocket

Millinocket Regional Hospital *(15)*
200 Somerset St.,
Millinocket, ME 04462
207-723-5161

Norway

Stephens Memorial Hospital *(50)*
181 Main St., Norway, ME 04268
207-743-5933

Pittsfield

Sebasticook Valley Hospital *(25)*
99 Grove Hill, Pittsfield, ME 04967
207-487-5141

Quality Medical Care—Maine Hospitals, continued

Portland

New England Rehabilitation
Hospital *(100)*
335 Brighton Avenue, Unit 201
Portland, ME 04102
207-775-4000

Maine Medical Center *(605)*
22 Bramhall St., Portland, ME 04102
207-871-0111

Mercy Hospital *(200)*
144 State St., Portland, ME 04101
207-879-3000

Presque Isle

Aroostook Medical Center *(72)*
140 Academy St., Box 151,
Presque Isle, ME 04769
207-768-4000

Rockport

Penobscot Bay Medical Center *(109)*
6 Glen Cove Dr., Rockport,
ME 04856-4240   207-596-8000

Rumford

Rumford Community Hospital *(25)*
420 Franklin St., Rumford, ME 04276
207-364-4581

Sanford

Goodall Hospital *(55)*
25 June St., Sanford, ME 04073
207-324-4310

Skowhegan

Redington–Fairview General
Hospital *(65)*
46 Fairview Ave., P.O. Box 468,
Skowhegan, ME 04976
207-474-5121

South Portland

Spring Harbor Hospital *(100)*
175 Running Hill Rd.,
S. Portland, ME 04106
207-761-2200

Waterville

Inland Hospital *(45)*
200 Kennedy Memorial Dr.,
Waterville, ME 04901
207-861-3000

MaineGeneral Medical Center
(Seton and Thayer units) *(350)*
149 North Main St.,
Waterville, ME 04901
207-872-1000

Westbrook

Mercy Westbrook *(30)*
40 Park Rd., Westbrook, ME 04092
207-854-8000

York

York Hospital *(72)*
15 Hospital Dr., York, ME 03909
207-363-4321

APPENDIX 3:
Local Issues—Maine Newspapers

Data provided by *Down East* magazine.

DAILIES

Augusta

Kennebec Journal
274 Western Avenue,
Augusta, ME 04332
207-623-3811 www.kjonline.com

Bangor

Bangor Daily News
P.O. Box 1329, Bangor, ME 04402
207-990-8000 www.bangornews.com

Biddeford

Journal Tribune
P.O. Box 627, Biddeford, ME 04005
207-282-1535 www.journaltribune.com

Brunswick

The Times Record
P.O. Box 10, Brunswick, ME 04011
207-729-3311 www.timesrecord.com

Lewiston

The Sun-Journal
P.O. Box 4400, Lewiston, ME 04243
207-784-5411 www.sunjournal.com

Waterville

Central Maine Morning Sentinel
31 Front Street, Waterville, ME 04901
207-873-3341 www.onlinesentinel.com

Portland

Portland Press Herald
390 Congress St., Portland, ME 04104
207-791-6650 www.pressherald.com

WEEKLIES AND OTHERS

Augusta

Capital Weekly
P.O. Box 2788, Augusta, ME 04338
207-621-6000 www.courierpub.com

Bar Harbor

The Bar Harbor Times
P.O. Box 68, Bar Harbor, ME 04609
207-288-3311 www.courierpub.com

Bath

Coastal Journal
P.O. Box 705, Bath, ME 04530
207-443-6241 www.coastaljournal.com

Belfast

Republican Journal
P.O. Box 327, 71 High St., Belfast, ME
04915 207-338-3333
www.courierpub.com

The Waldo Independent
P.O. Box 228, Belfast, ME 04915
207-338-5100 www.courierpub.com

Village Soup Citizen
48-4 Marshall Wharf, Belfast, ME 04915
207-338-0484 http://waldo.villagesoup.com

Bethel

The Bethel Citizen
P.O. Box 109, Bethel, ME 04217
207-824-2444 www.bethelcitizen.com

Biddeford

Biddeford–Saco–Old Orchard Beach Courier
P.O. Box 1894, Biddeford, ME 04005
207-282-4337

Blue Hill

The Weekly Packet
P.O. Box 646, Blue Hill, ME 04614
207-374-2341 www.weeklypacket.com

Boothbay Harbor

The Boothbay Register
P.O. Box 357, Boothbay Harbor,
ME 04538, 207-633-4620
www.boothbayregister.maine.com

Bridgton

The Bridgton News
P.O. Box 244, Bridgton, ME 04009
207-647-2851

Bucksport

The Enterprise
P.O. Box 829, Bucksport, ME 04416
207-469-6722

Calais

The Calais Advertiser
P.O. Box 660, Calais, ME 04619
207-454-3561
www.the-calais-advertiser.com

Downeast Times
332 North Street, Calais, ME 04619
207-454-2884 www.downeastwebs.com

Camden

The Camden Herald
56 Elm Street, Camden, ME 04843
207-236-8511 www.courierpub.com

Village Soup Times
21 Elm Street, Camden, ME 04843
207-236-8468
http://camden.villagesoup.com

Cape Elizabeth

The Cape Courier
P.O. Box 6242,
Cape Elizabeth, ME 04107
207-767-5023 www,capecourier.com

Caribou

Aroostook Republican & News
P.O. Box 608, Caribou, ME 04736
207-496-3251

Castine

Castine Patriot
P.O. Box 205, Castine, ME 04421
207-326-9300 www.castinepatriot.com

Cutler

The Downeast Coastal Press
2413 Cutler Rd., Cutler, ME 04626
207-259-7751

Damariscotta

Lincoln County News
P.O. Box 36, Damariscotta, ME 04543
207-563-3171
www.mainelincolncountynews.com

Lincoln County Weekly
P.O. Box 1287,
Damariscotta, ME 04543
207-563-5006 www.courierpub.com

Dexter

The Eastern Gazette
P.O. Box 306, Dexter, ME 04930
207-924-7402

Dover-Foxcroft

Piscataquis Observer
P.O. Box 30, Dover-Foxcroft, ME 04426
207-564-8355

Eastport

The Quoddy Tides (twice monthly)
P.O. Box 213, Eastport, ME 04631
207-853-4806 www.quoddytides.com

Ellsworth

The Ellsworth American
P.O. Box 509, Ellsworth, ME 04605
207-667-2576
www.ellsworthamerican.com

Falmouth

Falmouth Forecaster
317 Foreside Rd., Falmouth, ME 04105
207-781-3661 www.theforecaster.net

Farmington

Franklin Journal (twice weekly)
P.O. Box 750, Farmington, ME 04938
207-778-2075

Gorham

Gorham Times
P.O. Box 401., Gorham, ME 04038
207-839-8390 www.gorhamtimes.com

Gray

The Gray News
P.O. Box 433, Gray, ME 04039
207-657-2200
www.graynews.maine.com

Greenville

Moosehead Messenger
P.O. Box 400, Greenville, ME 04441
207-695-3077
www.moosemessenger.com

Houlton

Houlton Pioneer Times
P.O. Box 456, Houlton, ME 04730
207-532-2281

Islesboro

Islesboro Island News (six per year)
P.O. Box 104, Islesboro, ME 04848
207-734-6921 www.islesboronews.com

Kennebunk

York County Coast Star
P.O. Box 979, Kennebunk, ME 04043
207-985-2961
www.seacoastonline.com/news/yorkstar

Kingfield

The Irregular
P.O. Box 616, Kingfield, ME 04947
207-265-2773
www.news.mywebpal.com/index.cfm?pn
pid=282

Lincoln

Lincoln News
P.O. Box 35, Lincoln, ME 04457
207-794-6532
www.mainelincolncountynews.com

Livermore Falls

Livermore Falls Advertiser
P.O. Box B,
Livermore Falls, ME 04254
207-897-4321

Lubec

The Lubec Light
R.R. 2, Box 380, Lubec, ME 04652
207-733-2939

Machias

The County Wide
P.O. Box 497, Machias, ME 04654
207-564-7548

Machias Valley News Observer
P.O. Box 357, Machias, ME 04654
207-255-6561

Madawaska

Saint John Valley Times
P.O. Box 419, Madawaska, ME 04756
207-728-3336

Millinocket

Katahdin Times
202 Penobscot Ave., P.O. Box 330,
Millinocket, ME 04462
207-723-8118

New Gloucester

New Gloucester News
P.O. Box 102, New Gloucester, ME 04260
207-926-4036
www.newgloucesternews.com

Norway

Advertiser Democrat
P.O. Box 269, Norway, ME 04268
207-743-7011 www.advertiserdemocrat.com

The Bear Facts (twice monthly)
P.O. Box 718, Norway, ME 04268
207-583-2851

Old Town

Penobscot Times
P.O. Box 568, Old Town, ME 04468
207-827-4451

Portland

Maine Sunday Telegram
390 Congress Street,
Portland, ME 04101
207-775-6601 www.portland.com

Presque Isle

The Star-Herald
P.O. Box 510, Presque Isle, ME 04769
207-768-5431

Rangeley

Rangeley Highlander
P.O. Box 542, Rangeley, ME 04970
207-864-3756

Rockland

The Courier Gazette (three/week)
P.O. Box 249, Rockland, ME 04841
207-594-4401 www.courierpub.com

The Free Press
8 North Main Street, Suite 101
Rockland, ME 04841
207-596-0055 www.freepressonline.com

Rumford

Rumford Falls Times
P.O. Box 490, Rumford, ME 04276
207-364-7893
www.rumfordfallstimes.com

Sanford

The Sanford News
P.O. Box D, Sanford, ME 04073
207-324-5986

Scarborough

Current
27 Gorham Rd., Suite 3
Scarborough, ME 04074
207-883-3533

Leader
180 Main St., Biddeford, ME 04976
207-474-0606

South China

The Town Line
P.O. Box 89, South China, ME 04358
207-445-2234

Stonington

Island Ad-Vantages
P.O. Box 36, Stonington, ME 04681
207-367-2200 www.islandadvantages.com

Westbrook

The American Journal
4 Dana Street, Westbrook, ME 04092
207-854-2577

Windham

The Lake Region Suburban News
733 Roosevelt Trail, P.O. Box 790
Windham, ME 04062
207-892-1166

Wiscasset

Wiscasset Newspaper
P.O. Box 429, Wiscasset, ME 04578
207-882-6355
www.wiscassetnewspaper.maine.com

York

York Independent
P.O. Box 6, York, ME 03909
207-363-8484 www.yorkindependent.com

The York Weekly
P.O. Box 7, York, ME 03909
207-363-4343
www.seacoastonline.com/news/yorkweekly

APPENDIX 4:
Chambers of Commerce

Data provided by the Maine Office of Tourism.

[Augusta]
Kennebec Valley Chamber of Commerce
P.O. Box 676, Augusta 04332-0676
207-623-4559

Bangor Region Chamber of Commerce
519 Main Street, Bangor 04402-1443
207-947-0307

Bar Harbor Chamber of Commerce
P.O. Box 158, Bar Harbor 04609
207-288-5103

[Bath]
Chamber of Commerce of the
    Bath–Brunswick Region
45 Front Street, Bath 04530
207-443-9751

Belfast Area Chamber of Commerce
P.O. Box 58, Belfast 04915
207-338-5900

Bethel Area Chamber of Commerce
P.O. Box 1247, Bethel 04217
207-824-2282

Biddeford–Saco Chamber of Commerce
110 Main Street, Suite 1202,
    Saco 04072
207-282-1567

[Bingham]
Upper Kennebec Valley Chamber
    of Commerce
P.O. Box 491, Bingham 04920
207-672-4100

Boothbay Region Information Center
P.O. Box 187, Boothbay 04537
207-633-4743

Boothbay Harbor Region
    Chamber of Commerce
P.O. Box 356, Boothbay Harbor 04538
207-633-2353

[Bridgton]
Greater Bridgton Lakes Region
    Chamber of Commerce
P.O. Box 236, Bridgton 04009
207-647-3472

[Brunswick]
Chamber of Commerce of the
    Bath–Brunswick Region
59 Pleasant Street, Brunswick 04011
207-725-8797

Bucksport Bay Area
    Chamber of Commerce
P.O. Box 1880, Bucksport 04416
207-469-6818

Calais Regional Chamber of Commerce
P.O. Box 368, Calais 04619
207-454-2308

Camden–Rockport–Lincolnville
    Chamber of Commerce
P.O. Box 919, Camden 04843
207-236-4404

Caribou Chamber of Commerce
111 High Street, Caribou 04736
207-498-6156

Sugarloaf Area Information Center
RR 1 Box 2151,
  Carrabassett Valley 04947
207-235-2100

Damariscotta Region
  Chamber of Commerce
P.O. Box 13, Damariscotta 04543
207-563-8340

Damariscotta Region
  Information Bureau
P.O. Box 217, Damariscotta 04543
207-563-3175

[Dover-Foxcroft]
Southern Piscataquis County
  Chamber of Commerce
P.O. Box 376, Dover-Foxcroft 04426
207-564-7533

Eastport Area Chamber of Commerce
P.O. Box 254, Eastport 04631
207-853-4644

Ellsworth Area Chamber of Commerce
P.O. Box 267, Ellsworth 04605
207-667-2617

[Farmington]
Greater Farmington
  Chamber of Commerce
RR 4 Box 5091, Farmington 04938
207-778-4215

Fort Fairfield Chamber of Commerce
128 Main Street, Suite 4,
  Fort Fairfield 04742
207-472-3802

[Fort Kent]
Greater Fort Kent Area
  Chamber of Commerce
P.O. Box 430, Fort Kent 04743
207-834-5354

Freeport Merchants Association,
P.O. Box 452, Freeport 04032
207-865-1212

[Greenville]
Moosehead Lake Region
  Chamber of Commerce
P.O. Box 581, Greenville 04441
207-695-2702

Houlton Chamber of Commerce
109 Main Street, Houlton 04730
207-532-4216

[Island Falls]
Northern Katahdin Valley Regional
  Chamber of Commerce
P.O. Box 374, Island Falls 04747
207-463-2077

Jackman–Moose River Region
  Chamber of Commerce
P.O. Box 368, Jackman 04945
207-668-4171

Kennebunk–Kennebunkport
  Chamber of Commerce
P.O. Box 740, Kennebunk 04043
207-967-0857

[Kittery]
Gateway to Maine
P.O. Box 526, Kittery 03904
207-439-7545

[Lewiston]
Androscoggin County
  Chamber of Commerce
P.O. Box 59, Lewiston 04243-0059
207-783-2249

Limestone Chamber of Commerce
291 Main Street, Limestone 04750
207-325-4025

Lincoln Chamber of Commerce
P.O. Box 164, Lincoln 04457
207-794-8065

Machias Bay Area
   Chamber of Commerce
P.O. Box 606, Machias 04654
207-255-4402

[Madawaska]
Greater Madawaska
   Chamber of Commerce
378 Main Street, Madawaska 04756
207-728-7000

Maine Chamber and Business Alliance
7 University Drive, Augusta 04330-9412
207-623-4568

[Millinocket]
Katahdin Area Chamber of Commerce
1029 Central Street, Millinocket 04462
207-723-4443

Naples Information Center
P.O. Box 412, Naples 04055
207-693-3285

Mount Desert Chamber of Commerce
P.O. Box 675, Northeast Harbor 04662
207-276-5040

Ogunquit Chamber of Commerce
P.O. Box 2289, Ogunquit 03907
207-646-2939

Old Orchard Beach
   Chamber of Commerce
P.O. Box 600, Old Orchard Beach 04064
207-934-2500

[Portland]
Convention and Visitors Bureau of
   Greater Portland
305 Commercial Street, Portland 04101
207-772-5800

Presque Isle Area
   Chamber of Commerce
P.O. Box 672, Presque Isle 04769
207-764-6561

Rangeley Lakes Region
   Chamber of Commerce
P.O. Box 317, Rangeley 04970
207-864-5571

Rockland–Thomaston Area
   Chamber of Commerce
P.O. Box 508, Rockland 04841
207-596-0376

[Rumford]
River Valley Chamber of Commerce
P.O. Box 598, Rumford 04276
207-364-3241

St Francis Chamber of Commerce
P.O. Box 123, St Francis 04774
207-398-3431

Sanford-Springvale
   Chamber of Commerce and
   Economic Development
261 Main Street, Sanford 04073
207-324-4280

Skowhegan Area
   Chamber of Commerce
P.O. Box 326, Skowhegan 04976
207-474-3621

Oxford Hills Chamber of Commerce
P.O. Box 167, South Paris 04281
207-743-2281

Southwest Harbor–Tremont
   Chamber of Commerce
P.O. Box 1143,
   Southwest Harbor 04679
207-244-9264

Deer Isle–Stonington
   Chamber of Commerce
P.O. Box 459, Stonington 04681
207-348-6124

[Unity]
Waldo County Regional
   Chamber of Commerce
P.O. Box 577, Unity 04974
207-948-5050

[Van Buren]
Greater Van Buren
   Chamber of Commerce
65 Main Street, Van Buren 04785
207-868-5059

Waldoboro Town Office
P.O. Box J, Waldoboro 04572
207-832-5369

[Waterville]
Mid-Maine Chamber of Commerce
P.O. Box 142, Waterville 04903-0142
207-873-3315

Wells Chamber of Commerce
P.O. Box 356, Wells 04090
207-646-2451

Wilton Chamber of Commerce
P.O. Box 934, Wilton 04294
207-645-3932

Windham Chamber of Commerce
P.O. Box 1015, Windham 04062
207-892-8265

Yarmouth Chamber of Commerce
158 Main Street, Yarmouth 04096
207-846-3984

Yorks Chamber of Commerce
571 US Route 1, York 03909
207-363-4422

Appendix 5:
Retirement Communities

Every year more retirement communities are being built or expanded. Please call or write the individual facilities for their latest information. (Data as of March 2000, provided by *Down East* magazine.)

The communities listed here all provide housekeeping services and at least one meal per day, and most can provide transportation.

Key to abbreviations in the Types of Units column:
IA = independent apartments; C = cottages;
A = Alzheimer's units; LT = long-term care beds;
AL = assisted living units.

FACILITY	Number of Residents	Distance to Hospital	Rent, Purchase or Both	Types of Units
Auburn				
Clover Health Care 440 Minot Ave., Auburn, ME 04210 207-784-3573 www.mainecare.com	270	3	R	IA, AL, LT, A
Schooner Retirement Community 200 Stetson Rd., Auburn, ME 04210 207-784-2900; 800-924-9997 www.schoonerestates.com	180	3	R	IA, AL, LT
Bangor				
Park East Retirement Villa 146 Balsam Dr., Bangor, ME 04401 207-947-7992 www.parkeastapts.com	22	1	R	IA
Boyd Place 21 Boyd St., Bangor ME 04401 207-941-2837	85	.5	R	IA, AL

FACILITY	Number of Residents	Distance to Hospital	Rent, Purchase or Both	Types of Units
Sunbury Village 922 Ohio St., Bangor ME 04401 207-262-9600 www.sunburyvillage.net	138	2	R	IA
Bar Harbor Birch Bay Village 25 Village Inn Rd., Bar Harbor, ME 04609 207-288-8014 www.birchbayinfo.com	130	4	B	IA, C AL, A
Belfast Harbor Hill 2 Footbridge Rd., Belfast, ME 04915 207-338-5307 www.sandyriverhealth.com	85	3	R	AL, LT A
Penobscot Shores 10 Shoreland Dr., Belfast, ME 04915 207-338-2332 www.penobscotshores.com	74	.25	B	IA, C
Blue Hill Parker Ridge Retirement Community 63 Parker Ridge Ln, Blue Hill, ME 04614 207-374-2306 www.parkerridge.com	71	3	B	IA, C, AL
Boothbay Harbor St. Andrews Village 145 Emery Lane, Boothbay Harbor, ME 04538 207-633-0920 www.standrewsvillage.com	150	1.5	B	IA, C, AL, LT, A

FACILITY	Number of Residents	Distance to Hospital	Rent, Purchase or Both	Types of Units
Brewer				
Ellen M. Leach Memorial Home P.O. Box 359, Brewer, ME 04412 207-989-7890 www.leachmemorialhome.org	66	1.5	R	IA
Brunswick				
Sunnybrook Village 25 Thornton Way, Brunswick, ME 04011 207-729-8033; 800-729-8033 www.sunnybrookvillage.com	51	1	R	IA, AL, LT
Thornton Oaks 25 Thornton Way, Brunswick, ME 04011 207-729-8033; 800-729-8033 www.thorntonoaks.com	175	4.8	P	IA, C, AL, LT, A
Camden				
Camden Gardens 110 Mechanic St., Camden, ME 04843 207-236-0154	12	5	B	IA, C
Quarry Hill 30 Community Dr., Camden, ME 04843 207-230-6116 www.quarryhill.org	225	6	B	IA, C, AL, LT, A
Cape Elizabeth				
Village Crossings at Cape Elizabeth 78 Scott Dyer Rd., Cape Elizabeth, ME 04107 207-799-7332; 888-860-6914 www.carematrix.com	54	4	R	AL

FACILITY	Number of Residents	Distance to Hospital	Rent, Purchase or Both	Types of Units
Damariscotta				
Chase Point Assisted Living 65 Schooner St., Damariscotta, ME 04543 207-563-5523 www.mileshealthcare.org/schooner	42	0	R	AL
Schooner Cove 65 Schooner St., Damariscotta, ME 04543 207-563-5523 www.mileshealthcare.org/schooner	59	.1	B	IA
Falmouth				
OceanView at Falmouth 20 Blueberry Ln., Falmouth, ME 04105 207-781-4460 www.oceanviewrc.com	250	6	P	IA, C, AL
Farmington				
Orchard Park Rehabilitation and Living Ctr. 12 North St., Farmington, ME 04938 207-778-4416, 800-260-4416	13	5	R	IA, AL
Gorham				
Gorham House 50 New Portland Rd., Gorham, ME 04038 207-839-5757 www.mainecare.com	165	12	R	IA, AL, LT, A
Hallowell				
Granite Hill Estates 60 Balsam Dr., Hallowell, ME 04347 207-626-7786, 888-321-1119 www.granitehillestates.com	150	2	P	IA, C
Hampden				
Avalon Village 50 Foxglove Dr., Hampden, ME 04444 207-862-5100, 800-950-0037 www.avalon-maine.com	93	4	B	IA, C

FACILITY	Number of Residents	Distance to Hospital	Rent, Purchase or Both	Types of Units
Houlton				
Madigan Estates 93 Military St., Houlton, ME 04730 207-532-6593 www.madiganestates.com	135	1.5	R	IA, AL, LT, A
Kennebunk				
Atria Kennebunk 1 Penny Ln., Kennebunk, ME 04043 207-985-5866 www.atriacom.com	82	7	R	AL, A
Huntington Common 1 Huntington Com. Dr., Kennebunk, ME 04043 207-985-2810; 800-585-0533 www.huntingtoncommon.com	200	4.5	R	IA, C, AL, A
The Farragut at Kennebunk 106 Farragut Way, Kennebunk, ME 04043 207-985-9740 www.thefarragut.com	70	4.5	B	IA, C
Lewiston				
Montello Heights 550 College St., Lewiston, ME 04240 207-786-7149	80	2	R	IA
Newcastle				
Lincoln Home 22 River Rd., Newcastle, ME 04553 207-563-3350	40	1	R	IA, AL
Orono				
Dirigo Pines Retirement Community 9 Alumni Dr., Orono, ME 04473 866-344-3400 www.dirigopines.com	98	.1	R	IA, C, AL, LT A

FACILITY	Number of Residents	Distance to Hospital	Rent, Purchase or Both	Types of Units
Portland				
The Atrium at Cedars 640 Ocean Ave., Portland, ME 04103 207-775-4111 www.thecedarsportland.org	60	2.5	P	IA, AL
The Park Danforth 777 Stevens Ave., Portland, ME 04103 207-797-7710 www.parkdanforth.com	170	4	R	IA, AL
Seventy-Five State Street 75 State St., Portland, ME 04101 207-772-2675 www.75state.org	170	.1	R	IA, AL
The Woods at Canco 257 Canco Rd., Portland, ME 04103 207-772-4777	148	5	R	IA, C
Presque Isle				
Leisure Gardens Apartments 4 Dewberry Dr., Presque Isle, ME 04769 207-764-7322 www.ainop.com/lgardens/	140	.1	R	IA, AL
Rockland				
Bartlett Woods 20 Bartlett Dr., Rockland, ME 04841 207-594-2745 www.bartlettwoods.com	57	2.5	B	IA, C
Saco				
Atlantic Heights Retirement Community One Harbor Dr., Saco, ME 04072 207-283-3022, 800-874-6990 www.atlanticheightsretirement.com	231	4	R	C, LT, A

FACILITY	Number of Residents	Distance to Hospital	Rent, Purchase or Both	Types of Units
The Monarch Center 392 Main St., Saco, ME 04072 207-284-0900 www.themonarchcenter.com	40	5	R	AL, A
Wardwell Retirement Neighborhood 43 Middle St., Saco, ME 04072 207-284-7061	98	2.5	R	IA, AL
Scarborough Piper Shores 15 Piper Rd., Scarborough, ME04074 207-883-8700; 888-333-8711 www.pipershores.org	350	7	life care	IA, C, AL, LT,
Topsham The Highlands 26 Elm St., Topsham, ME 04086 207-725-2650; 888-760-1042 www.highlandsrc.com	300	5	B	IA, C, AL, A
Waterville Woodlands Assisted Living of Waterville 141 West River Rd., Waterville, ME 04901 207-861-5685 www.woodlandsofwaterville.com	129	1	R	IA, AL, A
Yarmouth Bay Square at Yarmouth 27 Forest Falls Dr., Yarmouth, ME 04096 207-846-0044, 888-374-6700 www.benchmarkquality.com	60	12	R	AL, A
York Sentry Hill 2 Victoria Ct, York, ME 03909 207-363-5116 www.sentryhill.com	160	.5	B	IA, C, AL, A

Index